Food Store Sanitation

Food Store Sanitation

Fourth Edition

Robert B. Gravani
Don C. Rishoi

Lebhar-Friedman Books
CHAIN STORE PUBLISHING CORP.
A Subsidiary of Lebhar-Friedman, Inc., New York

Chain Store Publishing Corp., 425 Park Avenue, New York, NY 10022

ISBN 0-86730-208-9

Contents

Preface

The first three editions of *Food Store Sanitation* have been widely used by the retail food industry and have provided associates with a great deal of practical information about this important subject.

Today, the field of food safety and sanitation has changed considerably since this book was first written. There has been an increase in the number and severity of foodborne illnesses, and as a result, a greater consumer and regulatory-agency concern about the safety and quality of the food supply. Some new guidelines and regulations have been published, several philosophies have changed, and newer, improved technologies are now available.

In preparing this edition, I have strived to update, modify, and improve the information in the book with practicality and the food retailer in mind. Knowledgeable, well-informed associates who understand and practice the principles in this book will be valuable assets to their companies because they will provide safe and wholesome foods to their customers!

I wish to acknowledge with gratitude the many individuals who provided advice, counsel, suggestions, and information for this fourth edition. Friends in the food retailing industry include Gale Prince of Kroger, David Richman of Giant, Bill Pool of Wegmans, Don Rung of Tops, Chuck Stoffers of Safeway, and Gary Bates of Publix, who all provided useful and practical advice as the book was being revised. Pest-management professionals including Dr. Austin Frishman, consultant, Robert Corrigan of Purdue University, and Ronald Gardner of Cornell University provided excellent suggestions for the chapters on controlling pests. Cornell University colleagues Dr. Richard Ledford, Janice Brown, and Donna Scott critiqued the chapters on microbiology and HACCP. Thanks are also extended to Dr. Bruce Tompkin of Swift-Eckrich and Dr. David Theno, consultant, for their comments on the HACCP chapter; Dr. Mark Banner of the Diversey Corporation for reviewing the cleaning and sanitizing chapter; and Maurice Guerrette of the New York State Department of Agriculture and Markets for sharing useful perspectives. I am indebted to all of these individuals who volunteered their time and talents to make this book a useful resource for the retail food industry.

I also want to thank three people who were most instrumental in the completion of this revision. My editor, Janelle Tauer, whose expertise is evident throughout this book, deserves thanks for her advice, assistance, and friendship during this project. Her gentle reminders of deadlines certainly moved the project to completion. Marcia Mogelonsky deserves thanks for her assistance with writing and for her sense of humor during this project. My administrative assistant, Mary Fraboni, also deserves thanks for word processing the many drafts of the book and for deciphering my handwriting. Her helpfulness was genuinely appreciated.

Last, but certainly not least, I'd like to express a very special "thank you" to my family. My wife Eileen, whose support, encouragement, and advice were invaluable, deserves special mention. Our children, Kristen and Steven, also deserve to be recognized for their understanding and patience when Dad had to work on the book. This book is dedicated to Eileen, Kristen, and Steven for their constant love, support, and understanding.

Robert B. Gravani, Ph.D.
Professor of Food Science
Cornell University

Memorial

Don C. Rishoi passed away suddenly and unexpectedly in 1982. It was a tremendous shock and loss to his family, friends, and colleagues. The many contributions that Mr. Rishoi made in his life will certainly be remembered by all persons in the retail food industry.

One of his major contributions was the original edition of this book, *Food Store Sanitation*, which was the first complete textbook written specifically for food retailers. His experiences from many years in the retail food business were embodied in that text, which continues to serve as a useful reference in the industry. Mr. Rishoi was especially proud that so many retailers read and used his book as part of the Cornell Home Study Program.

For those who weren't fortunate to know Don Rishoi, a short biographical sketch of this knowledgeable, well-versed, and dedicated man follows.

Don C. Rishoi received his bachelor of science degree in marketing and food distribution from Michigan State University and was active in the retail food industry most of his life. He was project director of the Supermarket Institute Sanitation System and was responsible for the organization and development of training materials and sanitation seminars. In this role, he played a major part in the development of the often-used film *The Spoilers*.

Early in his career, Mr. Rishoi spent five years in Copenhagen, Denmark, as staff consultant in store operations research and development to IRMA A/S, a retail food chain. He also served as a consultant to the United States Embassy Commissary in Copenhagen.

Prior to joining Chatham Supermarkets, Inc. in Warren, Michigan, as Director of Corporate Quality Control and Environmental Sanitation, Mr. Rishoi held the position of Director of Educational Services for the National Sanitation Foundation in Ann Arbor, Michigan.

His practical commitment to quality control and sanitation, as well as his dedication to the retail food industry, will long be remembered by his family, friends, and colleagues.

1

Introduction to Food Store Sanitation

Today's food shoppers are more aware of the quality, safety, and wholesomeness of their foods than ever before. The events that have made national news in recent years, including Alar® in apples, cyanide in Chilean grapes, pesticide residues on produce, food recalls, and several large foodborne illness outbreaks, have generated considerable interest in the safety and wholesomeness of the food supply. Customers need to feel confident that people who work in food stores are informed and educated about the safe handling of food products.

Knowledgeable, well-informed employees are the lifeblood of any successful food store. They need to understand how the principles of food safety and sanitation relate to all the foods that are handled, stored, prepared, merchandised, and sold in retail stores. This book is designed to help you understand the many areas of food safety and sanitation and why this information is so important to store operations, company image, sales, profitability, and the health and welfare of your customers.

The health, welfare, and satisfaction of customers should be the most important concern of every person working in a retail store. Why? Because food, when improperly handled, can cause foodborne illness. These illnesses can cause pain, discomfort, and sometimes, depending on the specific type of illness, even death. You can imagine the impact that a large outbreak of foodborne illness can have on your store, your company, and the entire industry. So, the main purpose of learning about the principles of food safety and sanitation is to provide safe and wholesome foods to your customers.

Today's food store has grown considerably from the neighborhood grocery store of the 1960s, when people would shop for a few items almost every day. The food store of the 1990s can have a number of different formats—conventional, superstore, and super warehouse store—with selling areas as large as 100,000 square feet and inventories of some 20,000 items. What a change from the early days of retailing!

With all the innovations in food marketing and food processing, the supermarket has also taken on the role of caterer, fast-food restaurant, food processor, and Euro-style gourmet food marketer. These innovations have necessarily brought about new food-safety problems and concerns.

This book is meant to address the *new* food store and to present up-to-date methods for assuring the quality, integrity, and safety of all food products sold in the supermarket.

Clean Is Not Always Sanitary

Before entering into a discussion of food store sanitation, it is necessary to clarify the terms we will be using. To many people, the term *sanitation* conjures up images of garbage trucks, landfills, sewer systems, and rest rooms. While these impressions are somewhat accurate, the concept of *food store sanitation* is defined by more limited guidelines.

Within the boundaries of the food store, *sanitation* refers to all of the factors that may influence the quality, safety, and wholesomeness of the food we sell. From store layout to trash disposal, from the deli counter to the produce storage areas, from the receiving dock to the front end, from food preparation to food packaging—all of the operations in a food store have an impact on sanitation.

When defining terms, it is important to differentiate between *clean* and *sanitary*. The term *clean* refers to the *visible*—dirt on the floor of the produce area, filthy countertops in the fresh-prepared food section, and

Knowledgeable, well-informed employees working in all areas of the food store—from the deli to the meat department—are the lifeblood of any successful store.

accumulated dirt that customers can see. *Sanitary,* on the other hand, refers to the *invisible,* such as microorganisms on preparation equipment in the deli department or those that have collected on improperly cleaned and sanitized equipment and utensils in the meat department. While these microorganisms cannot be seen with the naked eye, they can result in food spoilage, which reduces product shelf life, or worse. If they are harmful microorganisms, they can cause foodborne illnesses. Both of these situations are unacceptable.

Cleanliness reflects directly on a store's image. Shoppers consistently rate the cleanliness of a store as one of their top considerations when choosing a place in which to shop. In recent *Progressive Grocer* surveys, cleanliness was rated as the most important characteristic shoppers used to select their primary food store (*1*). Table 1.1 shows the top 20 characteristics that supermarket shoppers look for when selecting a store.

Table 1.1   What Shoppers Want in a Food Store

Rank	Characteristic	Score	% Ranking Extremely Important
1	Cleanliness	94.3	77
2	Low prices	92.8	76
3	All prices labeled	92.5	75
4	Accurate, pleasant checkout clerks	91.4	67
5	Freshness date marked on products	89.6	68
6	Good produce department	89.0	60
7	Unit-pricing signs on shelves	87.7	66
8	Good meat department	87.1	66
9	Shelves usually kept well stocked	86.4	53
10	Good layout for fast, easy shopping	85.3	49
11	Short wait for checkout	85.1	51
12	Convenient store location	84.8	51
13	Good dairy department	84.5	52
14	Frequent sales or specials	83.9	52
15	Does not run short of items on special	83.4	55
16	Helpful personnel in service departments	83.3	48
17	Good selection of nationally advertised brands	80.2	42
18	Good frozen food department	78.3	41
19	New items I see advertised are available	76.5	38
20	Not usually overcrowded	76.4	35

Source: *Progressive Grocer*, April 1992, p. 44.

A recent survey conducted by the Food Marketing Institute went a few steps further. It indicated that issues of food safety hinged on a number of issues related to food store sanitation—spoilage, germs, improper packaging, and unsanitary handling by supermarket employees (2). A clean, bright store, one in which good-quality food products are attractively displayed and properly handled, is an instant crowd-pleaser and will consistently attract a loyal clientele. Obviously, customer loyalty is one of the most important prizes a supermarket can hope to win. With shoppers spending nearly three-quarters of their food dollar in their primary store, it is also a prize that stores can ill afford to lose through poor sanitary practices (3).

Food store sanitation involves not only cleanliness, it also affects the health of the store's customers. Illnesses that are related to improper sanitary practices in the supermarket can have lasting effects on a store's reputation. Although microorganisms such as bacteria and viruses are invisible, the amount of damage they can cause is huge. An outbreak of salmonella resulting from improperly handled raw poultry products can ruin the reputation of even the most spotless supermarket.

The goal of an effective sanitation program is *to control harmful microorganisms* (ones that cause foodborne illness) throughout the store. To be effective, a sanitation program should be designed, documented, and implemented by food store professionals who have learned to identify trouble spots, to control harmful microorganisms, to educate and train employees in safe food-handling practices, and to monitor sanitation procedures at all times.

As the food industry moves into the twenty-first century, it is undergoing great changes resulting from newly developing technologies, innovative product introductions, and changes in the composition and needs of our consumers. As the food store works to meet the needs of its diverse clientele, many operational aspects of the store must also be brought up-to-date. Maintaining good sanitation practices and assuring the safety of all foods is of paramount importance, especially as fresh and prepared food items become more popular with busy consumers.

The Changing Face of the Grocery Shopper

Today's grocery shopper is well informed, demanding, and aware of the importance of safe and wholesome food products. These knowledgeable shoppers can be single parents, working women, full-time homemakers, senior citizens, male heads of households, or members of ethnic minorities.

Women are still the primary food shoppers, but this will change as more women enter the workforce. By the year 1995, it is predicted that only about one in seven women younger than age 45 will be a full-time homemaker (4). These busy working women will rely more on convenience items to save time.

The interest in food, diet, health, and fitness during the last decade has become a way of life for many Americans. As a result of these lifestyle changes, as well as advances and breakthroughs in nutrition and modern medicine, people are living longer than ever. A male baby born in 1990 has an estimated life expectancy of 71.9 years compared to a male child born in 1950, who had an expected lifespan of only 65.6 years (5). As a result of this phenomenon, many of the supermarket's customers are older Americans who have special dietary needs and food preferences, and who require easy-to-prepare items that are available in smaller portions.

Today's food store must be able to meet the needs of all its customers— working woman, singles, teenagers, seniors, people on the go, people from a variety of ethnic heritages, those interested in nutrition, and those looking for convenience.

The "New" Supermarket

How do all of these changes in the U.S. population affect the food store? The retail food industry has responded to these many changes in consumer trends, behavior, and lifestyles by making more convenience items available to customers and by providing more service and self-service areas in the store.

A deli/fresh-prepared foods department, in which customers can purchase ready-to-eat hot and cold entrées, soups, salads, sliced meats and cheeses, and desserts, is one example of the retail food store's response to the customer's need for convenient, nutritious food. Fish and shellfish departments have also been expanded, and many of them now provide precooked surimi (imitation crab, lobster, or shrimp) products, as well as fish salads and prepared fish entrées like fried haddock or cod. The meat department almost routinely sells premade hamburger patties, kabobs, marinated products, and cuts of meat stuffed with a variety of fillings. Many produce departments have recently begun to provide prewashed, microwave-ready vegetables and sauces as well as ready-to-eat, precut fruits and vegetables. Many stores have eat-in cafés or restaurants and feature ethnic products like Italian, Mexican, or Asian foods. Soup-and-salad bars in stores appeal to busy customers, too. Each of the supermar-

Today's food store reflects the tremendous changes that have taken place in food merchandising since the neighborhood grocery stores of the past.

ket departments, therefore, is responding to customers' needs for convenient foods.

The need for wholesome and safe foods cannot be ignored. The only way in which a supermarket can ensure that food products meet the highest standards of quality and safety is through a comprehensive food-protection program with food store sanitation as a key component. While many retailers think that merchandising, sales, profitability, or customer satisfaction are among their most important concerns, food-safety and sanitation procedures must be in place first. Food sanitation has a direct bearing on profits *and* customer satisfaction. Assuring the safety of foods is not just the job of supervisors, managers, the cleanup crew, or individuals who have the title of Director of Sanitation or Quality Assurance, but is a job that must be carried out by *every store employee.* Each employee—from the person most recently hired to the individual who has been at the store for a long time—plays a key role in assuring the safety and wholesomeness of the foods that are sold.

A well-designed and well-implemented food-protection program can assist retailers in meeting consumer needs. The direct benefits from such a program are increased profits from

- cost reduction possible in labor, materials, and equipment maintenance and replacement
- increased shelf life of products
- reduced product losses
- increased sales through an improved store image

Savings can also result by reducing the risk of great loss due to

- customer foodborne illness, resulting in legal costs, lawsuits, adverse publicity, permanent loss of business, store closure, increased insurance premiums, and bankruptcy
- regulatory-agency inspections, resulting in temporary or permanent closure, fines, or loss of sales from adverse publicity

The Aim of a Comprehensive Food-Protection Program

This book was designed to provide the basic knowledge needed to plan and implement a workable food-protection program, and to assist employees in all departments of the food store in understanding the important role that effective sanitation programs play in today's supermarkets.

Shoppers want foods that meet their changing lifestyles and are willing to pay to make sure that the foods they buy meet their expectations. They want foods that are

- clean and wholesome
- of high quality
- tasty
- nutritious
- safe
- protected from contamination
- readily available
- convenient
- economical

A comprehensive food store sanitation program addresses all the issues of health and safety, and is directed at every department in the store. Its overall aim is to provide customers with foods they can eat with enjoyment and with confidence.

A manager of regulatory compliance for a national supermarket chain said "Sanitation is one of the building blocks of the corporation. A lack of a good sanitation program would allow for costly problems. We have a moral and legal responsibility to deliver a safe, wholesome, and quality product to our customers. You must protect the consumers you serve!" Sanitation is an integral aspect of the running of a supermarket. It is up to you, the food store employee, to ensure that the products you sell are wholesome and safe.

Sanitation Quiz: How Much Do You Know Right Now?

The following quiz is provided as a quick test of your current knowledge. The answers are provided on page 12.

1. To best control the growth of harmful bacteria, the temperature of most perishable products should be kept:
   a. below 40°F, above 110°F (below 4.4°C, above 43.3°C).
   b. below 50°F, above 130°F (below 10.0°C, above 54.4°C).
   c. below 40°F, above 140°F (below 4.4°C, above 60.0°C).
   d. below 32°F, above 98°F (below 0.0°C, above 36.7°C).

2. The shelf life of perishable products can be extended considerably by:
   a. keeping temperatures close to the freezing point.
   b. cleaning and sanitizing processing areas regularly.
   c. processing only what is needed.
   d. all of the above.

3. *Salmonella* is most likely to be associated with:
   a. canned foods.
   b. raw poultry and eggs.
   c. undercooked pork.
   d. infected cuts on the hand.

4. Most foodborne-illness outbreaks in the United States are caused by:
   a. viruses.
   b. parasites.
   c. bacteria.
   d. chemicals.

5. The store is closing in one hour and you have a large kettle of hot soup to put in the cooler. Would you:
   a. pour soup into shallow containers and then refrigerate.
   b. place the kettle directly into the refrigerator.
   c. pour soup into shallow containers, set on the counter to cool for one hour, and then refrigerate.
   d. set the kettle on the counter to cool for one hour and then refrigerate.

6. Which of the following statements is false?
   a. Bacteria cannot go from place to place unless carried.
   b. The food temperature danger zone is between 40°F and 140°F (4.4°C and 60.0°C).
   c. Bacteria multiply by splitting in two.
   d. At freezing temperatures (below 32°F, 0.0°C) bacteria are eventually destroyed.

7. What do the initials HACCP stand for?
   a. Health Assistance Cooperative Company Plan.
   b. Hazard Analysis Critical Control Points.
   c. Headquarters Acceptable Consolidated Cheese Processing.
   d. one of the most popular food employees unions.

8. Products containing harmful food-poisoning microorganisms can always be detected by a:
   a. change in color.
   b. change in odor.
   c. both of the above.
   d. none of the above.

9. Hepatitis A is most likely associated with:
   a. improperly processed canned foods.
   b. undercooked pork.
   c. raw poultry, meat, and eggs.
   d. an infected worker who handles ready-to-eat foods.

10. You have thoroughly cooked a product, cooled it properly, and now want to reheat it. You should:
   a. reheat food until the product is just warm to prevent cooking damage.
   b. reheat food completely to an internal temperature of 165°F (73.9°C).
   c. reheat food completely to an internal temperature of 220°F (104.4°C) for twice the time it took to cook it originally.
   d. reheat food completely to an internal temperature of 140°F (60.0°C).

How well did you score on this quiz?

References

1. "Annual Report of the Grocery Industry." *Progressive Grocer*, April issues.
2. Food Marketing Institute. *1991 Trends*.
3. "60th Annual Report of the Grocery Industry." *Progressive Grocer*, April 1993.
4. Russell, Cheryl. *100 Predictions for the Baby Boom: The Next 50 Years*. New York: Plenum Press, 1987.
5. National Center for Health Statistics. U.S. Department of Health and Human Services and the Metropolitan Life Insurance Company.

Answers to the Quiz:

1.	c
2.	d
3.	b
4.	c
5.	a
6.	d
7.	b
8.	d
9.	d
10.	b

2

The Comprehensive Food Store Safety Assurance Program

With all of the changes in the layout and scope of the modern retail food store, it is no longer sufficient simply to mop the floors and wipe the counters in order to have a "sanitary" food store. A comprehensive food store safety assurance program must be established that presents general guidelines for all departments, as well as specific rules for each area of the store in which food is prepared, processed, displayed, and stored.

If safe food-handling practices are not carried out by all employees, especially when preparing ready-to-eat foods, the results can be disastrous. In the late 1980s, for example, a foodborne-illness outbreak involving at least

27 people was traced to a gourmet delicatessen of a major supermarket chain (1). One of the deli's specialty foods, baked lasagna, was contaminated with *Salmonella enteritidis,* a type of bacteria that caused the outbreak which sent 4 victims to the hospital.

Health department investigators isolated the *Salmonella* from food samples and from eight deli workers who also had become ill. During the investigation, it was learned that the store had a practice of culling cracked eggs from cartons on the shelves and using them in food preparation. This practice probably resulted in the *Salmonella* contamination of the food. The lasagna was cooked "until golden brown and bubbly," and then left at room temperature for some time. The cooking time and temperature were not sufficient to destroy the *Salmonella* that were present, and leaving the lasagna at room temperature allowed the microorganisms to grow.

This outbreak could have been easily prevented if the internal temperature of the lasagna had been checked with a thermometer instead of employees relying simply on the color of the cooked product. The company discontinued the practice of using potentially hazardous culled eggs, changed the cooking directions to include a temperature check, and installed a blast cooler so cooked foods could be cooled rapidly (1).

All food store workers need to handle foods properly, cook foods thoroughly, cool them quickly, and merchandise them safely. By practicing the rules of safe food preparation, foodborne-illness outbreaks can be prevented.

Poor Sanitation Practices

Even the most well intentioned sanitation efforts can be compromised by out-of-date equipment, poor working conditions, untrained or poorly trained associates, or the unwillingness of employees to comply with established sanitation practices and procedures.

Motivating personnel to participate in activities that may be complicated, time-consuming, or tedious may indeed be one of the most difficult challenges facing department heads trying to set up or maintain effective sanitation programs. Low morale, a passive staff, or a half-hearted attitude toward sanitation practices can all undermine the best of efforts. And it is not only the staff that may have a casual approach. Assistant managers or managers who think that cleaning and sanitizing are chores better left to others can also be hard to involve in a comprehensive, store-wide sanitation program.

Some common attitudes (2) that lead to poor sanitation practices include

- complacency
- the excuse of distractions
- a way to economize
- "it will never happen here"
- quick fixes
- pass the buck

These attitudes can create an atmosphere in the store that will undermine any sanitation program. When things are going well, *complacency*, or the feeling of self-satisfaction, can occur and people sometimes forget about how important sanitation is to food quality and safety. When people are complacent, they often fail to pay attention to details, mistakes are often made, and problems quickly result. Sanitation tasks must be performed properly and routinely.

The *excuse of distractions* is also typical. Although the department's personnel realize that sanitation programs must be followed, they may look for excuses to invest time in other aspects of the day-to-day job and

Good Sanitation   **Safe Food**

Food store associates are the vital link between good sanitation and safe food.

leave important tasks undone. Sanitation practices may not be the most glamorous part of their daily routines, and having distractions makes it easy to run out of time before tending to sanitation tasks.

Some department managers may try to find *a way to economize* on sanitation by "cutting corners" and not following through on sanitation practices. This is certainly a very poor way to economize. Product will spoil more quickly, customers will become dissatisfied, the risk of causing foodborne disease will increase, and the few dollars saved on sanitation procedures will never balance with the hundreds or possibly thousands of dollars that will be lost.

Another false perception that stands in the way of a comprehensive sanitation program is the attitude that "*it will never happen here.*" This kind of gambling with the store's reputation and the department's profits is very dangerous. Just because the department has had a good record to date does not necessarily mean that it will continue to operate without problems. Sanitation is a continuous and demanding job, and in order for it to be effective, it must be done routinely and properly.

Once a sanitation protocol and standard operating procedures have been established, managers and employees must be reminded to follow them completely. If, for example, a display case is in need of temperature adjustment, do not allow department personnel to fix it themselves. It is important to call the store's electrician or engineer to check out the temperature controls and adjust them properly. If there is an insect or rodent problem in the store, the first reaction is to have an associate take care of it. Oftentimes modifications and *quick fixes* by nonspecialists can only lead to more problems. These efforts delay getting specialists involved who have the knowledge and expertise to solve the problem quickly and efficiently.

Sanitation must begin with the store manager and department heads, who should be familiar with all aspects of the program that have been established for their areas of responsibility. It is not sufficient for individuals to *pass the buck* and let the next person down the line take care of a specific situation or problem—the store manager is ultimately responsible. Only when the manager is satisfied that all associates in a department are properly trained, understand all of the principles of sanitation, and can perform sanitation tasks correctly can the delegation of specific tasks to others take place.

Vigilance is necessary at all times. All sanitation procedures must be checked and double-checked to see that they are being carried out properly and at the appropriate times. It is only in this way that all store personnel can be reminded of the importance of performing daily sanitation practices properly and that a department's integrity can be maintained (2).

Elements of an Effective Food-Protection Program

All employees in the food-preparation areas of a retail food store should be directly involved in implementing measures in which foods are processed, prepared, packaged, and displayed under strict sanitary conditions. A well-organized food-protection program can only be effective if all employees are actively involved in it.

Successful food-safety and sanitation programs have been implemented by a number of food stores, and all of these systems have some key points in common (3).

Total management participation. Any food-protection program, no matter how well organized, will fail without the support, total commitment, and involvement of top management. Everyone in the company, from the president down, needs to recognize the importance of food protection and the vital role that sanitation plays in it. This important message and attitude must be conveyed to all employees.

A Hazard Analysis Critical Control Point (HACCP)-based food safety assurance program for the entire store. HACCP, which is discussed in more detail in chapter 6, presents a new way of looking at food safety by identifying hazards, determining the critical points at which food-safety

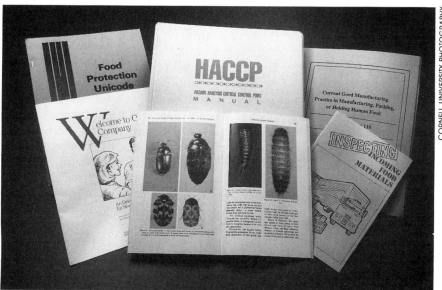

A company's sanitation manual, industry publications such as HACCP manuals, and copies of food-safety-related government regulations should be readily available to store managers and associates.

problems can occur, carefully monitoring these points, and verifying that product safety is being assured.

A company sanitation manual. Uniform and standard operations guidelines and procedures are essential. A sanitation manual is a "how-to" book that clearly states and illustrates what is expected, what specific jobs are to be done, and the frequency with which they should be performed.

A formal, documented education and training program. Sanitation programs can fall apart simply because there is no organized education and training program designed to acquaint new employees or refresh veteran staff with what is expected of them. A training program of continuing employee education can update knowledge and skills, provide important job information, improve communications, instill enthusiasm, and improve motivation. Top management should allow enough time for educating and training associates in the principles of food safety and sanitation. Remember that safe food depends on people who

- produce and process it
- transport and distribute it
- prepare it

Careful personal hygiene. Good health, personal habits, and work habits are vital to the safety of foods. The facts concerning personal hygiene, which are covered in chapter 9, should be clearly understood by all who work with food. The primary goal of the training program is to have associates throughout the store understand the vital link between good personal hygiene and the safety of food.

Effective communication and personnel relations. Almost by definition, an organization needs effective communications to prosper. Without it, the organization is prey to inaccurate messages, rumors, misunderstandings, and related problems. A comprehensive food-protection program can only be carried out when all employees are able to communicate with each other concerning the program's protocols and directives.

Proper supervision. Knowledgeable, well-trained supervisors are one of the most important elements of an effective food-safety and sanitation program. They can detect and correct problems while providing encouragement and instructions that can prevent hazardous situations from arising and recurring.

Effective pest control. When left uncontrolled, insects, rodents, and birds can enter a store and contaminate large volumes of food. A well-organized control program should keep pests out, reduce or remove their food and shelter, and be prepared to deal with them safely, quickly, and efficiently if they do manage to enter the store (see chapters 10 and 11).

INFLIGHT FOODSERVICE ASSOCIATION

Proper cleaning and sanitizing of equipment is an important component of an effective food safety assurance program.

Good working conditions and equipment. It is important that the store environment is properly equipped and that employees work together to produce high-quality, wholesome, and safe products (see chapter 12). Employees who feel that they are part of a winning team will excel and will be willing to go beyond what is normally expected (4).

Good Manufacturing Practices (GMPs). These are a collection of all of the correct procedures for preparing food that need to be followed in a food store. They should be part of a company sanitation manual, and they are also the law. During inspections, federal, state, and local regulatory agencies look for violations in food store manufacturing practices (see chapter 13 for more information on inspections).

Self-inspection procedures. A small group of knowledgeable people from several different departments in the store should develop and use a checklist of items to carefully inspect every department and area of the facility (see chapters 14 and 15). Vigilance is one of the best ways to catch problems and make any corrections before the problems become serious. Self-inspections, coupled with careful monitoring of critical points, will help assure the safety of foods. It is also a good way to train new staff and bring veteran food store employees up-to-date on the latest sanitation techniques and practices.

An attitude of respect for food products. After working in a food store for a few months, employees can forget that food is perishable and susceptible to harmful microorganisms. When people who work with food respect the product by realizing its value to the well-being of the store, their jobs, and customers, everyone will profit.

Customer satisfaction. The ultimate goal of every food store associate is to make sure that all of the store's customers are provided with safe and wholesome food products at all times. After all, customers are the main reason for a store's success. They must be assured that foods are handled, stored, processed, and prepared in a safe and sanitary manner, and that associates always have the health and safety of the customers in mind.

Conclusions

A workable comprehensive food safety assurance program is integral to every supermarket, whether it is a small, independently owned store or a component of a large chain. It is important to have a well-organized and effective sanitation program in place. A professional image is important, but the health and safety of customers, and the profitability of individual food departments are even more significant.

Food safety must be a concern of everyone in the company—from the chief executive officer of the chain to the part-time maintenance staff. The importance of food store sanitation should be communicated to every employee in the store. Only by working together on food-safety assurance can the necessary store-wide program be implemented and kept in place. Its importance to the health and welfare of everyone—consumers and store employees alike—cannot be emphasized enough.

References

1. "Salmonella Strikes Gourmet Market." *Food Protection Report* 3, no. 5 (May 1987).
2. Material in this section has been adapted from the *Cornell/NAWGA Warehouse Sanitation Program,* 1983.
3. Gravani, R. B., "Sanitation in the Food Industry." Food Science Fact Sheet 128. Department of Food Science, Cornell University, Ithaca, NY, 1983.
4. Conklin, D. M., and R. B. Gravani. "Welcome to Our Company: An Orientation Guide for New Employees." Institute of Food Science Fact Sheet 2. Cornell Cooperative Extension, Ithaca, NY, 1986.

3

Sanitation and Store Profits

Ensuring the quality and safety of the food sold through the retail supermarket outlet should always be the primary motivating factor in setting up sanitation systems in any area of the store. Equally important, however, is the impact food safety can have on a store's profits. Some of the most profitable departments in a food store, such as the deli/fresh-prepared, seafood, and meat departments, are those that may be most vulnerable to the dangers of poor sanitation.

Imagine discovering that the shrimp salad your seafood associates made yesterday at a net cost to the supermarket of $1.50 per pound has begun to spoil. Or that last week's "great buy" on scrod didn't attract quite enough customers, and the store still has more than 25 pounds of it on ice in the back room. Or five cases of milk left on the loading dock "for immediate refrigeration" were neglected in the confusion of a hot, busy day. Any one of these situations, which can have a devastating effect on store profits, can occur almost every day in some store, somewhere in the country.

As an economic issue, food store sanitation is gaining in importance. While some managers may still be reluctant to implement store-wide food-safety and sanitation programs, incorrectly thinking that such programs use up employees' valuable time and the store's financial resources, the issues of food quality and safety are forcing all food stores to take another look at this important situation.

For many food stores, the key to an effective food-protection program is not the purchase of new or more modern equipment. Instead, it involves establishing new procedures, educating and training all store employees in their implementation, and following up to be sure that they are being used routinely and correctly.

Sanitation in the Individual Departments of the Food Store

The retail food store is an important step in the delivery of safe, wholesome food products from their source (farmers, ranchers, or fishermen around the world) to the consumer. Whether that delivery chain is long, the marketing of shrimp from Thailand, for example, or short, as in the case of selling grapes grown by a local farmer, procedures to maintain the quality and safety of the product must be implemented every step of the way.

Different departments must implement different procedures based on the nature of the food being handled. Some general principles do carry through from department to department, such as general cleanliness, the personal-hygiene habits of store employees, and basic sanitation procedures for utensils and equipment. However, some departments are involved in food preparation as well as retailing (deli, fresh-prepared, fish, bakery, meat), while others market items that are processed elsewhere (dairy products) or are sold in their unprocessed state (produce). Despite these differences, profits in each of these departments can be affected by poor sanitation practices.

Studies have shown that in many instances the lack of good sanitation practices can be economically devastating. A study conducted by food-marketing specialists at Michigan State University, for example, highlighted losses in several supermarket department categories—meat, produce, dairy, dry grocery, frozen foods, bakery, and deli (1). The study pointed to a number of factors that contribute to product loss, the most important of which were directly related to sanitation:

- inadequate temperature control
- improper food handling

Sanitation and Meat Department Profits

Studies on the economic effectiveness of sanitation practices can take years to complete, and for that reason, it is often difficult to have the most up-to-date figures. A number of practical studies investigating the impact of sanitation on profitability in the meat department of retail stores have been conducted. These studies will be discussed later in this chapter.

Just as with any other department, the meat department must present an image of cleanliness and freshness. A good meat department, in fact, is one of the top ten criteria shoppers consider when choosing to shop at a specific food store (2). Consumers have a set of preconceived notions about the freshness of the meat they buy. To the shopper, freshness is indicated by a bright red color in the lean of the meat and a clean white color in the fat. Meat that is darker—dark-red or gray—will be rejected for being "old" or "past its prime." The prepacked cuts of meat that have discolored, therefore, will have to be pulled and reworked or discarded, and this financial loss (shrinkage) must be absorbed by the department.

Every time product is pulled and reworked, there is a substantial economic loss. More product must be trimmed and discarded, more trays and overwrap film are used, and more employee time is needed to get the product back on the shelves.

The losses can be astoundingly high. It is estimated that the total annual industry loss from meat spoilage and reworks is over $1 billion. About 50 percent of this loss ($500 million) could have been avoided with good sanitation management. Retailers *can* save money as a result of improved sanitation procedures. A brief example will help to illustrate this point.

Let's say that a meat department loses about $10,000 through spoilage and rewrap costs. At a 1 percent net profit rate, it would take an extra $1 million in meat sales to make up for this loss! It is certainly better to save this cost through the use of good sanitation and product-handling practices than to try to increase sales to compensate for the loss.

Improved sanitation in the meat department can also reap other benefits. The control of microbial growth that causes the discoloration and spoilage of meat products also extends the shelf life of these foods. This longer shelf life not only reduces rework and discard losses, but affords more flexibility in scheduling production time and allocating display space in the meat cases.

Meat departments—both service and self-service—that present an image of cleanliness and freshness will attract customers and contribute substantially to store profits.

While there are several factors that cause meat spoilage, bacteria are of primary concern (3). Some important facts about the bacterial spoilage of meat are listed below.

- Bacteria (microbes) cause spoilage.
- The more bacteria present, the faster the meat spoils.
- Meat spoilage is related to time and temperature.
- Bacteria grow most rapidly at warm temperatures (60° to 125°F; 15.6° to 51.7°C).
- The warmer the temperature, the faster the bacteria grow and multiply.
- The faster the bacteria grow and multiply, the faster the meat spoils and the shorter the shelf life.

Through the use of proper sanitation and product-handling procedures in the meat department, product quality can be maintained, meat spoilage can be reduced, and shelf life can be extended.

Meat Department Sanitation Studies

The Cornell University Study

One of the most recent studies of the meat department was undertaken at Cornell University in 1986 (4). This study demonstrated that there is an important relationship between the sanitation knowledge of employees and profitability in the supermarket meat department.

The primary way in which a store's profits are enhanced by proper sanitation is through a reduction of the losses incurred by spoilage of the meat products. When meat products become contaminated with bacteria as a result of improper sanitary procedures, the department head must assume the responsibility of discarding the ruined product. Given the high cost of meat—even at the wholesale level—a well-designed and well-implemented sanitation program is crucial to keeping profits high and minimizing losses from spoilage.

This Cornell study made the following important points:

- On-the-job experience *does* play a role in employee sanitation knowledge. This kind of experience, however, can only be gained through both formal *and* informal education and training programs.

PIGGLY WIGGLY, INC.

Proper product-handling procedures in the meat department help to maintain product quality and extend shelf life.

- Increased awareness of the importance of sanitation improves employee attitudes about following sanitation guidelines and also motivates them to correctly carry out sanitation procedures.
- Even though managers had a good understanding of sanitation principles, the full- and part-time meat department employees did not always possess this knowledge.

It is essential that managers be educated in the principles of food sanitation and that they be given the opportunity to properly communicate this information to staff members. The Cornell University study pointed out that there is a positive connection between department profits and the manager's level of sanitation knowledge. By ensuring that all employees are also aware of the importance of sanitation, the department's profits can increase even more.

The University of Missouri Study

The Cornell University study is the latest in a series of studies over the past three decades that have illustrated the relationship between sanitation knowledge, good sanitation procedures, and store profits. In the early 1960s, a team of meat scientists from the University of Missouri Cooperative Extension Service, under contract to the U.S. Department of

Agriculture (USDA), undertook a study on the effects of improved sanitation programs in two similar midwestern supermarket meat departments, one an independent and the other part of a national chain (5).

Specific areas of the meat departments of these two stores were monitored for several weeks, and then recommendations for improvement were made. The areas that were monitored were

- temperature in storage, processing, and display areas
- general operational procedures
- number and value of all fresh meats packaged, displayed, and rewrapped
- bacterial counts on products and equipment

After changes in some procedures were made, the departments were again studied for several weeks to see if any improvements could be noted. The thorough study of these two stores brought to light a host of poor sanitation practices, many of which led to lower profits. Among the changes made were the following:

- In one store, the meat department appeared to be relatively clean. Cleaning was done on a daily basis; equipment, however, was not dismantled. Hot water (an inadequate supply) and household bleach were being used. Although the department appeared to be clean, bacteria counts were relatively high. It should be noted that at this point the store was only three years old and the department had relatively new equipment.

  The study recommended the implementation of a daily cleaning program. Cleaning included dismantling saws, cubing machines, mills, and mixers, laying all knives on tabletops, and cleaning with cleaning and sanitizing agents premixed with hot water. Equipment was left to drain dry.

- In both stores, many of the problems stemmed from improper temperature settings in storage rooms, coolers, processing rooms, and display cases. When proper temperature adjustments were made, products had a longer shelf life and the bacteria present had less chance to grow.

It is a scientific fact that the bacteria which cause red meat to spoil grow slowly at temperatures under 40°F (4.4°C). When approaching the freezing point, growth is very slow. The information in Figure 3.1 clearly shows that the shelf life of fresh meat can be extended by lowering the temperature. Since meat freezes at about 28°F (–2.2°C), the ideal temperature to maximize shelf life is between 29°F and 32°F (–1.7°C and 0.0°C).

Figure 3.1   Fresh Meat Shelf Life

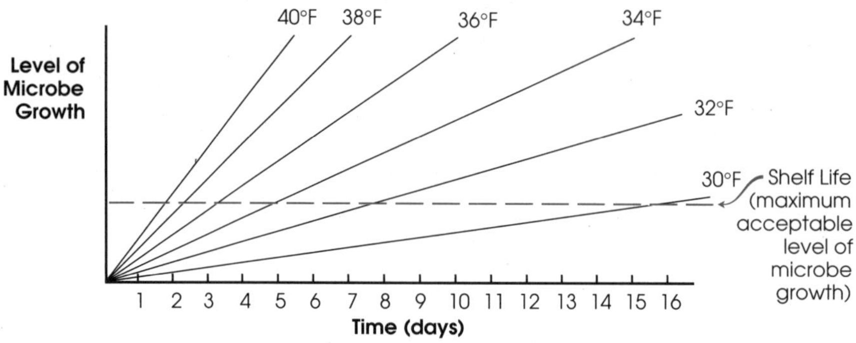

Source: Super Market Institute, Inc., "The War Against the Microbes," *SMI Sanitation System*, 1969.

From a practical standpoint, this can usually be accomplished in a storage and preholding cooler.

The study pointed out that another very important component of a good sanitation program is the thorough and frequent cleaning and sanitizing of all equipment and utensils that come in contact with meat products. Discoloration and spoilage of meat occur when meat surfaces are exposed to the bacteria that cause spoilage, primarily during slaughter, handling, cutting, and packaging. Prior to that time, the muscles of healthy animals are essentially free of microorganisms. The introduction of bacteria on meat surfaces is caused by air, equipment and utensils, people, as well as a number of other factors.

The study also concluded *that education of department personnel in basic sanitation knowledge is perhaps the most important single component of a store-wide sanitation program.* Without adequate education and training, employees could not be expected to understand the importance of sanitation and its relationship to product quality and safety. Only when they understood the importance of factors such as strict temperature control and thorough and frequent cleaning and sanitizing of equipment and utensils would they then be able to correctly perform and monitor these sanitation practices in the department.

Economically speaking, the University of Missouri study also demonstrated a direct correlation between good sanitary practices and department profits. Store A, for example, lost $230.56 in 1965 dollars weekly ($651.79 in 1989 dollars) to product loss from prepackaged meat pullouts. After the study, these losses were cut by 80 percent per week. In Store B, the before figure was $89.55 in 1965 dollars ($253.16 in 1989 dollars), and the losses were cut by one-third per week after it adopted the measures put forth in the study. The implementation of a well-designed sanitation program *can* reduce product losses.

The New Mexico State University Study

In 1967, scientists with the Cooperative Extension Service at New Mexico State University used the University of Missouri study as a basis to examine the workings of one specific supermarket meat department (6). This study made the following suggestions:

- Clean and sanitize thoroughly.
- Clean and sanitize work surfaces and equipment often (at a minimum, once every four hours).
- Use the correct detergent and sanitizer in the correct proportions.
- Properly educate and train employees, and closely monitor their work habits.
- Move product from the cooler to the display case as soon as possible.

When the store that participated in this study implemented these suggestions, the overall result was a reduction in the number of microorganisms on its equipment and in meat products. Bacterial counts in the meat products were reduced by 88 percent to 99 percent. By cutting down on the microorganisms that came in contact with the meat during preparation and packaging, the product's shelf life was extended and losses for the department were reduced. The study concluded that

- Good sanitation management can reduce the number of microorganisms that cause meat discoloration and spoilage.
- Savings in labor time, materials cost, and product loss more than make up for the additional cost of using an effective detergent and sanitizer.
- The case life of fresh meats can be extended economically.
- Lengthening shelf life provides greater management flexibility, both in allocating space in the display case and in merchandising, which ultimately results in greater sales and the possibility of increasing the share of total store sales for the meat department.

The Rutgers University Study

A third study, also conducted in 1967, reinforced the findings of the two earlier studies (7, 8). The University of Missouri method was again used to examine the workings of a single retail store's meat department. The Rutgers University study also considered labor savings and losses due to change of product. For instance, if steak had to be converted to hamburger for the product to be sold, the loss of profit (steak being more expensive than ground meat) and the added labor (unwrapping the product, reprocessing it, and rewrapping it) were also taken into account.

As a result of the improvements carried out by the meat department employees during the study,

- Rewraps were reduced by 58 percent, from 12 percent to 5 percent of product value.
- Discards were reduced by 84 percent, from 392 items to 64 items.
- Change in product form was reduced by 61 percent.

Once again, this study proved that proper sanitary practices can have a direct impact on profits. The store that participated in the study was able to save $8,808 in 1967 dollars annually ($24,812 in 1989 dollars) simply by adopting the sanitation procedures suggested by the researchers.

The Cornell University Deli Department Study

The meat department is obviously not the only area in a supermarket where profitability is compromised by poor sanitation practices. The deli/fresh-prepared section, with gross margins of 43.3 percent, accounted for a median 4.5 percent of total store sales and contributed a median 18.6 percent to total store profits in 1992 (9). Imagine the havoc one episode of foodborne illness in the deli department could wreak on these highly profitable numbers!

A 1992 Cornell University study demonstrated the relationship between employee food-handling practices, sanitation knowledge, and profitability in supermarket deli departments. This study included a 47-question survey that was administered to over 780 deli workers in a large chain-store operation (10). The survey focused on training, food sanitation, deli food-handling practices, spoilage and product loss, and food safety.

The results showed a *direct* correlation between employee food-safety and sanitation knowledge, and deli department profitability. Employees who scored well worked in deli departments that had higher net profit percentages. Scores also increased with education, on-the-job training, and employee status—from part-timers to managers.

The lessons learned from this study are important, especially as the deli department continues to be one of the more profitable areas in the retail

INFLIGHT FOODSERVICE ASSOCIATION

Proper temperature control is vital to product quality and safety.

food store. As the researcher pointed out, "The full potential of training cannot be realized unless it is conducted on a regular and continuing basis. Employees should be taught the theories as well as the associated safe food-handling practices."

Conclusions

These studies, as well as other independent research, demonstrate a direct correlation between sanitation practices and store profits. Factors such as temperature control in all stages of meat preparation and display, and the thorough and frequent cleaning and sanitizing of all equipment and utensils have a direct impact on the quality of the product being sold. While these measures were found to be important, equally essential is the proper education and training of store employees on basic sanitation knowledge.

Although the majority of sanitation studies have been carried out in meat departments, the results can just as easily be applied to other areas of the food store. Any department in which fresh food is handled can show the same kinds of profits and losses depending on the type of sanitation program it follows.

References

1. Pierson, T. R., J. W. Allen, and E. W. McLaughlin. *Food Losses: Overview and Summary.* Agricultural Economics Report 421. Department of Agricultural Economics, Michigan State University, 1982.
2. "60th Annual Report of the Grocery Industry." *Progressive Grocer,* April 1993.
3. Judge, M. D., E. D. Aberle, J. C. Forest, H. B. Hedrick, and R. A. Merkel. *Principles of Meat Science.* Dubuque, IA: Kendall/Hunt Publishing Company, 1989.
4. Edmiston, B. B., R. B. Gravani, and E. W. McLaughlin. "Sanitation Knowledge as It Relates to Employee Attitudes and Meat Department Profits in a Retail Supermarket Chain." Master of Professional Studies project report, Cornell University, 1986.
5. Nauman, H. D., W. C. Stringer, and P. F. Goulds. *Guidelines for Handling Prepackaged Meat in Retail Stores.* Manual 64. University of Missouri, Cooperative Extension Service, Columbia, MO, 1965.
6. Sneed, R., A. R. Stasch, and W. J. Vastine. *Costs and Returns of Improved Sanitation Management in a Retail Meat Market.* New Mexico State University, Las Cruces, NM, 1968.
7. Perkins, F. A. *Economic Impact of a Coordinated Sanitation Management Program on Improving the Efficiency of a Retail Meat Operation.* EIR 30. Rutgers University, Cooperative Extension Service, New Brunswick, NJ, 1969, 1972.
8. Perkins, F. A. "Showing a Retailer That Meat Sanitation Pays—An Economic Approach." *American Journal of Agricultural Economics* 51, no. 5 (1969): 1259.
9. Litwak, D., and Nancy Maline. "11th Annual Deli Operations Review." *Supermarket Business,* February 1993.
10. Thomas, Gene A. "The Impact of Employee Food Sanitation Knowledge and Handling Practices on Supermarket Deli Profitability." Master's thesis, Cornell University, Ithaca, NY, 1992.

4

The Microbial World

When retailers discuss the quality, safety, and wholesomeness of foods, the subject of microorganisms quickly surfaces. Microorganisms are "small living things" and include bacteria, yeasts, molds, viruses, and even a few parasites. In this chapter you will learn about the science of microbiology—that is, "the study of small living things"—and how microbiology relates to food quality, safety, customer satisfaction, and profitability.

Microorganisms are all around us and many carry out a number of processes that are vital to human society (1). The agriculture system, the health-care industry, and the food industry depend in many ways on microbial activities.

33

Microbes in Food

Microbes play several very important roles in foods—some are beneficial and are responsible for fermented dairy, meat, vegetable, and other products that we enjoy. Other microorganisms can cause food to spoil, and a small percentage are harmful to us (2). Some microorganisms are inert and do not have any effect on foods because they are unable to grow in them (3).

Fermented Foods

Beneficial microbes are used in the manufacture of many foods and produce desirable changes in these products. These microorganisms impart characteristic flavors and textures to a wide variety of fermented foods, including yogurt, buttermilk, sour cream, and cheeses, as well as sauerkraut, pickles, some sausages, beer, wine, and breads (2, 3, 4).

Milk is converted into yogurt, sour cream, cheeses, and several other products by the action of certain bacteria that are added during manufacture. Also, cabbage is converted into sauerkraut by bacterial action. Yeasts are used in the production of beer, wine, and bread, while molds are used in the manufacture of several mold-ripened cheeses. Very specific types of microbes are used and the environmental conditions are carefully controlled to produce the desired product characteristics.

Food Spoilage

Other microorganisms cause food to spoil (2, 3, 4, 5). Foods are composed of a combination of proteins, carbohydrates, and fats, and all of these compounds can support the growth of a wide variety of microbes. Once microorganisms find their way into foods and are given the proper conditions for growth, they can act in two ways: (1) they break down or degrade food constituents and use these products to grow and (2) they produce substances (metabolic by-products) such as acid, gas, or slime in a food as a result of their growth. Since microorganisms can ferment sugar and break down proteins, fats, and complex carbohydrates, the first signs of food spoilage are the undesirable changes in appearance, color, texture, odor, or flavor of the product. Sour milk, mold growth on cheddar cheese, the metallic taste of fruit juices, and slime produced on meats are all examples of microbial spoilage. Spoiled food is usually decomposed and not acceptable for human consumption.

Food spoilage is of concern to retailers, especially when it occurs in products in the perishable departments like deli, dairy, meat, or seafood. When spoiled food is discarded, profits are lost. Food spoilage can also affect customer relations because customers who purchase foods that are spoiled may be very reluctant to shop at that store again.

Foodborne Illness

Certain disease-producing microorganisms, known as pathogens, can cause foodborne illness in humans (3). These illnesses are characterized by the general symptoms of gastrointestinal distress—nausea, vomiting, diarrhea, and discomfort. Foodborne illness can range from very mild to life-threatening, depending on the specific microorganism involved. Contrary to what many people believe, the growth of most foodborne pathogens does not necessarily produce any noticeable changes in the appearance, color, odor, texture, or flavor of the food. Only laboratory testing can determine whether harmful bacteria are present in the food. Remember, there is a difference between spoiled food and food that will cause foodborne illness. Since the safety of foods is very important to food retailers, the causes and prevention of foodborne illnesses will be discussed more thoroughly in chapter 5.

Fortunately, most microbes are not harmful to humans and, in fact, most microorganisms cause no harm at all (1). In the retail food industry, the primary concern with microorganisms is to reduce the spoilage of foods and to prevent foodborne illness. So, sanitation, microbiology, food quality, and safety are *very* closely interrelated and should be a top priority for every individual working in food retailing.

Let's look at the different types of microorganisms, discuss factors that influence their growth, and focus on their specific importance to food retailers.

Bacteria

Bacteria are of primary concern in all segments of the food industry. Unlike animals and plants that are composed of many cells, bacteria are single-celled organisms (1, 2). Each bacterium is self-sufficient. Bacteria come in a variety of shapes, including those that are round, rod-like, and spiral, and their size varies somewhat. But one thing is for sure, they are *very* small. Since they are about 1/25,000th of an inch long, they are impossible to see without a microscope and must be magnified about 1,000 times to be identified. To illustrate how small they really are, consider that 1,000 bacteria could be placed end to end across the period at the end of this sentence. Because bacteria are invisible to the naked eye, their existence and activities are often overlooked or ignored until problems occur.

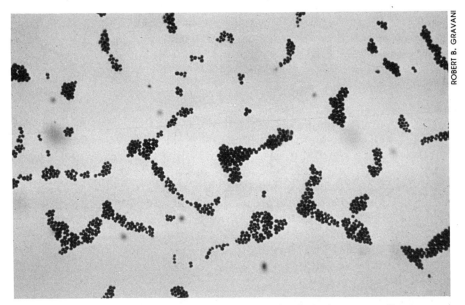

A typical example of what bacteria look like under the microscope. These round bacteria are stained with a blue dye to make them more visible.

A close-up photo of a single bacterial cell that was taken with a powerful electron microscope. Note the thread-like structures that are used by the bacterium for motion.

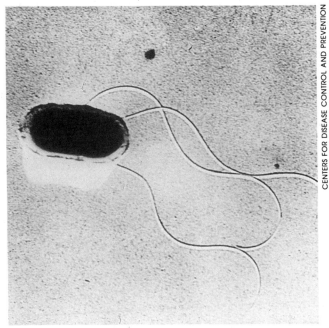

Bacteria are found everywhere—in the air, soil, and water, on the skin, and in the intestinal tracts of humans and animals. They are found on the skins and peels of fruits and vegetables, and on the hulls of grain, the shells of nuts, and on insects and rodents. They are also found on all unsanitized food-processing equipment and utensils, as well as on the hands, skin, hair, and clothing of people (4).

Bacteria get from place to place by "hitchhiking." Let's look at an example of how bacteria are transferred from one place to another. A tray that has been used to hold raw chicken and is not properly cleaned and sanitized contains millions of bacteria. If this equipment is used to hold some ready-to-eat foods like sliced luncheon meats, the bacteria are transferred to these products. If the foods are temperature-abused—that is, kept for long periods at room temperature or inadequately refrigerated—a foodborne-illness outbreak can occur after the foods are consumed.

The transfer of bacteria can be reduced through attention to such details as good personal hygiene, proper food-handling practices, cleaning and sanitizing of all equipment and utensils, and good temperature control. More information on these important subjects will be discussed later in the book.

Bacterial Reproduction and Growth

Bacteria grow and reproduce in a very interesting way. When environmental conditions are favorable, the bacterial cell enlarges and then divides into two cells; these two cells divide into four cells; these four cells divide into eight cells; and the process continues in this fashion (1).

The division results in a doubling of bacterial cells every time it occurs, so there can be a tremendous increase in the number of bacteria. If you started with one bacterial cell (and you very rarely, if ever, start with only one), after 12 hours, there would be billions of bacteria present. The rate at which bacteria grow is different for each type of organism and is affected by many environmental factors. Under favorable conditions, some bacteria can double in as short a time as 8 minutes, while others can take days. The average time for most bacteria to double in number is about 20 to 30 minutes when growth conditions are favorable. Figure 4.1 illustrates the process of cell division and the tremendous numbers of bacteria that can result.

Spores

Certain bacteria have the ability to produce a special structure, called a spore, that serves as a means of protection against unfavorable environmental conditions (1, 6). A spore is a thick-walled structure that is formed

Figure 4.1 Bacterial Reproduction

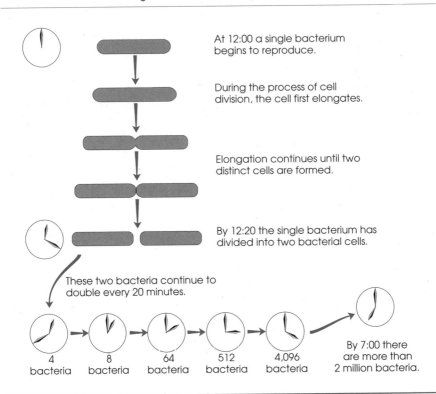

At 12:00 a single bacterium begins to reproduce.

During the process of cell division, the cell first elongates.

Elongation continues until two distinct cells are formed.

By 12:20 the single bacterium has divided into two bacterial cells.

These two bacteria continue to double every 20 minutes.

4 bacteria

8 bacteria

64 bacteria

512 bacteria

4,096 bacteria

By 7:00 there are more than 2 million bacteria.

within the bacterial cell when unfavorable conditions occur. The spores are an inactive or dormant form of actively growing, vegetative bacterial cells, and they are able to remain alive for many years. When growth conditions are favorable, the spores change back into active, vegetative bacterial cells.

Let's consider an example. When a large pot of stew is prepared in the deli, the cooking process destroys growing vegetative bacterial cells and some of the spores that are present. However, heat-resistant spores can survive. These spores can survive in the product and cause no problem as long as the food is handled properly. If the large quantity of stew is temperature-abused—left at room temperatures for a long period of time, slowly cooled, or inadequately refrigerated—the spores will grow into active, vegetative cells that could cause foodborne illness. So, to prevent problems, the food must be adequately cooked, quickly cooled, properly refrigerated, and rapidly reheated to proper temperatures. Spores are more resistant to heat, drying, freezing, and chemicals than vegetative bacterial cells.

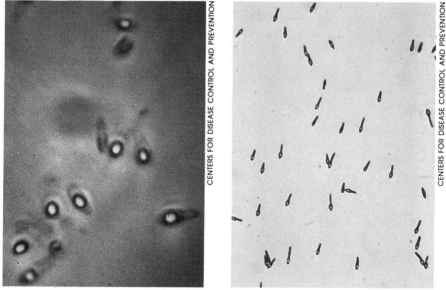

The round spores can be seen within these rod-shaped vegetative bacterial cells.

Pattern of Growth

Whenever bacteria are introduced into a food and conditions are favorable, the organisms will follow a distinct pattern of growth (1, 2, 6, 7). This characteristic pattern is called a bacterial growth curve, which can be seen in Figure 4.2.

When bacteria come in contact with a food, growth does not begin immediately. As the organisms adapt to their new environment, it takes some time for them to adjust their cellular machinery to break down food constituents, absorb the nutrients that are present in the food, and grow. This portion of the growth curve is known as the *lag phase*. The length of this lag phase depends on the numbers of bacteria present as well as on several environmental factors, including the moisture and temperature of the food. By reducing the initial number of microorganisms through the use of good sanitary practices, the lag phase can be extended, and entry into the next phase can be deferred.

As the bacteria begin to absorb nutrients, they grow rapidly and increase in numbers. This phase of maximum growth is known as the *log phase* and is affected by the number and characteristics of the microorganisms, as well as environmental factors such as temperature and nutrient availability.

Figure 4.2 A Bacterial Growth Curve

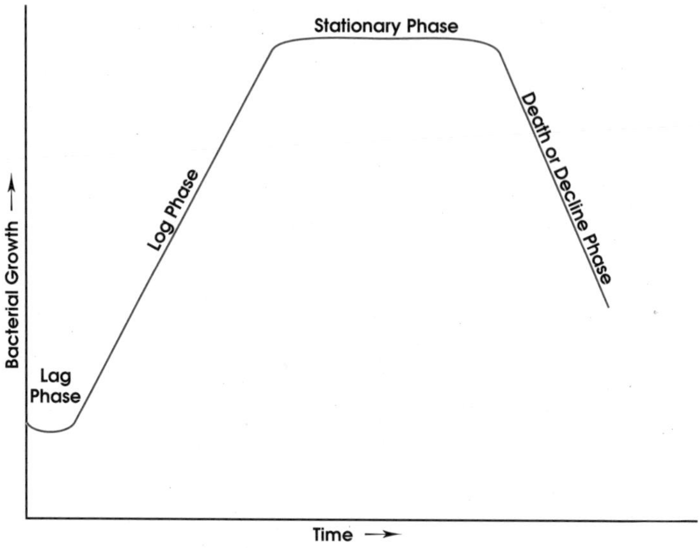

The *stationary phase* occurs when growth slows down and tapers off. This is due to the depletion of nutrients or the production of inhibitory substances by the bacteria. In this phase no growth occurs, but many cell functions continue.

The last phase, known as the *death (or decline) phase,* occurs when nutrients are exhausted and/or metabolic by-products build up to inhibitory levels and cause cell death.

It is important to keep bacteria in the lag phase as long as possible and not allow them to grow rapidly. This can be accomplished by minimizing bacterial contamination, thereby reducing the number of bacteria present, and through proper temperature control.

Factors Affecting Bacterial Growth

There are several very important factors that affect the growth of bacteria in foods (2, 3). These factors include nutrients, moisture, temperature, pH (acidity/alkalinity), and oxygen.

Nutrients

All bacteria require a source of nutrients to live and grow. Food constituents such as carbohydrates, protein, fats, vitamins, minerals, and other factors provide the nutrients necessary for bacterial growth. The composition of foods influences the types of microorganisms that will grow, as well as the products that are produced during growth (8).

Moisture

Bacteria need water to dissolve the food they use for energy and growth. This moisture allows the food to get into the bacterial cells, is used for the many chemical reactions necessary for life and growth, and allows waste products to be eliminated (3). The availability of water in food is described as *water activity* and is identified by the letters A_w. Pure water has a water activity of 1.00, while most fresh foods (like fruits and vegetables, meats, poultry, and fish) have water activity values that are in the range of 0.98 to over 0.99 (3, 6, 8). As the water activity is lowered so that less water is available ($A_w < 0.85$), the ability of bacteria to grow is reduced.

Foods that have low water activities are dried foods like cereals, flour, and dried fruits, and foods that are preserved with high levels of sugar or salt, like jams and jellies (3, 6). Most of the bacteria that cause spoilage and foodborne illness cannot grow in these products. Foods like meats, fish, poultry, salads, and other products handled in fresh-prepared food departments in the store have water activities that will easily support the growth of most bacteria. These products must be handled carefully.

Temperature

Temperature is one of the most important environmental factors affecting the ability of bacteria to grow and survive. Bacteria are capable of growing over a wide range of temperatures and are usually classified according to the temperature at which they grow (1, 3, 7, 8).

- *Psychrotrophs* are cold-tolerant bacteria that are capable of growing at temperatures ranging from 32° to 45°F (0.0° to 7.2°C). However, optimum growth of these organisms occurs at temperatures from 68° to 86°F (20.0° to 30.0°C). Most of these bacteria are responsible for food spoilage and cause off-flavors, odors, and colors in foods stored under refrigeration.

- *Mesophiles* are bacteria that grow in medium or middle temperature ranges, 77° to 113°F (25.0° to 45.0°C). Most bacteria that cause foodborne illness and other human infections grow at these temperatures.

- *Thermophiles* are hot-temperature-loving bacteria that grow at temperatures over 113°F (over 45.0°C). These are the types of organisms that produce spores and are of real concern in the canning industry.

Temperature is the most widely used method of controlling bacterial growth. This concept is illustrated in Figure 4.3.

Bacteria grow slowly at temperatures below 40°F (4.4°C). While the freezing of foods may reduce the number of microorganisms, bacterial cells survive. Bacteria will be killed at temperatures of 140°F (60.0°C) and higher, but spores will survive. Most bacteria grow and multiply rapidly at temperatures between 40°F and 140°F; this range is known as the *temperature danger zone*. As temperatures increase to room temperature and above, bacterial cells grow rapidly and populations can increase to tremendous numbers. This is why regulatory agencies are concerned about food that is left at room temperature (or elevated room temperature) for over two hours.

Since temperature control is vital to assuring the quality and safety of foods that are prepared, handled, and sold in retail stores, more information about this subject will be discussed in chapter 7.

pH (Acidity/Alkalinity)

pH is a measure of the acidity or alkalinity in a food product (1, 3, 6, 7, 8). It is expressed on a scale from 0 to 14, with 7 being neutral. Below pH 7 is considered acid, while above pH 7 is alkaline. Foods like sauerkraut, pickles, and citrus fruits are acidic in nature, while products like green beans, peas, corn, seafoods, and meats are considered low-acid foods and are in the pH range from 5.3 to 7.0. One food that is alkaline is egg white. It has a pH of 7.6 when the egg is freshly laid, but increases to about 9.5.

Most bacteria can survive in a pH range from 4.6 to 9.0, with the best growth at pH values between 6.6 and 7.5 (near neutral pH). Most bacteria will not grow at pH values below 4.6.

The pH of a food, along with other environmental factors, usually determines the types of bacteria that are able to grow and eventually cause a desired fermentation, a spoilage, or a potential health hazard.

Oxygen

Some bacteria require oxygen to grow and are called *aerobes,* while others grow only in the absence of oxygen and are known as *anaerobes.* Anaerobes can grow in vacuum-sealed cans, jars, and pouches, in large pots of food, and other conditions that exclude air (6). Many bacteria grow under either condition (with or without oxygen) and are called *facultative anaerobes.*

It is important to remember that bacteria can live in a variety of places and under many different environmental conditions. Most bacteria grow best in a warm, moist, protein-rich, pH neutral or low-acid environment. Minimizing bacterial contamination through proper product handling and inhibiting growth by good temperature control will help retailers provide wholesome and safe foods to their customers.

Figure 4.3   The Effect of Temperature on Bacterial Growth

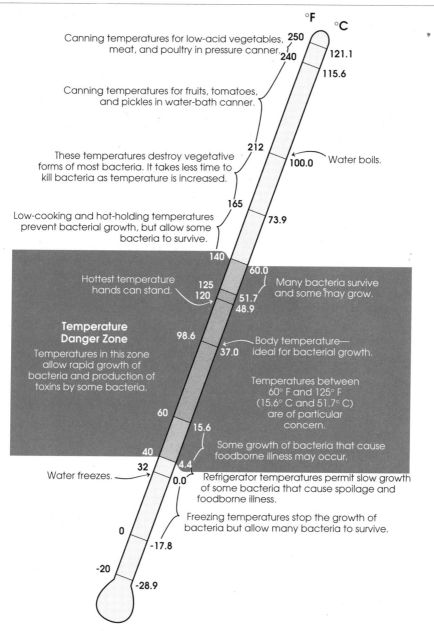

Canning temperatures for low-acid vegetables, meat, and poultry in pressure canner.

Canning temperatures for fruits, tomatoes, and pickles in water-bath canner.

These temperatures destroy vegetative forms of most bacteria. It takes less time to kill bacteria as temperature is increased.

Low-cooking and hot-holding temperatures prevent bacterial growth, but allow some bacteria to survive.

Hottest temperature hands can stand.

Temperature Danger Zone

Temperatures in this zone allow rapid growth of bacteria and production of toxins by some bacteria.

Water freezes.

°F   °C

250
240   121.1
       115.6

212
       100.0   Water boils.

165
       73.9

140
       60.0
125   Many bacteria survive
120   51.7   and some may grow.
       48.9

98.6
       37.0   Body temperature— ideal for bacterial growth.

               Temperatures between
               60° F and 125° F
60   (15.6° C and 51.7° C)
               are of particular
       15.6   concern.

               Some growth of bacteria that cause
40   foodborne illness may occur.
32   4.4
       0.0   Refrigerator temperatures permit slow growth
               of some bacteria that cause spoilage and
               foodborne illness.

               Freezing temperatures stop the growth of
               bacteria but allow many bacteria to survive.
0
       -17.8

-20
       -28.9

Source: Adapted from *Preventing Foodborne Illness: A Guide to Safe Food Handling*, Home and Garden Bulletin no. 247, U.S. Department of Agriculture, Food Safety and Inspection Service, September 1990.

Other Microorganisms

In addition to bacteria, other microorganisms play important roles in foods. Yeasts, molds, viruses, and some parasites can also affect the quality, safety, and wholesomeness of the foods offered by retailers.

Yeasts

Most yeasts are beneficial and are widely used in the production of bread, beer, wine, and many other foods (*1, 3, 6, 7, 8*). They are found in the soil and air, on plants, grains, fruits, and other foods containing sugar, as well as in many other places.

Yeasts are single-celled organisms that are usually larger than bacteria. Individually, they are invisible to the naked eye, but large masses can be easily seen.

Yeasts need less moisture than bacteria but more moisture than molds to grow. Yeasts can grow over a wide temperature range—from 32° to 117°F (0.0° to 47.2°C), with the optimum for most yeasts being between 68°F and 86°F (20.0°C and 30.0°C). Yeasts are easily destroyed by heat. Most yeasts grow best in the presence of oxygen and in an acid environment. Yeasts are of primary concern in the retail food industry because they can cause spoilage of foods such as sauerkraut, fruit juices, syrups, jellies, and other

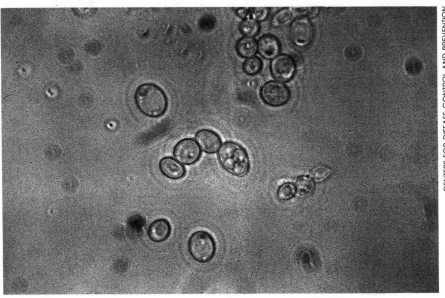

CENTERS FOR DISEASE CONTROL AND PREVENTION

An example of typical yeast cells under the microscope.

foods. While some yeasts are capable of causing disease in humans and plants, they have not been known to cause foodborne illness.

Molds

Molds are frequently seen growing on the surface of a wide variety of foods and other items (*1, 3, 6, 7, 8*). They are found everywhere and are easily spread by air currents, insects, and animals. Like bacteria and yeasts, molds are often involved in food spoilage, but they also have many beneficial uses.

Molds are larger than bacteria and yeasts, and their fuzzy, cottony, or velvet-like appearance is easily visible to the naked eye. Molds do not grow as single cells but are groups of cells that are very complex in structure. They are made up of hair-like filaments that form tangled masses which spread rapidly on food surfaces. These filaments send up branches that produce spores.

Unlike bacterial spores that are formed when environmental conditions are unfavorable, molds form spores to reproduce. Mold spores are small and lightweight, and are produced in large numbers. They detach from mold filaments and are carried by air currents to locations where favorable conditions allow new molds to grow.

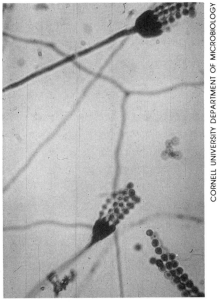
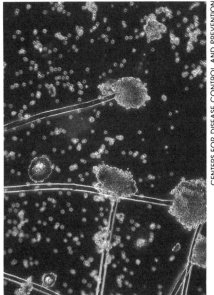

CORNELL UNIVERSITY DEPARTMENT OF MICROBIOLOGY

CENTERS FOR DISEASE CONTROL AND PREVENTION

A microscopic view of two typical molds.

Molds require less moisture than bacteria and yeasts to grow, but require a plentiful supply of oxygen. They grow over a wide temperature range of 14° to 131°F (−10.0° to 55.0°C) and a pH range of (2.0 to 9.0).

Molds are frequently used in the manufacture of many foods, including cheeses such as Blue, Roquefort, Camembert, and Brie. They are also used in the production of food ingredients, industrial chemicals, and pharmaceuticals (penicillin, for example).

Many types of molds are involved in food spoilage and they grow on bread, cheese, fruits, vegetables, grains, and many other products. Some molds can cause more severe problems when they grow on foods. The poisonous substances that are produced by certain molds are called *mycotoxins*. Mycotoxins have been detected primarily in grains and nuts. The best way to avoid mycotoxin production is to prevent mold growth in these food products.

Viruses

Viruses differ from bacteria in that they are not complete cells. They are genetic material inside a protein coat (*1, 3, 6, 7, 8*). Because of this unique structure, viruses cannot carry out any functions outside of a cell of a living organism.

Viruses invade a living cell and then reproduce. They vary in size, shape, and the cells that they infect. They can infect bacteria, insects, plants, animals, and humans. In humans, they cause a variety of diseases, including colds, influenza, mononucleosis, rabies, measles, and infectious hepatitis. Viruses that can be transmitted through foods, especially the hepatitis A virus, will be discussed in chapter 5.

Parasites

Parasites are organisms that depend on a living host to provide nutrients for growth and survival. There are several parasites that can live in animals used for food and cause foodborne disease in humans (*5, 8*). The best-known parasite is the roundworm, *Trichinella spiralis*, which can cause trichinosis in humans. Information on this parasitic foodborne illness can also be found in the next chapter.

Conclusions

What does all this information on microorganisms have to do with merchandising and selling foods to consumers? The answer is—a great deal!

To minimize spoilage, reduce shrinkage, increase profitability, and re-duce the risk of foodborne illness, all of these microorganisms need to be properly controlled. This control can be accomplished by understanding where microorganisms come from, how they are carried from place to place, how they grow and reproduce, and what can be done to minimize contamination and prevent their growth. Understanding these basic principles is the first step toward providing safe, wholesome, and high-quality foods to your customers.

References

1. Brock, T. D., and M. T. Madigan. *Biology of Microorganisms*. 5th ed. Englewood Cliffs, NJ: Prentice-Hall, 1988.
2. Gravani, R. B. "Bacteria." Food Science Fact Sheet 101. Department of Food Science, Cornell University, Ithaca, NY, 1981.
3. Banwart, G. W. *Food Microbiology*. New York: Van Nostrand Reinhold/AVI, 1989.
4. Gravani, R. B. "Food Deterioration and Spoilage Caused by Microorganisms." Food Science Fact Sheet 114. Department of Food Science, Cornell University, Ithaca, NY, 1982.
5. Potter, N. N. *Food Science*. 4th ed. New York: Van Nostrand Reinhold/AVI, 1986.
6. National Restaurant Association. Educational Foundation. *Applied Foodservice Sanitation*. New York: John Wiley & Sons, Inc., 1992.
7. Marriott, N. G. *Principles of Food Sanitation*. 2d ed. New York: Van Nostrand Reinhold/AVI, 1989.
8. Frazier, W. C., and D. C. Westhoff. *Food Microbiology*. 4th ed. New York: McGraw-Hill, Inc., 1988.

5

Foodborne Illness

In the last few years there have been several outbreaks of foodborne illness reported by the media (1), including:

- an outbreak involving more than 16,000 confirmed cases of salmonellosis in northern Illinois and surrounding states due to contaminated milk
- a botulism outbreak from dried, salted whitefish that caused the death of two people in New York
- a listeriosis outbreak in southern California from Mexican-style cheese that involved 86 people and caused 29 deaths

These incidents highlight the importance of food safety and serve as a constant reminder that problems can occur anytime and anywhere that foods are improperly processed, transported, distributed, stored, or prepared.

Foodborne illness is a major concern of food retailers. Associates in the deli and other prepared-food departments are involved in many food-preparation tasks, including handling raw foods; cooking a wide variety of entrées and specialty items; preparing salads; holding foods hot/cold in display cases, steam tables, and on salad bars; cooling prepared foods; and reheating foods. All of these important jobs require an understanding of safe food-preparation practices as well as knowledge of how to prevent foodborne illnesses.

Since there are many steps involved in preparing, holding, merchandising, and storing foods, associates need to know how foodborne illnesses are caused and ways to prevent them from occurring. The information in this chapter will provide you with these facts.

Although the *exact* number of people who get foodborne illnesses in the U.S. is unknown, it has been estimated that up to 81 million cases occur each year (2). Foodborne illnesses are widespread and can have serious health consequences, including death. It is estimated that about 9,000 deaths occur annually as a result of foodborne illnesses, and foodborne-illness outbreaks are thought to cost between $7.7 billion and $8.4 billion per year (2).

Think about how a foodborne outbreak could ruin the reputation and business of a supermarket. If a highly publicized foodborne illness is traced back to your store, it could be *very* costly. In addition to expenses for medical care, lost wages, public-health investigations, lost business, and legal fees, there could be fines or criminal action from regulatory agencies, as well as lawsuits, store closure, increased insurance premiums, adverse publicity, and embarrassment in the community. There certainly is a lot to lose!

Foodborne illnesses result from eating foods that contain

- pathogenic bacteria or their toxins (poisons)
- poisonous chemicals
- parasites
- viruses

Most food-related illnesses can be further classified as either intoxications or infections (3, 4). *Intoxications* are caused when food-contaminating toxins (or poisons) produced by the growth of bacteria or molds are eaten. These toxins are generally odorless and are capable of causing disease, even after the microorganisms have been killed. Toxins may also be naturally present in certain foods, like some types of poisonous mushrooms, as well as in specific plants and animals. A foodborne *infection* occurs when food containing living pathogenic microorganisms is consumed.

Another type of illness results from eating food that contains large numbers of certain types of bacteria that produce toxins in the human intestinal tract. These are known as *toxin-mediated infections* or *toxicoinfections (3, 4)*.

Examples of intoxications, infections, and toxin-mediated infections will be given when the causes of foodborne illnesses are discussed later in this chapter.

Bacterial Intoxications

Bacterial agents cause by far most of the outbreaks that occur in the U.S. each year. Although there are many different bacteria that cause foodborne illness, this text focuses only on the most important ones for food retailers. Keep in mind that the presence and growth of foodborne pathogens do not necessarily produce any noticeable changes in a food's appearance, smell, texture, or flavor.

There are three bacterial foodborne illnesses that are classified as intoxications: staphylococcal intoxication, botulism, and *Bacillus cereus* gastroenteritis. Each of these intoxications is discussed below (also see Table 5.1).

Staphylococcal Intoxication

Staphylococcal intoxication (3, 4, 5, 6) is one of the most frequently occurring foodborne illnesses in the United States. This foodborne illness is caused by the bacterium *Staphylococcus aureus* (*S. aureus*), known simply as staph. As they grow, these bacteria produce toxins in food. Even after the bacteria die or are killed, the toxin can still cause illness.

Source of the organism. The principal source of *S. aureus* associated with foodborne outbreaks is humans. Staphylococci are found in the noses of up to 60 percent of healthy people; they also occur in the throat; on the skin, especially the hands; on hair; in feces; and in infected cuts, burns, abrasions, pimples, and boils.

Foods involved. *S. aureus* can grow in a wide variety of foods, especially protein foods or mixtures of foods containing protein that provide a favorable pH range (pH 4.5 to 9.3). Any food that requires a great deal of hand preparation is a possible source of staphylococcal intoxication. These bacteria are also capable of growing in foods that contain high levels of salt or sugar, and can grow at the lowest water activity (A_w) of any bacterial foodborne pathogen (A_w 0.85). They prefer temperatures between 95.0°F and 98.6°F (35.0°C and 37.0°C), but they can grow at temperatures as low as 44°F (6.7°C) and as high as 118°F (47.8°C). Because staphylococci do not compete well with other microorganisms that may be present in foods, illness is most commonly associated with cooked foods that are contaminated after cooking has killed the other microorganisms.

Foods that have been involved in staphylococcal outbreaks include

- cooked meats, such as ham
- meat and vegetable salads, such as potato, macaroni, and chicken and tuna salads
- bakery products containing custard or cream fillings, such as eclairs, filled doughnuts, pastries, pies, and other protein foods

The disease. The symptoms of staphylococcal intoxication can occur from 1 to 6 hours after eating the food containing the bacterial toxin; most symptoms appear within 2 to 4 hours. The most common symptoms are nausea, followed by a violent onset of vomiting, abdominal cramps, and diarrhea. Victims may experience headache, sweating, chills, and prostration, and are usually very uncomfortable. The illness usually lasts one to two days and recovery is complete. Staphylococcal intoxication is rarely fatal. Figure 5.1 shows the typical sequence of events that is needed for a staphylococcal outbreak to occur.

Figure 5.1 Sequence of Events Needed for a Staphylococcal Intoxication to Occur

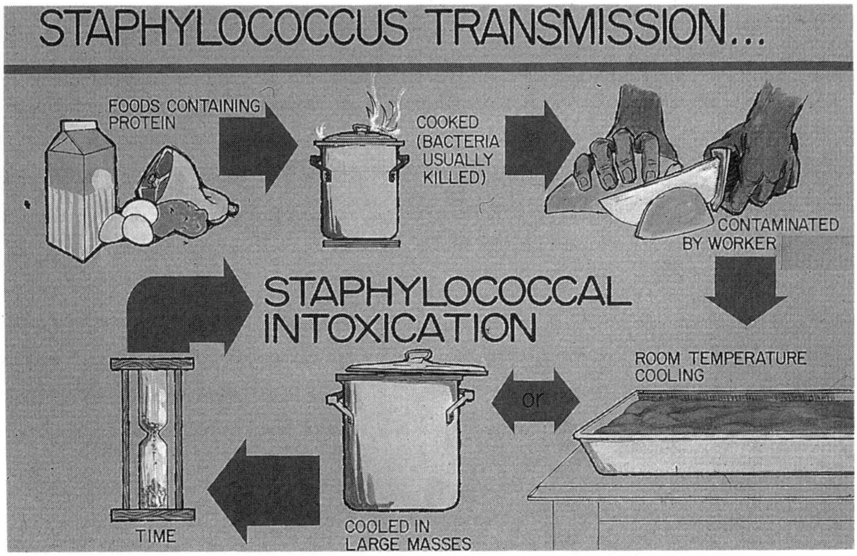

Source: Centers for Disease Control and Prevention.

Prevention. The cells of *S. aureus* are killed by normal cooking procedures, but the toxins produced by this organism are very heat resistant and are not inactivated by normal cooking, cooling, or freezing practices. To prevent staphylococcal food intoxication, efforts must be directed at preventing the organism from contaminating food products and inhibiting the organism from growing and producing toxin in foods. Prevention strategies include

- minimizing hand contact with foods; using clean and sanitized utensils and disposable gloves to handle foods
- making sure that associates with respiratory infections, pimples, boils, and infected cuts and burns do not work with foods
- avoiding hand contact with hair, face, nose, mouth, and other parts of the body
- cleaning and sanitizing equipment, utensils, and food-contact surfaces
- not allowing prepared foods to stay at room temperatures for any longer than necessary and for no more than two hours
- cooling and refrigerating cooked food rapidly to 40°F (4.4°C) or below, in shallow pans, and maintaining this temperature
- protecting cooked foods from cross contamination with raw foods

Botulism

Botulism (3, 4, 5, 6) is the most severe bacterial foodborne illness because if it is not diagnosed and treated quickly, it can result in death. Fortunately, botulism outbreaks rarely occur, but retailers need to be aware of how to prevent them from occurring.

Botulism is an intoxication caused by eating improperly processed (usually home-canned) foods that contain the toxins produced by the bacterium *Clostridium botulinum*, or *C. botulinum*.

Sources of the organism. *Clostridium botulinum* bacteria are present throughout the environment and are found in soil, water, plants, and in the intestinal tracts of animals and fish.

This organism produces spores that can contaminate foods during production, harvesting, or processing. If the foods are not properly processed, the spores will germinate, grow, and produce toxins in food. *C. botulinum* grows in the absence of air and is usually associated with low-acid canned foods that have been improperly processed or stored, or have been consumed without appropriate heating. Although the toxin is very potent, it can be inactivated by boiling for 10 to 15 minutes.

Foods involved. Foods that have been involved in a majority of botulism outbreaks include improperly processed, usually home-canned, low-acid foods like green beans, corn, spinach, asparagus, beets, peppers, pimentos, mushrooms, fruits, and condiments; and improperly processed, vacuum-packaged, fermented or smoked fish and fishery products.

The risk of botulism has long been associated with home-canned foods that are not processed to a high-enough temperature, or for a long enough time, to destroy the spores. More recently, botulism outbreaks have been reported in cooked foods held at room or warm temperatures for an extended time under conditions where oxygen was limited. These foods include baked potatoes wrapped tightly in foil, sautéed onions, potato salad made from leftover baked potatoes, meat pies, vacuum-packaged foods, and garlic in oil products. In each case, the foods were cooked and held in environments and at temperatures that allowed the growth of *C. botulinum* and then served. The lesson learned from these outbreaks is that foods potentially contaminated with *C. botulinum* or their spores need to be handled carefully, processed properly, and kept at appropriate temperatures.

The disease. Botulism toxin affects the nervous system and can be fatal if not treated. Symptoms usually appear 12 to 48 hours after eating the contaminated food and first include nausea, vomiting, and possibly diarrhea. Blurred or double vision, weakness, trouble swallowing and speaking, and difficulty breathing are common symptoms. Death usually occurs due to respiratory failure. Successful treatment of botulism requires quick medical attention and diagnosis of the disease, prompt administration of antitoxins, and close medical supervision.

Prevention. Botulism can be prevented by following some simple rules:

- Never use any home-canned foods in a retail store.
- Never use foods in cans that are bulging, swollen, leaking, or severely damaged. Likewise, foods from cracked jars or jars with loose or bulging lids should never be used. If the contents of a can are foamy, spurt when opened, or have an abnormal odor or appearance, these foods should not be used. Suspect food should *never* be tasted—it should be discarded immediately and reported to your supervisor.
- Divide large portions of cooked foods into small portions for cooling (40°F, 4.4°C).
- Keep hot foods at 140°F (60.0°C) or above.
- Reheat leftovers thoroughly to an internal temperature of at least 165°F (73.9°C).
- Make sure that cooked foods are moved through the temperature danger zone (40° to 140°F, 4.4° to 60.0°C) as quickly as possible.

Bacillus cereus Gastroenteritis

Bacillus cereus (*B. cereus*) is a spore-forming bacterium that produces two different types of toxin that cause two distinct forms of foodborne illness (3, 4, 5, 6). These illnesses differ in the foods involved, the time of onset, and symptoms. One *B. cereus* toxin causes a diarrheal illness, while the other causes a vomiting illness after the consumption of contaminated food.

Source of the organism. *Bacillus cereus* produces spores that are common in soil, dust, plant products (like rice, cereal, flour, and starch), bakery products, spices, animal products, and mixtures of ingredients (like soup mixes, gravy mixes, puddings, and spaghetti sauces). Foods from the soil or foods produced or prepared in dusty environments will contain the organism.

Foods involved. Foods involved in the diarrheal type *B. cereus* outbreaks have included vegetables, salads, meat dishes, casseroles, puddings, sauces, and soups. The main food involved in the vomiting type of *B. cereus* outbreaks is rice, although other starchy foods, such as macaroni and cheese, and vanilla slices (a product similar to cream puffs), have also been implicated.

The disease. The diarrheal form of *B. cereus* gastroenteritis occurs 6 to 16 hours after the consumption of contaminated foods. The symptoms include abdominal pain and watery diarrhea. The illness commonly lasts about 12 to 14 hours.

The vomiting form of the illness usually includes nausea and vomiting that occurs 30 minutes to 6 hours after eating food containing the toxin. The symptoms usually last about 24 hours.

Prevention. *B. cereus* can be a problem in food establishments where large batches of food are prepared ahead of time and not properly cooled prior to reheating and serving. Since *B. cereus* is frequently found in or on many foods, and because the spores can survive ordinary cooking procedures, steps should be taken to handle foods properly. In particular, cooked rice and other starchy foods should not be stored at room temperature for long periods of time.

Specific prevention measures include

- not holding food in the temperature danger zone for more than 2 hours.
- cooling foods to 40°F (4.4°C) within 4 hours of preparation.
- storing food in shallow pans that are less than 4 inches deep. Product in the pans should be less than 3 inches deep.
- using foods as quickly as possible.

Bacterial Infections

Foodborne illnesses caused by bacterial infections include salmonellosis, shigellosis, and listeriosis (Table 5.1).

Salmonellosis

Salmonellosis is an illness caused by any one of the more than 2,000 different types of salmonellae. Salmonellosis is an infection caused when food containing living organisms is consumed. It is one of the most frequently reported foodborne illnesses and cases of salmonellosis continue to increase.

Source of the organism. Salmonellae are very common in nature and are found wherever there are humans and animals. These bacteria occur in the intestinal tracts and fecal matter of animals. Food animals such as chickens, turkeys, pigs, and cattle are the most important sources, but dogs, cats, turtles, frogs, birds, and many other animals are also infected. Salmonellae have also been found in human carriers (people that don't show signs of the illness but carry the organism in their intestinal tracts), and in rodents and insects, as well as in soil, water, and sewage.

Salmonellae are facultative bacteria and can grow with or without the presence of oxygen. They are mesophiles and grow best at temperature ranges of 95.0° to 98.6°F (35.0° to 37.0°C), but reports indicate that they can grow between 41.0°F and 116.6°F (5.0°C and 47.0°C). Salmonellae are killed by temperatures of 130°F (54.4°C) and higher after two hours, or 165°F (73.9°C) in a few seconds. They can also be killed at lower temperatures with a longer exposure time (4).

Foods involved. A variety of foods have been involved in salmonellosis outbreaks, but foods of animal origin or those contaminated by foods of animal origin are most frequently involved. Foods such as meat and poultry products, unpasteurized milk and dairy products, eggs and egg products, and meat and vegetable salads have often been involved in salmonellosis outbreaks.

It has been recently shown that one type of salmonella, *Salmonella enteritidis*, can be present in Grade A uncracked eggs, and many outbreaks traced to raw or undercooked shell eggs have been reported. If hens are infected with *Salmonella enteritidis*, they can pass these organisms through their bodies into the eggs. Therefore, eggs should be kept refrigerated and be *thoroughly cooked* before they are eaten.

The disease. The symptoms of salmonellosis usually occur 12 to 48 hours after eating contaminated foods (3, 4, 5, 6). The gastroenteritis is characterized by diarrhea, abdominal cramps, and frequent nausea and vomiting the first day of illness. Mild fever sometimes follows and lasts for a few days. Headache, chills, dehydration, and prostration sometimes occur. The illness usually lasts from 2 to 6 days, and deaths are uncommon except in the very young, very old, or persons who are already weakened by illness.

Salmonellae can be transmitted in a variety of ways. Since these bacteria occur in the intestinal tract of animals and some humans, they are shed in fecal matter and a cycle of infection is always present in the environment. The disease is usually transmitted from animals to humans by ingestion of foods of animal origin that have been contaminated with these bacteria. There can also be direct transmission from person-to-person and from animal-to-person. Figure 5.2 shows the typical sequence of events that are needed for salmonellosis to occur.

Prevention. Salmonellosis often occurs when there is cross contamination or recontamination of cooked foods from raw foods that contain the bacteria (3, 4, 5, 6).

Figure 5.2   Sequence of Events Needed for Salmonellosis to Occur

---

SALMONELLA TRANSMISSION...

BUILD UP in TRANSIT/PENS

CONTAMINATION of FEEDS or FARM

INFECTED ANIMALS

SPREAD of CONTAMINATION in PROCESSING PLANTS

HUMAN SALMONELLOSIS

MISHANDLED in HOME or RESTAURANT

RESTAURANT

CONTAMINATED PRODUCTS

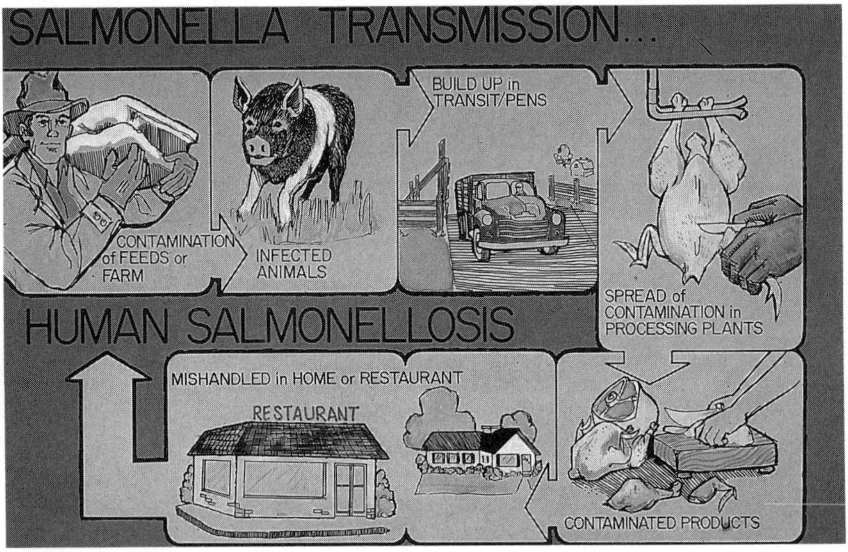

Source: Centers for Disease Control and Prevention.

Since it is very difficult to eliminate salmonellae from raw foods of animal origin, extreme care must be taken when handling these products. Some methods to prevent salmonellosis include

- Follow the rules of good personal hygiene and wash hands thoroughly after using the toilet.
- Be sure to cook animal foods to minimum internal temperatures appropriate for each food.
- Cool foods to 40°F (4.4°C) quickly (within 4 hours), and hold foods at proper temperatures during display.
- Prevent cross contamination of raw and cooked foods. Always use clean and sanitized equipment and utensils when handling raw and cooked foods.
- Use commercially pasteurized, frozen, or liquid eggs in recipes.

Shigellosis

Shigellosis, also known as bacillary dysentery, is an infection that is caused by several types of bacteria known as shigella (3, 4, 5, 6). The illness is associated with poor personal hygiene and poor sanitation and is spread by fecal contamination of food and water.

Source of the organisms. Shigellae are found in the intestinal tracts of humans. The main source of these bacteria involved in outbreaks is humans who are symptomless carriers or persons recovering from the illness. Shigellae can remain in the intestinal tract and fecal matter of about 50 percent of recovering persons for a month. When these infected people fail to wash their hands properly, they transmit bacteria to food and others can then become infected.

Foods involved. Foods that have been involved in outbreaks include raw produce; foods that receive much handling such as salads (including potato, tuna, shrimp, macaroni, and chicken); and cut, diced, chopped, and mixed foods that are not cooked. The ingredients may be clean, but during preparation the food is contaminated by hand manipulation or mixing. The organisms can easily multiply in most foods held at room temperatures and cause an outbreak of shigellosis.

The disease. The symptoms of shigellosis usually occur 1 to 7 days after eating contaminated food. Shigellosis is characterized by diarrhea, abdominal pain, and fever. Vomiting, chills, and headache frequently occur. The illness usually lasts about two weeks.

Prevention. Shigellosis can be prevented by using good personal hygiene, including the thorough washing of hands after using the toilet, not working with food when ill, and by practicing good sanitation on the job.

Listeriosis

Listeriosis is a foodborne infection caused by the bacterium *Listeria monocytogenes*, or *L. monocytogenes* (3, 4, 5, 6). Years ago, this organism was considered a veterinary pathogen, but recent foodborne outbreaks have highlighted its importance as a cause of human illness.

Source of the organism. *Listeria monocytogenes* is found in soil, decaying plant materials, water, the intestinal tracts of domesticated wild animals and birds, and sewage. It is a facultative organism that grows well in damp environments, including standing water and condensate (liquid that forms and drips) on pipes and ceilings, and in coolers, air-conditioning systems, and floor drains. It grows best at 98.6°F (37.0°C) but can grow slowly at refrigerator temperatures.

Foods involved. Raw, soil-grown vegetables, dairy products (especially raw milk, cheeses made from unpasteurized milk, and soft-ripened cheeses), raw meats, poultry, and seafoods are often contaminated with *L. monocytogenes*. Foods that have been incriminated in listeriosis outbreaks include milk, coleslaw, and a type of mexican-style soft cheese.

The disease. Although listeriosis is a rare disease, it can be fatal. Symptoms in healthy adults include the sudden onset of flu-like symptoms—nausea, vomiting, diarrhea, fever, chills, and headache. In people with weakened immune systems, such as the elderly and those with cancer, AIDS, kidney disease, chronic liver disease, and diabetes, listeriosis can cause such serious complications as meningitis, which affects the tissues around the brain and spinal cord, and blood poisoning. Pregnant women are also at risk since this disease can cause spontaneous abortions and stillbirths. Newborns and young children are vulnerable because of their underdeveloped immune systems. The symptoms of listeriosis can develop from 1 day to 3 weeks after eating foods contaminated with *L. monocytogenes*.

Prevention. Thorough cooking of foods will destroy *L. monocytogenes*, so proper food-handling practices and appropriate cooking temperatures should be used. Because *L. monocytogenes* can grow slowly at refrigeration temperatures, it is also important to practice good control in your cooler. The first-in, first-out (FIFO) system should be used, and all food items should be dated upon receipt so that older stock can be identified and used first.

Also, make sure that facilities are clean and dry, and be on the lookout for condensate on ceilings, pipes, and other areas within fresh-prepared food departments. Eliminate standing water and make sure that your coolers are functioning properly and checked by maintenance on a regular schedule.

Other Bacterial Infections

There are several other bacteria that also cause foodborne illness. Organisms such as *Yersinia enterocolitica*, *Campylobacter jejuni* (*C. jejuni*), *Escherichia coli* (*E. coli* 0157:H7), and *Vibrio parahaemolyticus* have all been in the news in recent years and are briefly described in Table 5.1. This table is a quick reference chart on the causes, symptoms, foods involved, and prevention of bacterial foodborne illness.

Toxin-mediated Infections or Toxicoinfections

Toxin-mediated infections or toxicoinfections are caused by eating food that contains large numbers of bacteria that reach the intestinal tract, multiply, and produce toxins that cause illness. There are several bacteria that cause toxicoinfections, but the bacterium that is frequently involved in causing foodborne illness is *Clostridium perfringens* (see Table 5.1).

Clostridium perfringens Gastroenteritis

The bacterium *Clostridium perfringens* (*C. perfringens*) causes a mild gastrointestinal illness and is classified as a toxicoinfection. This foodborne illness lasts a short time, seldom requires medical treatment, and often is not reported to health authorities.

Source of the organism. *C. perfringens* grows in the absence of air and produces spores. This organism is found in soil, dust, air, sewage, human and animal feces, and many food products. *C. perfringens* is so common in the environment that meat, poultry, soil-grown vegetables, and spices are frequently contaminated with the organism.

Foods involved. Foods involved in *C. perfringens* gastroenteritis usually include protein foods that have been boiled, stewed, or lightly roasted (3, 4, 5, 6). Meat and poultry stews, gravies, sauces, meat pies, casseroles, and bean dishes can support the growth of *C. perfringens* and have all been involved in outbreaks. The majority of reported outbreaks usually occur where foods are cooked several days in advance, allowed to cool slowly, and then held for long periods before reheating and serving. When these foods are first cooked, the heating lowers the oxygen content of the food and provides an airless environment for the bacteria to grow.

C. perfringens causes illness in a very unique way. The cooking of foods contaminated with the organism destroys growing bacterial cells and some spores, but heat-resistant spores can survive. When these foods are cooled slowly or inadequately refrigerated, the spores germinate into vegetative cells and these vegetative cells multiply. Under ideal conditions, they can multiply rapidly, doubling their numbers in as little as 7.1 minutes (5). When foods containing large numbers of *C. perfringens* are ingested, the organisms reach the small intestine, where they multiply and form spores. The sporulating cells produce toxins that cause illness.

The disease. The symptoms of this illness usually occur from 8 to 24 hours after eating the contaminated food. The symptoms are watery diarrhea and abdominal pain, with nausea and headache sometimes occurring. Vomiting and fever are rare. The illness is relatively mild, and the symptoms commonly last from 12 to 24 hours.

Prevention. Prevention of *C. perfringens* gastroenteritis depends on the adequate cooking, rapid cooling, and proper reheating of foods like stews, meats, and gravies. Effective control measures include

- cooking foods thoroughly
- holding cooked foods at 140°F (60.0°C) or higher
- cooling foods quickly in shallow pans
- reheating foods to 165°F (73.9°C) or higher within two hours
- planning food preparation; not preparing foods too far in advance

By following the rules of good sanitation, practicing personal hygiene, and using proper temperature control, all foodborne illnesses can be prevented.

Chemical Foodborne Illnesses

Chemical foodborne illnesses are caused when people consume poisonous substances that occur naturally in some foods or that may be intentionally or accidentally added to foods during harvesting, processing, transportation, storage, or preparation. Five types of chemical foodborne illness are caused by metals, poisonous chemicals, intentional food additives, poisonous plants, and poisonous animals. Each of these types of chemical foodborne illnesses will be briefly discussed.

Metals

Although small quantities of mineral elements are necessary for human health, excessive amounts of some metals can be toxic (7). These toxic metals can get into food through the use of equipment and utensils that are made from unsuitable materials. Acid foods, such as fruit juice, fruit punches, carbonated beverages, sauerkraut, tomato juice, and fruit gela-

Table 5.1 A Quick Reference to Bacterial Foodborne Illnesses

Illness and Bacterium that Causes It	Source of Organism	Onset (Duration) of Illness	Characteristics of Illness	Common Foods Involved	Prevention
Intoxications					
Staphylococcal intoxication *Staphylococcus aureus*	Hands, throats, nasal passages, and sores of humans.	1–6 hours (1–2 days)	Heat-resistant toxin causes nausea, vomiting, diarrhea, and abdominal cramps.	Reheated foods, ham, and other meats; meat, vegetable, and egg salads; cream-filled pastries and other protein foods.	Practice good personal hygiene and sanitary habits; avoid contamination of food from bare hands; heat, cool, and refrigerate foods properly.
Botulism *Clostridium botulinum*	Soil, water sediment, and intestinal tracts of animals and fish.	12–48 hours, up to 72 hours (Depends on speed of diagnosis; can last several days to a year.)	Neurotoxin causes dizziness, blurred vision, and difficulty swallowing, speaking, and breathing. Can be fatal without antitoxin.	Low-acid canned food, especially home-canned products; meats, fish, smoked and fermented fish; vegetables.	Do not use home-canned foods in retail stores; avoid using foods from severely dented or bulging cans.
Bacillus cereus gastroenteritis *Bacillus cereus*	Soil, dust, water, and a variety of foods, such as cereals, rice, dried foods, spices, milk and dairy products, meats, and vegetables.	Two types of illness: (1) diarrheal type 6–16 hours (12–14 hours) (2) vomiting type 30 minutes – 6 hours (1 day)	(1) Watery diarrhea; abdominal cramps; no fever or vomiting. (2) Nausea and vomiting; abdominal cramps and diarrhea occasionally occur.	(1) Meat and vegetable dishes; casseroles, puddings, sauces, and soups. (2) Fried, boiled, or cooked rice; other starchy foods, such as macaroni and cheese.	Good sanitation. Keep foods hot (>140°F, 60.0°C); cool leftovers quickly; reheat foods to 165°F (73.9°C).

Table 5.1   A Quick Reference to Bacterial Foodborne Illnesses (continued)

Illness and Bacterium that Causes It	Source of Organism	Onset (Duration) of Illness	Characteristics of Illness	Common Foods Involved	Prevention
Infections Salmonellosis *Salmonella* species	Intestinal tracts of animals, especially poultry and pigs; birds and insects; also human carriers.	12–48 hours (2–6 days)	Nausea, vomiting, abdominal cramps, diarrhea, fever, and headache.	Poultry and poultry products, shell eggs and egg products; milk and dairy products; meat salads; shellfish; and other protein foods.	Cook animal foods thoroughly; prevent cross contamination; cool food quickly; practice good personal hygiene.
Shigellosis (bacillary dysentery) *Shigella* species	Intestinal tracts of humans and polluted water.	1–7 days (Up to 14 days or longer; recovery is slow.)	Diarrhea with bloody stools, abdominal cramps, and fever. There may be complications in severe cases.	Foods that receive much handling, including meat, vegetable, and pasta salads, and raw vegetables.	Good sanitation and personal hygiene; minimize hand contact with food; prevent cross contamination.
Listeriosis *Listeria monocytogenes*	Soil, silage, decaying plant matter, water, other environmental sources; intestinal tracts of animals.	1 day–3 weeks (Depends on treatment, but has a high fatality rate in immuno-compromised individuals.)	Mild flu-like symptoms in healthy individuals; in immuno-compromised individuals, meningitis and blood poisoning can occur; spontaneous abortion in pregnant women.	Raw milk and cheese made from raw milk; raw meat and poultry; raw vegetables.	Good sanitation; use only pasteurized milk and dairy products; cook food thoroughly; keep foods below 40°F (4.4°C); prevent cross contamination.

Table 5.1 (continued)

Illness and Bacterium that Causes It	Source of Organism	Onset (Duration) of Illness	Characteristics of Illness	Common Foods Involved	Prevention
Infections (continued)					
Yersiniosis *Yersinia enterocolitica*	Soil; untreated water; intestinal tracts of animals, especially pigs.	24–28 hours (2–3 days; some longer)	Fever, abdominal pain, diarrhea, nausea and vomiting; pseudo-appendicitis; complications can occur in severe cases.	Meat and meat products, especially pork; milk and dairy products; seafoods; fresh vegetables.	Good sanitation; use only pasteurized dairy products; cook foods thoroughly; keep foods below 40°F (4.4°C); prevent cross contamination.
Campylobacteriosis *Campylobacter jejuni*	Soil; sewage; untreated water; intestinal tracts of chickens, turkeys, cattle, pigs, rodents, and some wild birds.	2–5 days (5–10 days; relapses are common)	Fever, headache, nausea, muscle pain, and diarrhea (sometimes bloody).	Undercooked meat and poultry; raw milk.	Cook animal foods thoroughly; cool foods quickly; prevent cross contamination.
Hemorrhagic colitis *E. coli* 0157:H7	Intestinal tracts of animals, particularly cattle, chickens, pigs, and sheep.	3–9 days (2–9 days)	Severe abdominal pain, watery diarrhea which becomes bloody, and vomiting may occur; dehydration; severe complications can result.	Raw or rare meats, especially ground beef; raw milk and dairy products.	Cook meats thoroughly; prevent cross contamination; keep food below 40°F (4.4°C).

Table 5.1 A Quick Reference to Bacterial Foodborne Illnesses (continued)

Illness and Bacterium That Causes It	Source of Organism	Onset (Duration) of Illness	Characteristics of Illness	Common Foods Involved	Prevention
Infections (continued)					
Vibrio parahaemolyticus gastroenteritis *Vibrio parahaemolyticus*	Estuaries and salt water.	2–48 hours (2–3 days; can be longer)	Diarrhea, abdominal cramps, nausea, vomiting, headache, fever, and chills.	Raw fish or inadequately cooked seafood: clams, oysters, crabs, shrimp, and lobster.	Cook all seafood thoroughly; prevent cross contamination; keep foods below 40°F (4.4°C).
Toxin-mediated Infection (Toxicoinfection)					
Clostridium perfringens gastroenteritis *Clostridium perfringens*	Intestinal tracts of humans and animals; soil, dust, and water.	8–24 hours (12–24 hours)	Diarrhea; intense abdominal pain; occasional vomiting.	Improperly prepared, held, cooled, or reheated meat and poultry dishes, stews, gravies, soups, sauces, and casseroles.	Cook foods thoroughly; cool foods quickly; hold hot foods above 140°F (60.0°C); reheat leftovers to 165°F (73.9°C).

Source: Adapted from *Dairy and Food Sanitation, Applied Food Service Sanitation,* and *Foodborne Bacterial Pathogens* (3, 4, 5).

tin, have been involved in chemical poisonings. When these acid foods are prepared or stored in equipment containing antimony (gray enamelware), cadmium (plated utensils, refrigerator shelves), lead (glazed earthenware or pottery), tin (uncoated tin containers), and zinc (galvanized containers), the metals dissolve in the food.

Other metals such as copper, which is used to carry potable water safely, can cause gastric disturbances when acid foods or carbonated liquids come in contact with it. This has occurred in vending machines and carbonated-beverage dispensers that were equipped with faulty backflow-preventer valves.

The incubation period of metal poisonings ranges from 5 minutes to 8 hours, but is usually less than 1 hour. Although the symptoms of each type of metal poisoning vary, vomiting usually occurs. There may also be nausea, diarrhea, abdominal pain, and a metallic taste associated with the poisoning.

Metal poisoning can be prevented by

- using only approved equipment and utensils for preparing, storing, transporting, or cooking foods
- being sure that backflow-preventer valves are installed and properly functioning in carbonated-beverage dispensers

Poisonous Chemicals

Since a wide variety of chemicals is used in retail stores, it is important to recognize the tremendous benefits and hazards of some of these products. Chemical compounds (such as cleaners, detergents, sanitizers, pesticides, and food additives) used for their intended purposes and in the recommended amounts can be beneficial; however, when used for the wrong purpose or in excessive amounts, they can cause illness and sometimes death (7).

Cleaning compounds. Detergents, cleaning compounds, polishes, and sanitizers should be handled properly. When these and other chemicals find their way into food, it is usually through inadequate training, neglect, poor housekeeping practices, or a variety of other reasons. People working with food should use these products with care.

Pesticides. Today, many types of specialized pesticides are used to kill insects and rodents where food is grown, processed, stored, prepared, and sold. Most pesticides are toxic chemicals, and many can be harmful to humans. They should be handled carefully and safely; in retail stores, they should be applied only by state-certified applicators. Improperly used pesticides have caused poisonings when they were accidentally mixed in flour and sprayed on oatmeal. The indiscriminate use of aerosol pesticides around foods, packaging materials, and in food-preparation areas should not be overlooked as a source of potential problems (7).

Intentional Food Additives

Food additives are used to enhance the flavor, texture, nutritive quality, and appearance of foods, as well as to ensure their keeping quality (7). One example is the food additive monosodium glutamate (MSG), commonly used to enhance the flavor of foods. MSG has been reported to cause illness when used in excessive amounts.

When people who are sensitive to MSG eat foods containing excessive amounts of this additive, they can develop the symptoms of MSG poisoning. These symptoms appear from a few minutes to 2 hours (usually less than 1 hour) after ingestion. The symptoms include burning sensations in the chest, neck, abdomen, or extremities; sensations of lightness; numbness and pressure on the face; and a feeling of chest pains. Flushing of the face, tingling sensations, dizziness, headache, and nausea have also been reported. Duration of the illness is usually less than 24 hours and is commonly 2 to 7 hours. No lasting adverse effects have been reported. It is important that associates follow all recipes carefully and use only the exact amounts of MSG specified.

Another food additive that can cause problems in some individuals is a class of compounds called sulfites. Sulfites are used to maintain the freshness and color of vegetables, fruits, frozen potatoes, and certain wines. Sulfites have caused allergic reactions in individuals who are sensitive to these compounds, especially asthmatics (4). The symptoms caused in allergic individuals include nausea, diarrhea, and asthma attacks, and sometimes loss of consciousness. Symptoms can be quite severe and life threatening, and several deaths have been reported.

To protect people who have these allergies, the U.S. Food and Drug Administration (FDA) prohibits the addition of sulfites to fresh fruits and vegetables in retail food stores. Although processed foods have sulfites added, they are clearly labelled to alert consumers to this fact. It is important that retail store associates in all departments avoid the use of sulfites (including sulfur dioxide, sodium and potassium bisulfite, sodium and potassium metabisulfite, or sodium sulfite) on any foods.

Foodborne disease caused by poisonous chemicals and intentional additives can be prevented by (7)

- using all chemicals for their intended purposes and in the amounts recommended on the label
- reading and following label directions carefully and accurately

- storing toxic chemicals in a separate place, away from food-preparation and storage areas
- keeping toxic chemicals properly labeled and in their original containers
- not storing or transporting chemicals in containers used to hold food
- having state-certified applicators handle and apply pesticides

Poisonous Plants and Animals

When thinking of chemical foodborne illness, it is easy to overlook the fact that many plants and animals used for human food contain natural substances that have toxic properties (7). In most cases these foods are avoided, but through lack of understanding, carelessness, or misuse, the food may be consumed and illness can occur.

A large number of plants are known to cause illness in humans, but most of them are not commonly eaten. Most serious plant intoxications occur when people gather wild food in the woods. Remember, only food from approved and inspected sources can be used in retail stores.

The tissues of some animals, particularly certain fish and shellfish, can be naturally toxic to humans due to toxins produced in the fish or through consumption of toxic organisms in their diets (4, 7). Paralytic shellfish poisoning, scombroid fish poisoning, and ciguatera fish poisoning are types of chemical foodborne illnesses that have been reported and are discussed below.

Although poisonous plants and animals are present in our environment, proper vigilance keeps them from becoming a significant threat to public health.

Paralytic Shellfish Poisoning

Paralytic shellfish poisoning is caused by a potent neurotoxin produced by certain algae called dinoflagellates (7). When the right environmental conditions occur, these organisms reproduce rapidly. Filter-feeding shellfish, such as mussels, clams, scallops, and oysters, feed on the toxic algae, concentrate the neurotoxin in their digestive glands, and become toxic to humans. The amount of toxin in the shellfish depends upon the number of poisonous dinoflagellates in the water and the amount of water filtered by the shellfish. The toxin is bound in the shellfish and causes them no harm but is released when the shellfish are eaten by humans. Usual methods of shellfish cookery (including steaming, boiling, baking, or frying) do not destroy the toxin.

The symptoms of shellfish poisoning usually become apparent in less than 1 hour (often within 30 minutes) after eating the toxic mollusks (7).

The symptoms begin with a numbness in the lips, tongue, and fingertips. This is followed by numbness in the legs, arms, and neck, with a general lack of muscular coordination. Other symptoms include dizziness, weakness, drowsiness, incoherence, and headache. Respiratory distress and muscular paralysis become more severe as the disease progresses, and death can result from respiratory paralysis.

Health agencies monitor the level of toxin in shellfish during the danger periods (May through October) by collecting samples of mollusks and testing them in the laboratory. If shellfish exceed the safe levels for toxin, the growing area is quarantined and their sale is prohibited.

In the U.S. most victims of paralytic shellfish poisoning are tourists and picnickers who gather shellfish for their own consumption. Commercially harvested shellfish have seldom been involved in outbreaks.

Since poisonous shellfish cannot be detected by appearance, odor, or any method other than chemical analysis, the best way to prevent paralytic shellfish poisoning is to follow public health agency restrictions on the harvesting of shellfish and buy seafoods from reputable distributors and wholesalers.

Scombroid Fish Poisoning

This foodborne illness is caused by the products of bacterial action on the muscles of certain fish after they are caught (4, 7, 8). Scombroid fish poisoning can be caused by scombroid fish, such as tuna, mackerel, bonito, mahi-mahi (dolphin fish), and bluefish, that are improperly handled and stored. These fish normally contain large amounts of the amino acid histidine in their muscle tissues. When the fish are held at warm temperatures for several hours after they are caught, the bacteria present can convert the histidine in the muscle to histamine. High levels of histamine, as well as other heat-stable byproducts of bacterial action, are responsible for this foodborne illness.

The symptoms of scombroid poisoning begin within a few minutes to an hour (usually within 30 minutes) after the toxic fish is ingested (7). The illness is characterized by a variety of symptoms that vary in frequency and occurrence. The symptoms can affect the skin (rash, edema, and local inflammation), gastrointestinal tract (abdominal cramps, nausea, vomiting, and diarrhea), and the neurological system (headache, palpitations, tingling, flushing, or burning and itching). Most people suffering from scombroid poisoning will experience only a few of these symptoms. The illness is generally short-lived and recovery usually occurs within 8 to 12 hours, although some deaths have been reported.

Scombroid toxin is heat resistant, so cooking does not destroy it. To assure both safety and quality, fresh fish should be kept at temperatures as close to 32°F (0.0°C) as possible. Frozen fish should be properly thawed in the refrigerator or under cold running water. Prompt and proper temperature control from the time the fish are caught until they are processed, prepared, or sold is essential to prevent scombroid fish poisoning.

Ciguatera Fish Poisoning

Ciguatera fish poisoning is caused by a neurotoxin called ciguatoxin that is sometimes found in tropical and subtropical coral reef fish (4, 7, 8). Fish such as barracuda, snapper, grouper, amberjack, and sturgeonfish have been reported to cause this type of foodborne illness.

These reef fish acquire the ciguatoxin through the food chain by eating toxic marine organisms. The toxin becomes concentrated in the muscle, skin, and viscera of the fish, and the larger the fish, the greater the amount of toxins present (8). The first symptoms of ciguatera poisoning usually occur from a few minutes to 30 hours (average is 1 to 6 hours) after eating the toxic fish (7). The symptoms vary greatly but include abdominal cramps, nausea, vomiting, and watery diarrhea. In some cases, initial symptoms include numbness and tingling of the lips, tongue, nose, and throat, and a metallic taste. Headache, chills, fever, sensory disturbances, and general muscular pain also result. Unusual temperature sensitivities and temporary paralysis have also been reported. Most symptoms subside within a few days, but weakness and sensory disturbances may persist for long periods, depending on the severity of the poisoning. Some deaths have been reported.

Ciguatoxin is heat stable and moves through the food chain without affecting the fish that carry it. There is no reliable method of detecting poisonous fish by their appearance, and ciguatoxin cannot be destroyed by cooking, freezing, drying, or smoking.

The key to preventing seafood poisoning and to providing safe and wholesome seafood products is proper temperature control along with good handling procedures. Retailers must also purchase fish and shellfish from reputable distributors and wholesalers who comply with all local, state, and federal regulations. After the seafood is received, careful attention to good sanitation and proper temperature control is essential to maintaining safety and quality (8).

Parasites

Parasites are organisms that depend on a living host to provide nutrients and shelter (9). There are several parasites that can live in animals used for food and cause foodborne illness in humans. Although parasites are not responsible for a great number of outbreaks, illnesses resulting from them can cause discomfort and in some cases even death.

Trichinosis

Probably the best known and most important foodborne parasite is *Trichinella spiralis*, which causes trichinosis in humans (9). This parasite is a delicate, threadlike worm.

Source of the organism. This parasite is found in pigs, bears, walruses, rats, dogs, cats, and other domestic and wild animals (4, 9). Among the meat-producing animals, pigs are the greatest single source of trichinosis in humans. Although much progress has been made in reducing *Trichinella spiralis* in pigs and human cases are on the decline, food store associates still need to handle and cook pork properly.

Foods involved. Pigs become infected with *Trichinella spiralis* by eating scraps of meat from infected animals that harbor the live worm in their

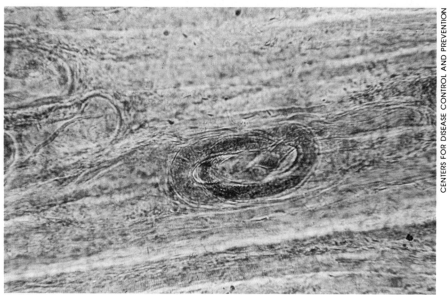

CENTERS FOR DISEASE CONTROL AND PREVENTION

A microscopic view of *Trichinella spiralis* in muscle tissue.

Table 5.2   Storage Time and Temperature Required for the Destruction of
Trichinella spiralis in Pork

	Days of Storage Required	
Temperature	Pork Less Than 6" Thick	Pork 6" to 27" Thick
5°F (–15.0°C)	20	30
–10°F (–23.3°C)	10	20
–20°F (–28.9°C)	6	12

Source: "Prescribed Treatment of Pork and Products Containing Pork to Destroy Trichinae," *Code of Federal Regulations*, 1990.

muscles. After slaughter, when the infected and inadequately cooked or raw pork is consumed, trichinosis occurs.

The disease. The symptoms of trichinosis usually appear about 4 to 9 days after eating the infected meat, but this time can vary from 2 to 28 days (*4, 9*). The first symptoms are nausea, vomiting, diarrhea, and abdominal pain. Later, fever, swelling of the tissues around the eyes, and muscular pain usually develop. Death may occur in severe cases.

Prevention. Trichinosis can be prevented by following a few simple rules (*4, 9*):

- Cook pork thoroughly—until it reaches an internal temperature of 160° to 170°F (71.1° to 76.7°C).
- Prevent cross contamination of raw pork with other meat products.
- Wash, rinse, and sanitize any equipment or utensils that are used to handle raw pork.

Freezing pork at certain temperatures for specific periods of time will also kill trichinae, as shown in Table 5.2 (*10*).

Remember, even though freezing will destroy the trichinae, pathogenic bacteria may still be present. At all times, avoid eating raw or undercooked pork.

Other Foodborne Parasites

Anisakiasis is an illness caused by Anisakis simplex, a roundworm contaminant of some marine fish. This roundworm can cause human illness if infected fish are eaten raw or are inadequately cooked. Anisakis larvae are inactivated by freezing at 4°F (–20.0°C) or lower for at least 24 to 48 hours, or by thorough cooking of the fish (*9*).

Viruses

Viruses are inert and do not carry out any functions outside of a living cell; they begin to grow and reproduce after invading living cells (9). New viruses are then liberated and infect other cells. Viruses vary in size, shape, chemical composition, cells they infect, and kind of damage they do to cells. They are very small and cannot be seen under an ordinary microscope but must be viewed under a powerful electron microscope.

Viruses are found in the intestinal tracts of infected humans and are transmitted from person to person through food or water that is contaminated with fecal matter. Infected persons who have poor personal hygiene and handle foods are responsible for many viral foodborne illnesses (4, 9). While there are several viruses (Norwalk virus, Rota virus) that can cause foodborne illness, the one that is most common is hepatitis A virus.

Hepatitis A Virus

Hepatitis A virus causes a disease of the liver called infectious hepatitis.

Source of the organism. This virus can be found in water that has been contaminated with raw sewage and in shellfish (clams and oysters) harvested from fecally contaminated water. Infectious hepatitis can also be a problem in fresh-prepared food departments of retail stores, where foods

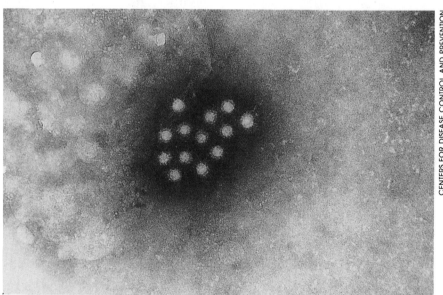

An electron micrograph of the hepatitis A virus.

CENTERS FOR DISEASE CONTROL AND PREVENTION

may be handled by an infected person and then consumed without cooking or reheating. Infected workers who do not wash their hands after using the rest room and then handle food can spread the virus to other individuals (4, 9).

Foods involved. Foods involved in viral foodborne disease outbreaks include water, dairy products, sliced luncheon meats, salads, sandwiches, fruits, raw clams and oysters, and bakery products (4, 9). The hepatitis A virus does not grow or multiply in food but is carried on food and is transmitted to people who consume the product.

The disease. The symptoms of infectious hepatitis can occur 15 to 50 days (usually 28 to 30 days) after eating the contaminated food (4, 9). The symptoms include fever, nausea, vomiting, and abdominal pain, followed by enlargement of the liver. Jaundice, a yellowing of the skin, occurs in many cases and is due to the way the virus affects the liver. Prolonged disability is common, but death is rare.

Prevention. Infectious hepatitis and other viral infections can be easily prevented by (4, 9)

- identifying people who are ill and not permitting them to work with food
- practicing good personal hygiene and instructing people to wash their hands often—*especially* after using the toilet
- handling foods with clean and sanitized utensils, and *clean* plastic gloves
- properly cooking foods
- obtaining shellfish from approved, certified sources (not from contaminated waters)

The foodborne illnesses described in this chapter are the most common ones that occur in the U.S. It is important to understand the causes of these illnesses and ways to prevent them from ever occurring in your store.

Remember, the safety of food depends on people: those who produce and process it, those who transport and distribute it, and last but not least, those who prepare it. Only through education, awareness, and following the rules of food safety and sanitation will the level of foodborne illness be reduced.

References

1. Gravani, R. B. "The Causes and Costs of Foodborne Disease." *Dairy and Food Sanitation 7*, no. 1 (1987): 20–25.
2. Bean, N. H., and P. M. Griffin. "Foodborne Disease Outbreaks in the United States, 1973–1987." *Journal of Food Protection* 53, no. 9 (1990): 804–17.
3. Gravani, R. B. "Bacterial Foodborne Diseases." *Dairy and Food Sanitation 7*, no. 2 (1987): 77–82.
4. National Restaurant Association. Educational Foundation. *Applied Foodservice Sanitation*. 4th ed. New York: John Wiley & Sons, Inc., 1992.
5. Doyle, M. P. *Foodborne Bacterial Pathogens*. New York: Marcel Dekker, Inc., 1989.
6. Banwart, G. J. *Basic Food Microbiology*. New York: VanNostrand Reinhold/AVI, 1989.
7. Gravani, R. B. "Chemical Foodborne Diseases." *Dairy and Food Sanitation 7*, no. 4 (1987): 192–97.
8. Arnold, R. E., and K. Gall. *Service Seafood Management and Operations*. Cornell University Home Study Program, Ithaca, NY, 1991.
9. Gravani, R. B. "Parasitic and Viral Foodborne Diseases." *Dairy and Food Sanitation 7*, no. 5 (1987): 244–46.
10. "Prescribed Treatment of Pork and Products Containing Pork to Destroy Trichinae." *Code of Federal Regulations*. 9 CFR 318.10. Washington, DC: U.S. Government Printing Office, 1990.

6

The Hazard Analysis Critical Control Point (HACCP) System

There are many hazards that can cause harm to people if they are present in foods. Biological, chemical, or physical hazards can cause foodborne illness or injury to people who consume foods that contain them. The biological and chemical hazards that cause foodborne illness have been discussed in chapter 5. Physical hazards include foreign objects or extraneous matter that are not normally found in foods. Items like metal fragments, nuts and bolts, small pieces of jewelry, wood splinters, glass, plastic, and many other foreign objects can cause injury to your customers when they are present in foods. Although biological hazards cause a majority of the reported foodborne illnesses, contamination of foods by chemical and physical hazards must also be prevented to assure the safety of foods in your store.

Factors Contributing to Foodborne Outbreaks

Investigations have shown that there are several important factors that contribute to foodborne-illness outbreaks (1). The ten most important contributing factors are listed in order of importance in Table 6.1. These factors relate to the contamination, survival, and/or growth of microorganisms, so the risk of foodborne illness is high whenever these improper practices occur during food preparation or storage.

Investigations of outbreaks have also found that certain foods are frequently involved in foodborne illnesses. These foods are called "potentially hazardous" foods because they can support the rapid and progressive growth of bacterial foodborne pathogens (2). These foods usually have several characteristics in common, including

- a pH in the low acid range (above pH 4.6)
- a water activity (A_w) of greater than 0.85
- a high protein content

Table 6.1 Factors that Contribute to Foodborne Illness

---

1. Improper cooling of foods:
   - Leaving cooked food at room temperature
   - Storing foods in large containers in the cooler
2. Lapse of 12 or more hours between food preparation and eating
3. Infected persons handling foods:
   - Infected persons may have skin infections, diarrhea, or sore throats.
   - Infected persons may also harbor pathogens in their bodies but show no signs of illness.
4. Inadequate reheating of foods
5. Improper hot-holding of foods
6. Contaminated raw foods or ingredients
7. Use of food from unsafe sources
8. Improper cleaning of equipment and utensils
9. Cross contamination from raw to cooked foods
10. Inadequate cooking of foods

Source: F.L. Bryan, "Risks of Practices, Procedures, and Processes that Lead to Outbreaks of Foodborne Diseases," *Journal of Food Protection* 51 (1988): 663–730.

Examples of some potentially hazardous foods (3, 4) are:

- meat and meat products (roast beef, ground meat and meat mixtures, ham, meat tacos and enchiladas)
- poultry and poultry products
- fish and shellfish
- eggs and egg products
- milk and milk products
- meat and vegetable salads (potato, macaroni, chicken, turkey, tuna, and egg salads)
- gravies
- soups (especially creamed soups)
- sauces (except those high in acid)
- dressings
- puddings, custards, and cream-filled products
- cooked or heated vegetables and plant products, including rice, mashed and baked potatoes, and tofu
- low-acid foods

In addition, some ethnic foods, such as Asian and Mexican-style foods, have been implicated in foodborne disease outbreaks and are also considered potentially hazardous foods (4). These foods are commonly prepared in departments throughout the store, so associates must take particular care and precautions during their preparation, storage, and display to prevent foodborne illness.

HACCP: A New Approach

While some food store sanitation programs have been more successful than others in controlling hazards and preventing foodborne illness, the food industry as a whole has realized the importance of implementing an across-the-board program that can be applied to all departments of the store. The education and training of employees, inspection of facilities and equipment, and microbiological testing of foods are examples of programs that have been used to control hazards and prevent foodborne illnesses. While all of these programs have had some positive results, foodborne illnesses still occur (5).

Today, many food-processing plants, foodservice establishments, and retail stores are using a novel, preventative approach to assure the safety of foods that are manufactured, prepared, and merchandised. This new approach is called the Hazard Analysis Critical Control Point system, or HACCP (pronounced hassip) system (6, 7, 8, 9, 10, 11, 12). The goal of an effectively designed and implemented HACCP system is to assure the safety of food that is prepared, merchandised, and sold.

HACCP is being promoted by federal government agencies such as the U.S. Food and Drug Administration (FDA), the U.S. Department of Agriculture (USDA), the U.S. Department of Commerce, National Marine Fisheries Service, and scientific advisory committees to these agencies; state and local regulatory agencies; and industry trade associations as an innovative way to prevent foodborne illness and assure the safety of foods. The Food Marketing Institute has developed a comprehensive HACCP manual and suggests that this system be used in all departments where raw or fresh products are handled (12). Many states are now conducting HACCP inspections in retail food stores, so you should know about this new system and understand how it functions.

This chapter is intended to serve as an introduction to the principles of HACCP and to provide food store employees with an understanding of the components of this important system. It is not intended to be a comprehensive guide to HACCP or to provide specific details of its implementation in all specialty departments. The principles and procedures outlined here will give you an understanding of what HACCP is, how it functions, and how a HACCP program is developed for retail stores.

Historical Perspectives

HACCP was developed in the late 1960s by scientists at the Pillsbury Company, who were asked by the National Aeronautics and Space Administration (NASA) to provide the first foods used by American astronauts in space (13). Faced with the challenge of producing foods that would be totally safe and free from contaminants, Pillsbury scientists needed to develop a new system to assure food safety. (Think about how a contaminated food could cause a foodborne outbreak in space, resulting in a failed or even catastrophic mission.) After much research and evaluation, the company established a system of assuring safety that could be applied to any point in the food chain—from harvesting to final preparation—and HACCP was born.

The HACCP system was first implemented in the food-processing industry in the early 1970s. Today, HACCP procedures are also being used to assure the safety of the diverse products produced and prepared in many foodservice establishments and supermarkets throughout the country.

What Is HACCP?

HACCP is an effective preventive approach to assuring the safety of foods. It is a systematic way of looking at food processing and preparation as an ongoing process, rather than as a set of isolated steps. In the HACCP system, a "flow chart" or "flow diagram" of the steps showing how a specific potentially hazardous food goes from raw ingredients to saleable merchandise is first established; then the hazards that could affect the product at each step are identified.

The procedures or steps in the process at which the safety of the finished product could be compromised are called *critical control points* (CCPs). Once these critical points are identified, control procedures or boundaries of safety must be established. The CCPs must be closely monitored to make sure that the processing or preparation is being carried out correctly and that the hazards present are being controlled. If a problem or deviation is found, action can be taken to correct it immediately—before a dangerous situation develops. In a HACCP program, effective recordkeeping systems must be established to document the results of measurements and to control the process. Procedures for verifying that the system is working must also be established.

Today, many regulatory agencies are conducting HACCP-based inspections. Inspectors are focusing on practices and procedures in the processing and preparation of foods that can lead to foodborne outbreaks (Table 6.1). In particular, they are concentrating on temperature control (during cooking, cooling, reheating, storage, and display), how raw and cooked foods are handled, personal-hygiene practices, and cleaning and sanitizing procedures. Well-developed HACCP plans identify these critical areas of concern and the steps that must be taken to assure the safety of the products that are being processed or prepared. In the grocery store, HACCP systems are particularly important in the deli department, the in-store restaurant, the soup-and-salad bar, and the seafood department (*8, 12*).

Developing a HACCP Plan

In order for a successful HACCP program to be planned and implemented in retail stores, top management must be *totally committed* to the HACCP approach. Once this occurs, then a HACCP plan can be developed for specific, potentially hazardous food items in departments throughout the store. The HACCP plan is a written document that is based upon the HACCP principles and that lists the procedures which will be used to assure the safety of foods (6, 7).

The HACCP Team and Flow Diagrams

The first step in developing an effective HACCP plan is to *assemble a HACCP team* (see Figure 6.1). This team should consist of people who have specific knowledge and expertise in the processing and preparation of foods, food microbiology, sanitation, quality assurance, or other related disciplines, and who understand and have experience with the HACCP concept. These individuals may already work for the company or can be outside experts brought in to provide advice on developing HACCP plans.

When your team is in place, the HACCP concept can be applied to the store operations by identifying departments where potentially hazardous foods are prepared and/or handled. Then a HACCP plan for each of these departments can be developed and implemented.

The next step is to *identify all the potentially hazardous foods* that are processed and prepared in each department and how they will be merchandised, sold, and used by the consumer. (Keep in mind the potentially hazardous foods that were mentioned earlier in this chapter.) After this is done, the *development of flow diagrams for the preparation or processing of these food products* can begin. These flow diagrams should provide a clear, simple description of all the steps required for the preparation or processing of each food item. The *diagrams should then be checked and verified* for completeness and accuracy.

Let's assume that your company's HACCP team has been assembled and has identified fried chicken as a potentially hazardous food that is prepared in your store's deli department. The HACCP team has developed and verified a simple flow diagram showing all of the steps in-

---

Figure 6.1   The First Steps Involved in Developing a HACCP Plan for Foods
Processed or Prepared in Grocery Stores

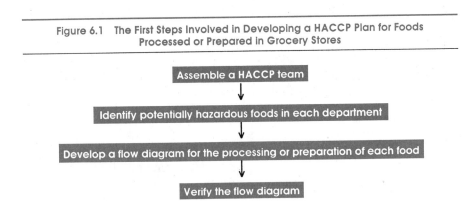

volved in the preparation, display, and storage of fried chicken (*12*), which is shown in Figure 6.2.

The Seven Basic HACCP Principles

The next step is to apply the seven basic HACCP principles to the flow diagram. These principles, identified by the National Advisory Committee for Microbiological Criteria for Foods (*7, 8*), are the key to developing an effective HACCP plan. The principles are

1. Identify potential food-safety hazards at each step in the flow diagram. (Conduct a hazard analysis.)
2. Determine where and when to prevent potential problems. (Identify which steps are critical control points.)

Figure 6.2   Flow Diagram for Fried Chicken

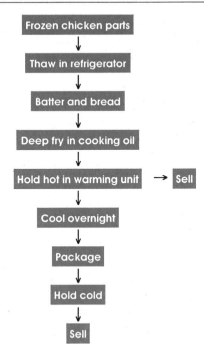

3. Establish control procedures at critical control points. (Set limits to control potential problems.)

4. Monitor critical control points. (Set up methods to monitor limits.)

5. Take corrective action when there is a deviation at critical control points. (Set up procedures to handle control problems.)

6. Establish effective recordkeeping systems that document the HACCP system. (Keep good records and review them to check that controls work.)

7. Verify that the system is working. (Conduct periodic audits to ensure that the HACCP plan works properly.)

At first glance, these seven principles may look quite technical, but they provide a systematic and practical approach to preventing foodborne illness.

To illustrate the HACCP approach, each principle will be applied to the preparation, display, and storage of fried chicken in the deli department, and will be explained in sequence. Refer to Table 6.2 (pages 84–85) throughout the following discussion.

Conduct a Hazard Analysis

Conduct a hazard analysis by identifying and listing the steps in the flow diagram for fried chicken where significant hazards occur. Some questions that should be asked during a hazard analysis include (7, 9, 12)

- What are the raw materials or ingredients? Are they likely to be contaminated by pathogenic microorganisms?

- Do any of the ingredients have toxic properties? How are they stored and handled?

- Can a contaminant reach the product during or after preparation and storage?

- Will pathogenic microorganisms or toxic substances be killed or rendered harmless during cooking, heating, or other processes?

- Is cross contamination between raw and cooked product likely?

- Could any pathogenic microorganism multiply during preparation or storage?

- How long will it take to prepare and store the food?

- After preparation, is the food going to be held hot, at room temperature, refrigerated, or frozen?

- How will the food be handled by the customer?

The answers to these questions and many others can help identify hazards and can be used to determine their severity and risks. For example, if the chicken is undercooked and a pathogen survives, it can cause illness. In this case, the severity of the hazard is very high and needs to be carefully controlled. Raw chicken is frequently contaminated with *Salmonella, C. perfringens,* and other pathogens, and should be handled with care. Most of the hazards in the fried chicken process (see Table 6.2) deal with time/temperature considerations of the product—thawing the raw, frozen chicken parts; cooking; hot-holding; cold-holding the cooked product for sale—and how these factors can influence the growth, survival, or destruction of bacteria that are present.

Identify Critical Control Points

A critical control point (CCP) is a point, step, or procedure where control can be applied and a food-safety hazard can be prevented, eliminated, or reduced to acceptable levels (6, 7). CCPs include steps such as cooking, cooling, reheating, specific cleaning and sanitizing procedures, prevention of cross contamination, and certain aspects of employee hygiene. Steps that are identified as CCPs should be given continuous attention and the highest priority since a hazard that is not controlled can lead to a foodborne illness (12).

There are four CCPs in the deli-prepared fried chicken example, including the cooking (frying) process (CCP #1), hot-holding the chicken in a warming unit (CCP #2), cooling the chicken (CCP #3), and holding the cold chicken in the display case (CCP #4) prior to sale. These critical control points are highlighted in Table 6.2.

Establish Control Procedures at Critical Control Points

It is important that control procedures be established at each CCP. These procedures need to be properly implemented to assure the prevention, elimination, or reduction of hazards. They are also referred to as criteria for control, or critical limits, and represent the boundaries of safety at the CCPs. Examples of control procedures are *specific* cooking, cooling, or reheating temperatures; time of a cooking or cooling process; specific sanitation procedures; and many others. Criteria for control are usually specified for every step in a process, but those at CCPs are of the greatest concern. The preventive measures for each step in the fried chicken process are shown in Table 6.2.

The first step in the process is to receive and store the chicken parts frozen (0°F or less; –17.8°C or less). The second preventive measure is to thaw the chicken in the refrigerator at less than 40°F (4.4°C) or, alterna-

Table 6.2   The Preparation, Display, and Storage of Fried Chicken in the Deli Department

Process Step	Hazards	Critical Control Points	Criteria for Control (Preventative Measures)
Receive frozen chicken parts Store frozen	*Salmonella* and other pathogens, as well as heat-resistant spores, are present.	—	Receive frozen product at temperature of 0°F (–17.8°C) or less; store at 0°F (–17.8°C) or less.
Thaw in refrigerator	Incomplete thawing can lead to insufficient cooking, and microbes can survive; keeping thawed items at room temperature for a few hours or in the refrigerator for several days can lead to bacterial growth.	—	Thaw in refrigerator at <40°F (<4.4°C); alternatively, thaw under cold, running water; use products within specified time; maintain internal temperature at <40°F (<4.4°C).
Batter and bread	Bacterial spores are present in batter and breading ingredients.	—	Discard batter and breading after use; don't hold used batter and breading for use with other batches of chicken.
Cook in oil	Undercooking may not kill bacterial pathogens; bacterial spores can survive.	CCP #1	Internal temperature must reach at least 165°F (73.9°C).
Hold hot in warming unit or on steam table Sell	Bacteria may multiply unless high temperatures are maintained.	CCP #2	Hold at internal temperature of at least 140°F (60.0°C); hold batch less than 5 hours; never cover steam table inserts with lids or pans and put cooked chicken on top; never keep chicken in bowls while on tables.
Cool in refrigerator	Bacteria may multiply unless chicken is cooled rapidly and held cold.	CCP #3	Cool rapidly at depth less than 3 inches (8 cm); do not use pans higher than 4 inches (10 cm); never stack pans; maintain refrigerator air temperature and chicken temperature at 40°F (4.4°C) or less.
Package (wrap and label)	Bacterial contamination during packaging is possible.	—	Don't touch cooked product with bare hands during wrapping; keep raw chicken away from cooked product.
Hold cold in display case Sell	Bacterial growth caused either by improper cold-holding or prolonged storage is possible.	CCP #4	Refrigerate promptly after wrapping; hold at 40°F (4.4°C) or below; keep display-case air temperature <40°F (<4.4°C).

Source: Adapted from the Food Marketing Institute HACCP Manual, 1989. Only the highlighted

Table 6.2 (continued)

Monitoring Procedures	Corrective Action (if criteria are not met)	Records	HACCP System Verification
Inspect product and check that temperature is 0°F (–17.8°C) or less.	Reject shipment if thawed.	Receiving log	Inventory control audit by deli department manager*
Observe thawing method; use promptly after thawing or keep in refrigerator for a short period of time; monitor product code dates.	Modify thawing procedure; modify time frame in which product is used.	Equipment and product temperature logs	Deli department manager*
Observe whether batter is being reused for other batches.	Discard used batter and breading.	Record of exception	Deli department manager*
Follow time/temperature cooking instructions carefully; measure temperature in thickest part of chicken.	Continue heating until criteria for control is met.	Deli department time/temperature log	Deli department manager*
Measure temperature in center of chicken every 2 hours.	Reheat to 165°F (73.9°C); cool to 40°F (4.4°C) in 4 hours or less, or discard.	Deli department time/temperature log	Deli department manager*
Measure depth of pan and fill; measure refrigerator air temperature every 4 hours.	Discard deep containers of food; modify cooling procedure; adjust thermostat setting.	Deli department time/temperature log	Deli department manager*
Observe whether cooked product is touched; make sure clean, disposable gloves are worn; observe whether raw chicken is kept away from cooked product.	Either discard or reheat to 165°F (73.9°C) items that are touched.	Record of exception	Deli department manager*
Measure depth of pan and fill; measure temperature of chicken and of display case every 2 hours.	Chill rapidly; adjust thermostat setting.	Deli department time/temperature log	Deli department manager* *Or designated individual

steps are elements of a true HACCP plan. The others are important, but not critical to product safety.

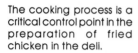

The cooking process is a critical control point in the preparation of fried chicken in the deli.

tively, under cold, running water. The chicken must be used within a specified period of time and have an internal temperature of less than 40°F (less than 4.4°C). The third preventive measure involves the batter-and-breading operation. The batter and breading should be discarded after use and should not be held over for use with other batches of chicken.

The control procedure for CCP #1 at the frying step of this process is that the internal temperature of the chicken must reach at least 165°F (73.9°C) to ensure doneness and to destroy any foodborne pathogens that may be present.

At the hot-holding step, CCP #2, the control procedure is to hold the cooked chicken in a warming unit at an internal temperature of at least 140°F (60.0°C) for no longer than five hours.

The preventive measure at the product-cooling step, CCP #3, is to cool the cooked chicken rapidly in small quantities (less than 3 inches, or less than 8 cm, in depth) to 40°F (4.4°C) within four hours. Pans should not exceed 4 inches (10 cm) in depth and pans should never be stacked on top of each other. The refrigerator temperature should be less than 40°F (4.4°C).

When wrapping the cold chicken, the chicken should not be touched with bare hands. The last preventive measure is at CCP #4, where the chicken is held cold in the refrigerated display case. The chicken must be refrigerated promptly after wrapping and held at 40°F (4.4°C) or below. Display-case air temperature must be less than 40°F (4.4°C) (12).

An important consideration throughout the entire preparation of this fried chicken is to prevent cross contamination. Always separate raw and cooked foods, and wash and sanitize all equipment and utensils between products.

Attention needs to be given to the temperature of the oil and the length of time the chicken is cooked.

Monitor Critical Control Points

To be sure that the HACCP system is functioning properly, the CCPs must be carefully monitored by those associates involved in the operation. Monitoring is simply checking to determine that procedures at each CCP meet the established criteria for control. It can be done by visual observations (for example, checking frozen food to see that it is frozen solid and that no thawing has occurred) or through measurements such as temperature of the food, time of a cooling procedure, pH of a product, or sanitizer strength. Monitoring helps to make sure that the system is in control. Monitoring results are frequently recorded and used later to verify that the system is working correctly.

The monitoring procedures of the fried chicken example are listed in Table 6.2. The frozen chicken should be checked to see that it is frozen solid; temperature of frozen product should be 0°F (–17.8°C) or less. The process of thawing the chicken in the refrigerator should be observed to make sure that it is done properly and that the chicken is used promptly after it is thawed or kept in the refrigerator for only a short period of time. The monitoring procedure at the batter-and-breading step is to observe that these ingredients are not held and used for other batches of chicken.

Cooking time and temperature must be carefully monitored at CCP #1 and should be done according to company or supplier instructions for the specific product and equipment that are being used. The temperature of the chicken is monitored by using a correctly calibrated, cleaned, and sanitized thermometer that is inserted into the thickest part of the product. If the temperature reaches at least 165°F (73.9°C), then the chicken has been properly and thoroughly cooked. The actual finished temperatures of each batch of chicken should be recorded in a time/temperature log book in the deli.

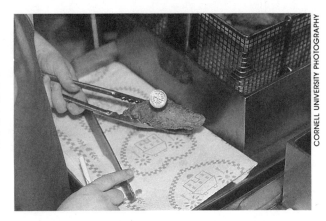

After cooking, the temperature of the chicken should be taken using a calibrated thermometer. The temperature in the thickest part of the chicken should be at least 165°F (73.9°C).

In the warming unit, CCP #2, the internal temperature of the chicken should be monitored every two hours. At CCP #3, the equipment used for cooling cooked chicken should be monitored every four hours for temperature compliance. Also, the pans used for cooling should be measured to be sure that they meet the criteria for control.

When packaging the cold, cooked chicken, it is important that associates wash their hands prior to beginning this job and then use clean and sanitized utensils or clean, disposable gloves to handle the product. The chicken should not be touched with bare hands. At CCP #4, during the cold-holding in the display case, the cooked chicken and display-case temperature should be monitored every two hours. The cooked chicken should be stored properly to prevent recontamination.

Take Corrective Action

When the results from monitoring indicate that there is a deviation from established procedures, action must be taken to correct the situation and assure that the CCPs are under control. Corrective actions that must be taken if criteria for control are not met in the fried chicken process are listed in Table 6.2.

For example, if the chicken parts are not frozen when they are received, the parts should be rejected. If there is a problem with the thawing of product, the thawing procedures should be modified. Likewise, if the batter and breading are being held and used for another batch of chicken, they should be discarded. If the chicken is removed from the fryer and the internal temperature is at 140°F (60.0°C), then it must be returned to the fryer until it reaches 165°F (73.9°C). Immediate corrective action is necessary for the chicken to reach appropriate temperatures to ensure doneness and the destruction of pathogens.

Another critical control point is the hot-holding of the fried chicken. The chicken should be kept at a minimum internal temperature of 140°F (60.0°C) in the warming unit.

If the temperature of the chicken in the warming unit falls below 140°F (60.0°C), then the food should be immediately reheated to 165°F (73.9°C) or rapidly cooled to 40°F (4.4°C). If the cooked chicken does not cool to 40°F (4.4°C) in four hours, the cooling procedure needs to be modified. Perhaps the thermostat on the cooling equipment needs to be adjusted. If chicken is found in pans deeper than 4 inches (10 cm), the food should be discarded. If cooked products are touched with bare hands during packaging, the product should be reheated to 165°F (73.9°C) or discarded. Control measures for holding the chicken cold include adjusting the thermostat of the display case to assure that the product is at 40°F (4.4°C) or below.

Establish Effective Recordkeeping Systems that Document the HACCP System

It is important that associates record all appropriate monitoring data and that supervisors review these logs to be sure that monitoring is being done effectively (*10*). Well-organized monitoring records provide evidence that food-safety assurance is being accomplished according to the HACCP principles. These records should include flow diagrams, monitoring procedures, deviations (if any), corrective actions, sanitation procedures, and other pertinent information. Specific individuals need to be responsible for monitoring the steps in the flow diagram, taking corrective actions, and recording this information. Associates who are involved in these activities need to initial and date each log when the work is completed. This information is later reviewed by a supervisor, who also signs the log. An example of a log for HACCP recordkeeping is shown in Figure 6.3. The records that need to be kept for the fried chicken are shown in Table 6.2.

The recordkeeping system for fried chicken is easy to set up and maintain. The receiving log is where pertinent information on the shipment of chicken is listed. A deli department time and temperature log is

---

Figure 6.3 Form for Monitoring Safety of Hot Foods in Warmers and Steam Tables

---

FOOD MARKETING INSTITUTE
FORM FOR MONITORING SAFETY OF HOT FOODS IN WARMERS AND STEAM TABLES

(1) Date _____

Activity	Food Temperature						Verification		
	1	2	3	4	5	6	#		I
(2) Cooking completed								T	
(3) Display/hot holding 10 am								T	
12:00 Noon									
2:00 pm									
4:00 pm									
6:00 pm									
8:00 pm									
(4) Cooling	Container depth (inches/cm)						Verification		
							#	D	I
(5) Completion of cooling	Food temperature							T	
(6) Reheating	Food temperature							T	

(7) Type of food:

1 _____   2 _____

3 _____   4 _____

5 _____   6 _____

Verification legend:
 # = Food number; T = Temperature; D = Depth of food in container; I = Initials of supervisor

(8) Comments: _____

_____

_____

Source: Food Marketing Institute, *A Program to Ensure Food Safety in the Supermarket—The Hazard Analysis Critical Control Point System: A HACCP Manual* (Washington, DC, 1989). Reprinted with permission.

an effective way to record and maintain the times and temperatures of products from thawing to final sale. A "record of exception" is kept only if there is an exception to the control criteria. For example, the standard procedure in a batter-and-breading operation is to discard the used material after the step is completed. Normally, records would not be kept; but if for some reason these materials are reused for another batch of chicken, this would be noted and kept on file. At first, completing the logs may seem time-consuming and unnecessary, but the assurance, as well as the evidence, that food is being prepared or processed safely will be very rewarding (12). These logs can also be invaluable should some problems occur later.

Verify that the System Is Working

The final step in the HACCP plan is to verify that the system is working correctly. Verification should first be done by the individuals who set up the HACCP plan, as well as by outside reviewers. The entire system needs to be examined and double-checked with a critical eye to making sure that everything is in place and working properly. Be sure that

- the product flow diagram is accurate and that food is being prepared exactly according to the recipe
- hazards have been properly identified throughout the entire process
- the appropriate critical control points have been carefully chosen
- effective control or preventive measures have been specified at each point
- these control measures are in place
- the most effective monitoring procedures possible have been chosen and these monitoring procedures are being followed
- if problems are found at any point in the process, appropriate corrective actions are taken to rectify them
- well-documented and orderly records are being kept

In addition to a thorough review of the written HACCP plan, careful and thorough observations of the entire preparation process (from raw ingredients to finished product) should be undertaken. The observations should not deviate from the written plan.

The verifications for each step in the fried chicken HACCP plan are listed in Table 6.2. HACCP verification can be done through department audits by supervisory personnel—store or department managers—or by responsible individuals that they designate. These supervisors should check time and temperature logs to see that they are being kept in an accurate and orderly manner. They should also make sure that associates are not filling out the logs until the tasks are actually performed; that is, *temperatures should not be listed until they are actually taken.* If all the information is present to their satisfaction, the supervisors should sign and date each log. These procedures verify that the system is working properly.

Remember that every time a new ingredient is used, a new recipe is tried, or new, potentially hazardous foods are added to your inventory or menu, a new HACCP plan needs to be developed. If ingredients and processing or preparation steps are changed without reviewing and reevaluating the HACCP plan, some new hazard(s) may be present and may not be properly controlled—foodborne illness can be the result. The HACCP plan needs to be reviewed and rewritten when any changes are made.

While all associates who work in specialty departments need to understand the HACCP principles, personnel at company headquarters will probably assist in developing the specific details of the HACCP plan for products in your store. Associates are usually responsible for carrying out the HACCP plan—especially for adhering to procedures, monitoring CCPs, taking corrective actions, and keeping complete records. Of course, the responsibilities of associates involved in a HACCP program will vary with each food retailer.

Applying HACCP in Store Departments

HACCP can be easily applied to foods prepared in many departments in the store. A few points to consider when developing HACCP plans for several specialty food departments are discussed below.

Deli/Fresh-prepared Foods

Among the deli/fresh-prepared items that should be prepared using HACCP principles are the following:

- hot foods like poultry, meat, fish, and vegetable dishes prepared and displayed on steam tables. Critical control points include cooking, keeping the product hot in warming units or on steam tables, preventing cross contamination, and rapidly cooling unsold product.
- cooked foods containing meat that are cooked and sold cold (lasagna, roast turkey, roast beef, pâté). Critical control points include cooking, cooling, slicing, and preventing cross contamination.

- salads containing cooked poultry, meat, or seafood. Critical controls should be put into place at the initial cooking and cooling stages, the addition of other ingredients, and the storage or display of the finished product. Preventing cross contamination is essential.
- pasta salads. The critical control points are located at the cooking and cooling steps, as well as during refrigerated storage or display of these salads. Preventing cross contamination of these foods is also essential.

Soup-and-Salad Bar

Food items on a soup-and-salad bar, often a component of the deli/fresh-prepared department, should also be prepared, displayed, and stored according to the HACCP principles. Especially important is the monitoring of temperatures of foods like soups, chili, rice, taco meat, and refried beans that are held hot on the steam table or in soup kettles (12). Cooling the products and their subsequent reheating are also critical control points in the operation.

Preparing raw vegetables for the salad bar presents many hazardous situations (12). The raw vegetables must be stored properly prior to preparation. They then must be washed, peeled, chopped, or grated with clean and sanitized utensils, and mixed without being touched with bare hands. The products must also be displayed in clean and sanitized containers in the salad bar, and properly cooled while on display and while stored.

The other elements of the salad bar—prepared chilled salads and canned items such as puddings, tuna, chickpeas, and kidney beans—must also be monitored carefully. Since the salad bar is usually in an area of the supermarket that sees a lot of traffic, it is essential to maintain strict controls to ensure the safety of the food displayed on it.

Seafood

Seafood, both fish and shellfish, requires extreme care when being processed, displayed, and stored, as it can transmit bacteria or harbor parasites (12). The HACCP flow chart that is drawn up for products in this department should take into account every step in the chain, from unpacking an order to displaying the product on the cold table. Don't forget the problems that can be caused by the cross contamination of bacteria from raw seafood products to cooked items. Keep raw and cooked foods separated, wash hands, and wash and sanitize all equipment and utensils between products.

Critical control points in the storage, handling, and display of fresh seafood include initial storage of the product as soon as it is received, display on the cold table, and storage of the unsold product. The same points should be monitored when frozen seafood products come into the department.

Shellfish must be checked upon arrival to make sure that they are properly tagged and were obtained from approved sources, not harvested from contaminated waters. Storage and display are also critical control points. Cooked shellfish must be monitored throughout the cooking and cooling process, display, packaging for sale, and storage of unsold product. Employees should never handle raw seafood and cooked seafood in succession without washing their hands, and displays of these products should always be kept separate.

Many seafood departments now sell processed products such as soups, chowder, stews, and gumbos, as well as fully cooked seafood and seafood-based salads. These items should also be prepared, handled, and stored with care. The same HACCP guidelines described above for fresh-prepared foods should be used by employees preparing and selling salad and soup items in the seafood department. There are several model HACCP plans currently being used in seafood departments throughout the food retailing industry.

HACCP Training Programs

The success of the HACCP system in a supermarket depends on *everyone* who works in the facility. Each person, especially those who work in the specialty departments, needs to be properly and thoroughly educated about the HACCP system and his or her important role in it. Although employee education and training programs will be discussed in detail later in this book, it is important to recognize that employees must first understand what HACCP is and then learn the skills necessary to make it function properly. Attention to detail when preparing or processing foods is very important.

Management must provide adequate time to thoroughly train associates. Management must then give associates the materials and equipment necessary to carry out their tasks. When this is done properly and in a spirit of cooperation, a close-knit team of people with a winning attitude develops and food-safety problems can be prevented.

HACCP and Sanitation

You are probably wondering exactly what the relationship is between HACCP and all of the sanitation programs that you now have in place. HACCP is a system that has been built on a strong foundation of key food-safety and sanitation components, including food temperature control, effective cleaning and sanitizing of equipment and utensils, good personal hygiene, proper work habits, and effective pest-control (insect and rodent) programs. To be effective, HACCP depends on the commitment of top management, a well-developed employee education and training program, and a thorough understanding of biological, chemical, and physical hazards and their control in foods. Figure 6.4 shows all of these important components, graphically illustrated in the shape of a pyramid.

Now that you have an understanding of HACCP, each of the key food sanitation components that provide the foundation for HACCP will be discussed in the next several chapters.

Figure 6.4 The HACCP Food Safety Assurance Pyramid

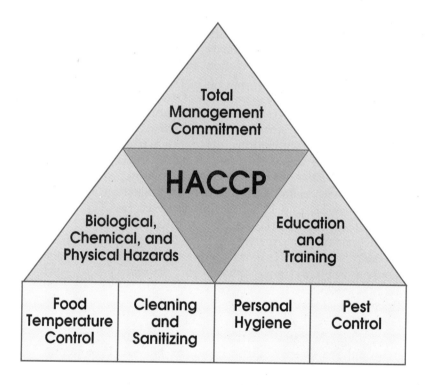

Developed by Robert B. Gravani, Cornell University.

Conclusions

HACCP is a preventive, state-of-the-art, systematic approach to assuring the safety of foods. It is rapidly becoming a vital part of many supermarket operations. Your understanding and familiarity with the concepts discussed in this chapter will enable you to be on the cutting edge of the latest information on preventing foodborne illness. Remember, a HACCP program is only as effective as the people who understand, develop, and implement it.

References

1. Bryan, F. L. "Risks of Practices, Procedures, and Processes that Lead to Outbreaks of Foodborne Diseases." *Journal of Food Protection* 51(1988):663–73.
2. U.S. Food and Drug Administration. Center for Food Safety and Applied Nutrition. *Proposed Food Protection Unicode.* 1988.
3. National Restaurant Association. Educational Foundation. *Applied Foodservice Sanitation.* 4th ed. New York: John Wiley & Sons, Inc., 1992.
4. Bryan, F. L. "Risks Associated with Vehicles of Foodborne Pathogens and Toxins." *Journal of Food Protection* 51(1988):498–508.
5. World Health Organization/International Commission on Microbiological Specifications for Food. *Report of the WHO/ICMSF Meeting on Hazard Analysis: Critical Control Point System in Food Hygiene.* Geneva, Switzerland: World Health Organization, 1982.
6. Pierson, M. D., and D. A. Corlett, Jr., eds. *HACCP: Principles and Applications.* New York: VanNostrand Reinhold, 1992.
7. U.S. Department of Agriculture. The National Advisory Committee on Microbiological Criteria for Foods. "Hazard Analysis Critical Control Point System." *International Journal of Food Microbiology* 16(1992):1–23.
8. Price, R. J., P. D. Tom, and K. E. Stevenson. *Ensuring Food Safety . . . the HACCP Way. An Introduction to HACCP and A Resource Guide for Retail Deli Managers.* U.S. Dept. of Agriculture, Extension Service, National Sea Grant College Program, NOAA, U.S. Dept. of Commerce, 1993.
9. Bryan, F. L. "Hazard Analysis Critical Control Point (HACCP) Concept." *Dairy, Food and Environmental Sanitation* 10(1990):416–18.

10. Bryan, F. L. "Hazard Analysis Critical Control Point (HACCP) Systems for Retail Food Stores and Restaurant Operations." *Journal of Food Protection* 53(1990):978–88.
11. International Association of Milk, Food and Environmental Sanitarians (IAMFES). *Procedures to Implement the Hazard Analysis Critical Control Point System.* Ames, IA: 1991.
12. Food Marketing Institute. *A Program to Ensure Food Safety in the Supermarket—The Hazard Analysis Critical Control Point System: A HACCP Manual.* Washington, DC, 1989.
13. Bauman, H. E. "Introduction to HACCP." In *HACCP: Principles and Applications,* edited by M. D. Pierson and D. A. Corlett, Jr. New York: VanNostrand Reinhold, 1992.

7

Food Temperature Control

Food temperature control is one of the foundation blocks of the HACCP food safety assurance pyramid. It is perhaps the most important concept to remember when receiving, storing, preparing, and displaying foods for sale. Many of the factors contributing to foodborne-illness outbreaks relate to the control of temperatures. Remember that the cooking, hot-holding, cooling, reheating, and cold-holding of foods are critical control points that must be carefully monitored and controlled in all fresh-prepared food departments in the store.

The recent foodborne-illness outbreak from improperly cooked hamburgers at a fast-food chain in the Northwest illustrates the critical role temperature control plays in assuring the safety of foods. The deaths and serious illnesses that occurred from this *E. coli* outbreak could easily have been prevented had the hamburgers been cooked to an internal temperature of at least 155°F (68.3°C) and held at 140°F (60.0°C) or above (1). Temperature control in this instance meant the difference between life or death. The baked lasagna outbreak mentioned in chapter 2 also involved improper cooking and provides another important example of

98

why food temperatures need to be carefully monitored and controlled to assure safety.

As you know, virtually all bacteria will multiply rapidly if they are kept at temperatures between 40°F and 140°F (4.4°C and 60.0°C). The reason for this is simple; most bacteria grow slowly or not at all at temperatures below 40°F and do not survive at temperatures above 140°F. This range of temperatures is known as the *temperature danger zone* (2). Food products left at temperatures in this range for an extended period of time will become unsafe and therefore unsalable.

A primary rule that many food professionals follow is known as the *time and temperature principle* (2). This rule requires that foods be kept at an internal temperature below 40°F or above 140°F during storage, display, and service. If during periods of preparation foods must be exposed to temperatures between these two crucial points, their exposure should be for as short a time as possible. The total accumulated time that potentially hazardous foods are in the temperature danger zone must not exceed four hours (3).

Thermometers

Before discussing the specific details of food temperature control, it is important for food store associates to understand how to measure temperature properly. There are a wide variety of thermometers on the market that are used to measure the temperature of equipment and foods in retail stores. Equipment such as refrigerators, freezers, warming units, and dishwashers usually have built-in thermometers. These thermometers should be monitored frequently (twice daily), properly maintained, and repaired by qualified personnel at the first sign of malfunction.

Several different types of thermometers are used to measure food temperatures—from digital types to the bimetallic stem or bayonet thermometers. Be sure that the thermometer you use in foods is approved by NSF *International* (Ann Arbor, MI). Since physical hazards are a major concern, glass and mercury-filled thermometers should never be used in or around foods. The bimetallic-stem thermometer is frequently used in food stores because it is easy to use, very versatile, and reasonably priced. The parts of a typical bimetallic-stem thermometer are shown in Figure 7.1.

The thermometer should be numerically scaled, easily readable, and accurate to within ± 2°F (± 1°C) (3). The thermometer should also have a calibration nut under the dial face so that it can be adjusted to maintain maximum accuracy.

Figure 7.1 Parts of a Typical Bimetallic-Stem Thermometer

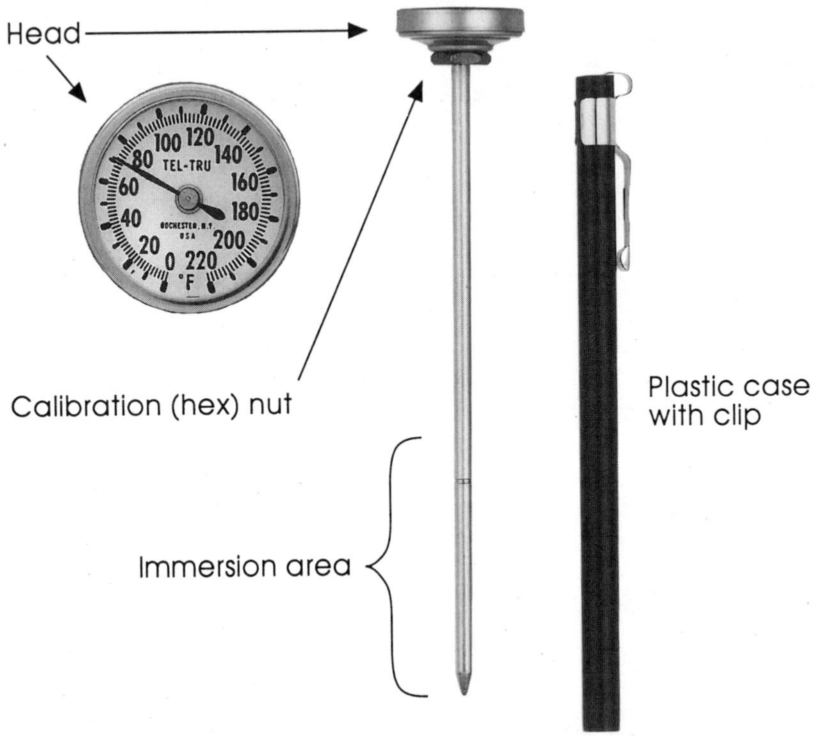

Head

Calibration (hex) nut

Immersion area

Plastic case
with clip

A pocket stem thermometer should be used for spot-checking the internal temperature of foods.

The actual size of the thermometer is: head = 1"
                                          stem length = 5"

Source: Tel-Tru Manufacturing Company, Rochester, NY.

Make sure that your thermometer is accurate and use it properly. Here are a few simple rules to follow:

1. Carefully read and follow the manufacturer's instructions for using and calibrating the thermometer that you use.

2. As with any instrument, thermometers should be handled with care and stored properly to prevent damage (4).

3. Prevent cross contamination by making sure your thermometer is clean and sanitized before putting it into a food product. Wash, rinse, sanitize, and air dry the thermometer before and after each use. An appropriate sanitizing solution or alcohol swab can be used to sanitize the thermometer. After sanitizing, return the thermometer to its clean plastic case or holder for storage (2).

4. Check the accuracy of the thermometer periodically and especially after extreme temperature changes or after the thermometer has been dropped; adjust it as necessary (4). There are two easy methods (or checkpoints) that are used to adjust or calibrate stem thermometers—the melting point of ice (32°F, 0.0°C) and the boiling point of water (212°F, 100.0°C). These two methods are explained in Table 7.1 (4).

5. Be sure to measure the temperature in the geometric center or thickest part of the food. This is usually the part of the food that will take the longest to reach doneness. Remember that the composition of the food will affect its heating characteristics, so take temperatures carefully and accurately. After inserting the thermometer into the food, let the indicator needle stabilize or stop moving. When it is stable for 15 seconds, you can record the temperature (2).

Measure the temperature of a food in its geometric center or thickest part.

Table 7.1 Thermometer Calibration

Melting Point of Ice Method

1. Place ice in a container and let it melt.

2. Stir to make sure that the temperature in the ice/water mixture is uniform throughout the container.

3. When the ice is partially melted and the container is filled with a 50/50 ice and water solution, insert the thermometer and wait until the needle indicator stabilizes. The temperature should be 32°F (0.0°C).

4. If the thermometer is not reading 32°F (0.0°C), it should be adjusted by holding the head of the thermometer firmly and using a small wrench to turn the calibration (hex) nut under the head until the indicator reads 32°F (0.0°C).

   An important item to remember as you are calibrating your thermometer using the melting point of ice is to never add tap water to ice because this will *not* be 32°F (0.0°C) but will be at a higher temperature. The calibration will be much more accurate if you use melting ice.

Boiling Point of Water Method

1. Bring water to a full boil.

2. Stir to make certain that the temperature is uniform throughout the container.

3. Insert the thermometer and observe the temperature. It should read the same as the boiling point of water in your area—(212°F; 100°C) at sea level.

   Remember, for each 1,000-foot increase in elevation above sea level, the boiling point will drop 1°F (0.6°C), so make the appropriate adjustment for your altitude level.

Source: Tel-Tru Manufacturing Co., "Calibration Check Points for Thermometers" (Rochester, NY, 1993).

A bimetallic-stem thermometer with a plastic dial face should never be used in foods during cooking in an oven, on a stove, or in a microwave oven. The plastic will melt! It should be used for spot temperature checks and not left in foods. Do not forget to follow the manufacturer's instructions for the proper use of your thermometer.

In a HACCP food safety assurance program, the importance of temperature control cannot be emphasized enough. Food temperatures should be controlled in the following areas:

- receiving
- handling and storage
- thawing
- cooking
- cooling
- reheating and hot-holding
- cold-holding
- display
- when brought home by the customer

It is essential that temperature control be a major concern of all associates in the store, but especially those in fresh-prepared food departments.

Receiving

All food products entering the supermarket should be carefully checked to make sure they have arrived in good condition (2, 5). Personnel working in receiving should verify that

- the vehicle carrying perishable foods was at the proper temperature, in good repair, and maintained in a sanitary condition.
- perishable products were not subject to temperature abuse during shipping. Refrigerated foods should not be warmer than 40°F (4.4°C); frozen foods should not be warmer than 0°F (-17.8°C). Check product temperatures and also check the recording thermometers inside the trucks, if they are so equipped.
- no out-of-condition, outdated, damaged, leaking, contaminated, or spoiled products are included in the shipment.
- items have not been contaminated by water or condensation, or by pests.
- canned foods are not leaking, badly dented, pitted with rust, or bulging at the ends.

If, for example, a shipment of milk comes to the food store after having been transported in an inadequately refrigerated truck, the shipment must be rejected. Refrigerating a product that has already been temperature abused will not improve it.

Handling and Storage

As soon as perishable or temperature-sensitive foods enter the supermarket, they must be handled carefully and quickly to make sure that they are maintained at proper temperatures to assure quality and safety. Frozen foods and foods that must be refrigerated should be stored at the correct temperature as soon as they arrive and have been checked by the receiving personnel. Raw and cooked products should be separated to prevent cross contamination.

Occasionally, products requiring refrigeration, such as milk or cream, must be removed from that environment for periods of time so they can be used in the preparation of other food items in the store. In these instances, it is essential that the products are returned to the refrigerated area as quickly as possible. For example, if an employee is preparing a cream-based soup for sale in the fresh-prepared department, he or she should measure the required quantity and immediately put the remaining cream back into refrigeration.

Foods requiring temperature control—either refrigeration or heat—may be handled at many other stages during the daily routine of a food store. Items may be moved from the steam table to cold storage at the end of the day; cooked product may be taken from the oven to hot-holding; and quantities of refrigerated product may be weighed, wrapped, and sold to customers. In all these cases, associates should maintain constant temperature control so that the quality and safety of the product is not compromised.

Thawing

When meat or poultry products are thawed improperly, pathogenic bacteria that may be present on the product will grow, increasing the risk of foodborne illness. Thawing procedures must have time and temperature controls that prevent this growth from occurring. In any fresh-prepared food department, the thawing temperature should be checked frequently. Several acceptable methods used to thaw frozen foods are listed below (2, 3, 5).

1. *Cooking them frozen*: Be sure to allow adequate time to cook the food thoroughly and always measure the temperature to assure doneness.

2. *Under refrigeration at 40°F (4.4°C) or less*: Be sure to plan ahead as large cuts of meat and poultry items take a long time to thaw. Also, be sure to provide adequate refrigeration space below cooked, ready-to-eat foods and a pan to catch juices that will drip from thawing foods. This practice will help prevent the cross contamination of ready-to-eat food products.

3. *Under potable, running water at 70°F (21.1°C) or below for no more than two hours*: This thawing method requires a cleaned and sanitized prep sink with an overflow device to allow the running water to remove loose food particles, etc. Care must be taken to prevent cross contamination of foods or food-contact surfaces near the sink.

   When thawing is completed, all equipment, including the sink and other utensils used in the process, should be thoroughly washed, rinsed, and sanitized. This method is not recommended for larger food items.

4. *In a microwave oven*: This method should be used only if the food is immediately transferred to conventional cooking equipment or if the entire uninterrupted process takes place in the microwave oven. It is not recommended for large frozen foods.

Never thaw a product at room temperature! Be sure to select the thawing method appropriate to the food item that you are preparing. If the item has been commercially frozen, follow the manufacturer's instructions for thawing and cooking.

Cooking

To make sure that any pathogens present on raw meat and poultry products are destroyed, appropriate cooking methods must be used and specified internal temperatures must be reached in the products. Oven temperatures, internal product temperatures, and cooking times should be monitored, recorded in a log, and verified by department or store management.

Associates must make sure after cooking that a product's internal temperature—a critical control point—reaches the recommended minimum temperature.

Cooking time and temperature will vary from recipe to recipe and from product to product. The first step in cooking is to check the recipe or instructions from the supplier carefully and to set the oven temperature and cooking timer accordingly. Associates must also make sure that the product has been thoroughly cooked by monitoring its internal temperature. Since cooking is a critical control point, it is vital that associates make certain that recommended minimum internal product temperatures be reached. Food store associates should never rely just on their instinct or experience, the appearance of the food, or the time in the oven (6). *Food temperature must be checked!*

The following general guidelines should be observed when cooking foods in the supermarket (2, 6):

- Never partially cook a food product and expect a warming or hot-holding table to finish the job.

- Never partially cook a food product ahead of time, store it, and then finish cooking it closer to when you need it. Warming the food in this manner gives bacteria an optimum environment in which to multiply. When some types of bacteria, like staph, have time to grow under these circumstances, they may produce a toxin that can cause illness. Even if the food is then cooked thoroughly, the toxin present in the food will not be destroyed and will eventually cause a food-borne illness.

- Be sure not to overload the cooking unit. Too much product may cause improper cooking. The heat may not be able to circulate around the unit thoroughly, and some items may not be adequately cooked.
- Do not cook all the product at the same time. Stagger cooking times to maintain a supply of freshly prepared product in the department.
- Check the accuracy of cooking equipment on a routine basis.
- Check the food's temperature with a clean and sanitized thermometer when the cooking time has elapsed. Take the temperature in several areas of the product. For poultry, it is recommended that the temperature be taken using the thigh meat. For the most accurate reading, insert the thermometer alongside, but not touching, the thigh bone.
- Avoid any chance of cross contamination. Make sure that equipment, utensils, or personnel that have come in contact with raw product are thoroughly cleaned and sanitized before they touch a cooked product.

Table 7.2 shows the required minimum internal temperatures for selected cooked foods.

Table 7.2 Minimum Internal Temperatures for Cooking, Reheating, and Hot-holding

Cooking

All poultry	165°F (73.9°C)	
Stuffed meats	165°F (73.9°C)	
Stuffing	165°F (73.9°C)	
Pork products	160°–170°F (71.1°–76.7°C)	
Pork products in a microwave	170°F (76.7°C)	
Potentially hazardous foods	145°F (62.8°C)	
Ground beef patties	155°F (68.3°C)	15 seconds
Meat mixtures	145°F (62.8°C)	3 minutes
	150°F (65.6°C)	1 minute
	155°F (68.3°C)	15 seconds

Reheating
Cooked and cooled foods that are reheated

Solids	165°F (73.9°C), within 2 hours	
Liquids	212°F (100.0°C)	

Hot-holding

Hot foods that are held hot	140°F (60.0°C)

Cooling

Because the improper cooling of foods is frequently implicated in foodborne-illness outbreaks, foods must be carefully cooled to prevent problems. Cooked products should be cooled rapidly in small quantities to 40°F (4.4°C) within four hours (3). It is important to remember that the thickness or distance to the center of the food greatly influences the cooling rate of the food. The thinner the food item or the smaller the distance to the center of the product, the faster the food will cool (6). The height of the storage pan should be less than 4 inches (10 cm), and the depth of the product should be less than 3 inches (8 cm). When cooling cooked product, the pans should never be stacked and the lids should be left ajar until cooling is accomplished—only then should the pan be completely covered. Do not overcrowd the refrigerator (2, 6).

There are several methods used to cool foods in less than four hours (2, 3, 6):

1. Use shallow pans and store in the refrigerator or quick-chill unit.

2. Use an ice-water bath and stir the food frequently.

As with any critical control point in a HACCP plan, the equipment used for cooling and the foods being cooled should be frequently monitored for temperature compliance.

Most people do not realize how long it takes food to cool. In an experiment conducted by the U.S. Food and Drug Administration in the early 1970s, 14 gallons (64 liters) of beef stew was made from scratch and cooked thoroughly in a 15-gallon pot (7). The beef stew, at a temperature of 150°F (65.6°C), was placed in a walk-in commercial refrigerator set at 40°F (4.4°C). (This practice is *not* recommended but was done for experimental purposes.)

How long do you think it took for the center of that pot of beef stew to cool to 45°F (7.2°C)? Experienced chefs, cooks, and food-preparation professionals were very surprised to hear that it took SIX DAYS for this product to cool to 45°F (7). Figure 7.2 graphically illustrates the cooling curve for the beef stew.

The important messages from this experiment are

1. Foods take a *long time* to cool.

2. Never cool foods in large quantities, but transfer product into shallow pans so cooling can take place quickly.

3. Cool foods as quickly as possible.

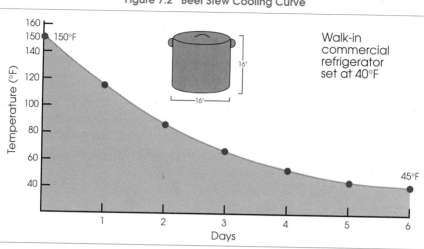

Figure 7.2 Beef Stew Cooling Curve

Source: Dickerson and Read (7) courtesy of O. P. Snyder.

4. There are many factors to consider when cooling foods (2, 6):

- The nature and composition of the food influences the cooling rate. A very thick product like beef stew will take longer to cool than a thin liquid.
- The thickness or the distance to the center of the food greatly influences the cooling rate.
- Stirring or shaking cooked foods will speed the cooling rate.
- Some food equipment cools food more rapidly than others. For example, stainless steel pans tend to transfer heat more quickly than plastic containers.
- The type and capacity of refrigeration is also important in cooling food.

For additional information about the cooling of foods, the reader should refer to an article entitled "Chilled Food Handling and Merchandising: A Code of Recommended Practices Endorsed by Many Bodies" (8).

Reheating and Hot-Holding

Cooked and refrigerated foods must be reheated rapidly to 165°F (73.9°C) or above within two hours, and then sold or held hot (2, 3). Equipment used for reheating and the foods being reheated should be monitored frequently to assure that the proper temperatures are maintained.

It is important to follow these simple rules when reheating foods:

1. Never mix leftover foods with fresh foods.
2. Never reheat previously prepared food more than once.

Department personnel should also keep accurate temperature records of the hot-holding equipment and the foods in them. Both should be monitored frequently (every two hours). All cooked foods including meat and poultry, as well as any dishes containing these items, should be maintained at a temperature above 140°F (60.0°C).

If any product falls below 140°F (60.0°C), take it out of the display, reheat it at once to 165°F (73.9°C), and put it back in the hot-holding display. This procedure should only be done once; after that, if the temperature of the food again falls below 140°F (60.0°C), it should be discarded.

Cold-Holding

For cooked products, the items should first be cooled to temperatures below 40°F (see the previous section on cooling) and then maintained at this temperature. Refrigerated display cases should be maintained at 40°F (4.4°C) or below at the warmest point in the case, and the products in the cases should be monitored periodically for temperature compliance (2, 3, 6).

Store personnel must monitor the amount of time a product has been kept in the cold-holding state, and "sell by" dates must be established and observed.

Display

Correct temperature monitoring must be conducted in the areas in which fresh food is displayed—refrigerated cases, steam tables, salad bars, soup crocks, and cold-display tables. Cold food should be kept cold (below 40°F, below 4.4°C) and hot foods should be kept hot (above 140°F, or above 60.0°C). Other general guidelines that should be followed when foods are displayed include the following (5):

- When the refrigerated display is being replenished, never add or mix product that has been on display with fresh product taken out of the cooler. Both products would be safe to eat if their temperature has been properly maintained, but the shelf life of the product that has been on display is probably shorter because it has been exposed to many factors that influence its deterioration.

- To fill the display, remove the food item on display and either put it in a smaller merchandising pan and put it back on display, or repackage it as a single-serving unit and place it in the self-service case.

- Check the temperature of the product removed from the cooler before putting it on display.

- Food temperatures should be checked every two hours. If a product is too warm, the equipment may be malfunctioning. Notify the department manager immediately, and seek the assistance of qualified heating and refrigeration professionals to repair the malfunctioning unit.

Taking the Product Home

Customer education is an important, although sometimes neglected, part of an effective sanitation program. Through their own mishandling and poor sanitation practices, your customers can cause the safe food products you sell to spoil before they should or become the source of foodborne illness. Potentially dangerous—and all-too-common—food-preparation practices customers use once they leave your store include

- leaving perishable foods in a warm automobile while doing other shopping

- leaving frozen food sitting on the kitchen counter at room temperature to thaw all day (or longer) for the evening meal

- leaving cooked food or leftovers at room temperature for long periods of time and then serving them again

- not cooking raw products to proper *internal temperatures* (see Table 7.2)

- using a cutting board or other preparation surface that has just been used for raw product to prepare ready-to-eat food without properly cleaning and sanitizing it

- storing food close to toxic chemicals

- not washing hands after using the toilet or touching anything that may contaminate food

Investigations of many cases of foodborne illness show that they resulted from customer mishandling of the food, either before or after preparation of the product.

What, then, can you do to educate your customers on safe food practices? Some stores place practical tips on food protection in their weekly newspaper advertisements. Retailers have also provided information to their customers through the use of

- stick-on labels
- store signs
- pamphlets and brochures
- bag stuffers

Examples of the types of information that can be communicated are shown in Figure 7.3 (9). Customers must also be told what the most potentially hazardous foods are so they will take extra care when handling them. As you already have learned in this textbook (chapter 6), such foods include

- egg and milk products, including custards, cream-filled pastries, and egg salads
- meat products
- poultry products
- fish and shellfish
- other low-acid foods

Proper food preparation and handling is particularly important at picnics. Customers should be warned about keeping potentially hazardous foods refrigerated on warm days if they are not consumed shortly after preparation. Thanksgiving, Christmas, and other holidays also pose hazards primarily due to incorrect handling procedures when large meals are prepared. "Grandma's recipe" that calls for thawing the turkey in warm water or at room temperature, or stuffing the bird the night before and letting it sit overnight in a "cool" basement can prove disastrous.

Store personnel must inform customers that perishable products can spoil quickly or cause illness if proper temperature control is not maintained after the product leaves the store. Customers should be encouraged to refrigerate cold foods at 40°F (4.4°C) or lower as soon as possible, and to maintain the temperature of hot foods at 140°F (60.0°C) or higher, or to consume these products immediately.

Figure 7.3   Consumer Guidelines for Safe Food Handling

When you shop:

- Buy cold foods last, get it home fast

When you store food:

- Keep it safe, refrigerate

When you prepare food:

- Wash hands thoroughly
- Use clean utensils and equipment
- Keep raw and cooked foods separated

When you're cooking:

- Cook food thoroughly
- Microwave foods for safety
- Use a thermometer to test doneness

When you serve food:

- Never leave it out over 2 hours

When you handle leftovers:

- Use small containers for quick cooling
- Cool foods quickly
- Reheat leftovers thoroughly
- When in doubt, throw it out
- Discard suspect foods

Source: "A Quick Consumer Guide to Safe Food Handling," Home and Garden Bulletin no. 248, U.S. Department of Agriculture, Food Safety and Inspection Service, September 1990.

Conclusions

Temperature control is one of the major critical control points of a well-structured HACCP food safety assurance program. It is essential to maintain careful temperature control of perishables. While the simple rule "keep cold foods cold and hot foods hot" is a basic rule of thumb for maintaining the integrity of prepared or perishable products, more careful monitoring is needed. At all stages in the marketing of food products the temperature should be checked and verified. The other important areas that make up the foundation of the HACCP food safety assurance pyramid—cleaning and sanitizing, personal hygiene, and insect and rodent control—are discussed in the following chapters.

References

1. U.S. Department of Agriculture. Food Safety and Inspection Service. *Report on the* Escherichia coli 0157:H7 *Outbreak in the Western States.* May 1993.
2. National Restaurant Association. Educational Foundation. *Applied Foodservice Sanitation.* New York: John Wiley and Sons, Inc., 1992.
3. U.S. Food and Drug Administration. Center for Food Safety and Applied Nutrition. *Proposed Food Protection Unicode.* 1988.
4. Tel-Tru Manufacturing Co. "Calibration Check Points for Thermometers." Rochester, NY, 1993.
5. Food Marketing Institute. *Food Handler's Pocket Guide for Food Safety and Quality.* 1989.
6. National Restaurant Association. Educational Foundation. *Managing a Food Safety System.* 1992.
7. Dickerson, R. W., Jr., and R. B. Read Jr. "Cooking Rates of Foods." *Journal of Milk and Food Technology* 36, no. 3 (1973): 167–71.
8. Farquhar, J., and H. W. Symons. "Chilled Food Handling and Merchandising: A Code of Recommended Practices Endorsed by Many Bodies." *Dairy, Food, and Environmental Sanitation* 12, no. 4 (1992): 210–13.
9. U.S. Department of Agriculture. Food Safety and Inspection Service. *A Quick Consumer Guide to Safe Food Handling.* Home and Garden Bulletin no. 248. September 1990.

8

Principles of Cleaning and Sanitizing

The principles of cleaning and sanitizing form another important portion of the foundation of the HACCP food safety assurance pyramid (see page 95). These principles are vital to the success of a food safety assurance program and must be practiced regularly as part of each department's standard operating procedure.

It is important to understand the difference between cleaning and sanitizing. *Cleaning* is the physical removal of soil from surfaces, while *sanitizing* (or sanitization) is the treatment of a cleaned surface to destroy disease-causing and spoilage microorganisms and to reduce them to safe levels. The compounds and equipment used in these two processes are different (1).

Effective sanitation *can only be accomplished on clean surfaces.* All surfaces that come in contact with food must be thoroughly washed (cleaned), rinsed, and sanitized to ensure the reduction of microorganisms.

To better illustrate the importance of removing bacteria from surfaces that come in contact with food, some important research conducted by scientists at the University of Minnesota must be mentioned (2, 3). By using a powerful electron microscope, these food scientists took a close look at a highly polished type of stainless steel that is frequently used in the food industry. What appears quite smooth to the naked eye actually contains many pronounced and irregular lines and grooves (see Figure 8.1). Bacteria that come in contact with this stainless steel can attach to these grooved surfaces (Figure 8.1) and form a biofilm. These attached bacteria can cause some real problems and must be removed by proper cleaning and sanitizing of all food-contact surfaces on a regular basis.

Figure 8.1   Electron Photomicrographs of Stainless Steel

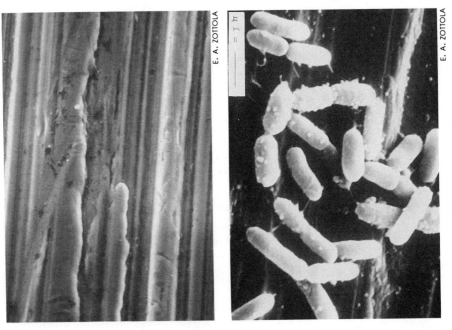

Electron photomicrographs show the grooves in a section of stainless steel (left) and the bacteria that can grow in these grooved surfaces (right) magnified 5,000 times.

Electron photomicrographs courtesy of E. A. Zottola, University of Minnesota.

The ultimate goal of an effective cleaning and sanitizing program is to have a clean and sanitary facility where HACCP principles are being used to prevent foodborne illness and assure the safety of foods. The objectives of the program are to

- remove soil from food equipment, utensils, and surfaces
- reduce the number of microorganisms on these surfaces
- eliminate food-contact surfaces as a source of spoilage and pathogenic organisms.

Factors involved in an effective cleaning and sanitizing program are

- use of the correct detergent (cleaner)
- use of the proper cleaning equipment
- use of the appropriate sanitizer
- development of uniform procedures
- proper scheduling of personnel
- proper training of personnel
- follow-up and control

Each of these important factors will be discussed in this chapter.

Detergents

Many cleaning agents are available for daily housekeeping chores, including hot water, steam, abrasive materials, and other agents that can be used to remove soil from surfaces. One of the most widely used agents, and the one most common to food retailers, is the detergent.

A detergent is a chemical agent manufactured specifically to remove soil so that a sanitizer can kill the bacteria remaining on surfaces. The soil becomes a part of the detergent solution and is rinsed away. In other words, the soil is transferred from the surface of the object being cleaned to the detergent solution itself through chemical action and friction caused by rubbing or scrubbing. Detergents break down food components like fat, protein, and carbohydrates left on equipment.

The following steps occur in effective detergent cleaning:

1. The detergent is brought in direct contact with the soil to be removed.
2. The soil is displaced from the surface being cleaned.

3. The soil is dispersed in the detergent solution.

4. The detergent solution containing the soil is rinsed away to prevent redepositing the soil on the surface of the object.

The detergent must possess the following qualities in order to be an effective cleaning agent:

- effective water conditioner in the presence of hard water
- noncorrosive
- nontoxic when used as recommended
- dissolves easily and rapidly in water
- rinses freely
- stable when stored for periods of time
- economical to use

Because it is so important to use the correct detergent to achieve an effective job of cleaning, it is recommended that a commercial supplier of detergents be contacted for the correct compound to use to meet your specific needs. A reputable commercial firm will consider the specific task and suggest the correct detergent, taking into account the types and conditions of soil involved, the local water conditions (hardness and temperature), and the composition of the equipment and surfaces to be cleaned.

Alkaline Detergents

Alkaline detergents are most commonly used for regular cleaning of equipment, tables, utensils, glassware, floors, walls, ceilings, and general-purpose areas. They are quite effective in breaking down proteins and decomposing fats, and are particularly well suited for applications where a sanitizing solution will follow the cleaning and rinsing steps.

Acid Detergents

Acid detergents can be used for special applications to supplement (not replace) alkaline detergents. Acid detergents are sometimes used where minerals in food or hard water leave deposits on equipment, utensils, and other surfaces that cannot be cleaned with alkaline products. They are also used to remove surface films and other encrusted soils. Acid detergents must be used with caution, however. They are extremely corrosive if used to excess, so be sure to follow the directions for using acid detergents carefully and accurately.

Detergent Sanitizers

Detergents that contain sanitizing agents are also referred to as detergent sanitizers. These products are effective, but cleaning and sanitizing must be done in two separate steps. That is, the detergent sanitizer must be used twice—first to clean the piece of equipment and then again to sanitize it (1). These products have very limited applications, so it is best to check with your chemical supplier and local regulatory agency regarding specific uses.

Cleaning Equipment

Detergents alone cannot always remove buildups of soil from utensils and surfaces. Cleaning equipment—everything from brooms to high-pressure washers—are also necessary to ensure that cleaning is done with a maximum of efficiency.

A retail store needs some basic equipment to do an effective cleaning job. The equipment itself must be kept clean, and all cleaning supplies and equipment should be properly stored in a designated room or equipment

Equipment must be thoroughly cleaned using the appropriate detergent.

closet in an orderly and neat fashion (1). Among the most useful pieces of cleaning equipment are the following:

- deck brooms (a wide variety)
- plastic brushes (a wide variety)
- scrubbing pads
- dustpans or shovels
- squeegees
- floor scrapers
- equipment scrapers
- putty knives
- disposable wipes
- plastic spray bottles
- water vacuum
- hoses
- high-pressure washer
- hot-water source (minimum 140°F or 60.0°C, 80- to 100-gallon capacity tank)
- buckets with wringers
- buckets (different sizes)
- mops
- waste containers
- heavy-duty rubber gloves
- disposable gloves
- plastic aprons
- rain suits
- boots
- goggles

Sanitizers

The definition of sanitizing is to render a surface, utensil, or object microbiologically clean. The object to be sanitized must first be washed with detergent and rinsed to ensure that no soil is left to prevent the sanitizer from working properly. After a piece of equipment or a food-contact surface is clean, it can then be sanitized.

There are several methods of sanitizing. *High-temperature/hot-water sanitizing* is commonly used in the beverage industry for sanitizing processing equipment. *Ultraviolet radiation* can be used in specific instances, such as water treatment. The most commonly used sanitation process for the food store is *chemical sanitation,* which involves the use of a chemical compound to reduce the level of microorganisms on the cleaned surfaces.

Chemical sanitizers are regulated by the U.S. Food and Drug Administration (FDA) and the Environmental Protection Agency (EPA). The FDA first approves the use of the sanitizer on food contact surfaces and then the EPA registers the product. The EPA mandates that all pertinent information about chemical products be listed on the product's label. The sanitizer label will contain an EPA registration number as well as information on what concentration to use, effectiveness, and warnings of possible hazards (1). By doing this, the government is able to monitor and control the toxicity of a product, as well as its efficiency as a sanitizer.

To determine whether a sanitizer is intended specifically for use in a food store, consult the *List of Proprietary Substances and Nonfood Compounds* authorized for use under U.S. Department of Agriculture (USDA) Inspection and Grading Programs. This publication lists all products that have been checked for toxicity and are authorized by the USDA for use in food-processing areas (4).

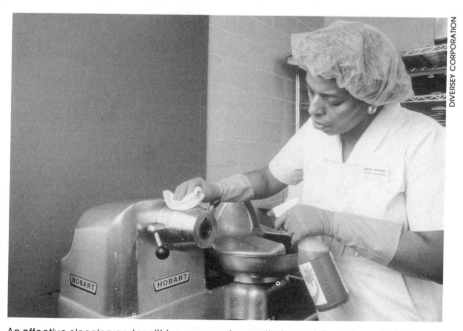

An effective cleaning and sanitizing program is essential in providing safe and wholesome foods to your customers.

Principles of Chemical Sanitizers

A chemical sanitizer is an agent used for the specific purpose of reducing the number of microorganisms to a level judged safe by public-health requirements or to a significant degree in areas where public-health standards have not been established (5).

Some generally accepted principles that influence the effectiveness of sanitizers are listed below.

- Sanitizers will lose their effectiveness if used on unclean surfaces.
- Sanitizers must be used in the right amounts (listed on the label) to be effective. Too little will not do the job, and too much can leave residues on equipment and utensils that may cause off-colors and disagreeable odors in food products. The use of too much sanitizer may also be mildly toxic or corrosive.
- It is important to know the type of water in your area. Some sanitizers will not work in the presence of hard water.
- It is also important to know the types of bacteria that may be present and need to be destroyed. Some bacteria are not affected by certain kinds of sanitizers.

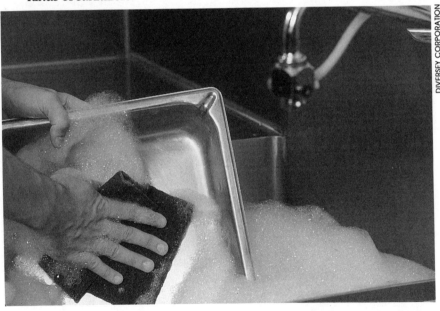

DIVERSEY CORPORATION

The thorough washing and rinsing of equipment removes soil and prepares the surface for sanitization.

- Surfaces in heavy use may have a much greater level of bacterial contamination after they have been cleaned than surfaces used less frequently. Either a heavier concentration of sanitizer or a second application may be needed in certain cases.

- The strength of the solution (usually expressed in "parts per million" or "ppm") is important. The label will give the strength to be used under each particular application. A reputable chemical supplier is the best resource for identifying the strength needed for various jobs. Since the strength of a sanitizer is depleted as it kills bacteria, be sure to test the strength of your sanitizer frequently using the appropriate test kit. Sanitizing solutions should be discarded when the strength falls below recommended levels or when the solution becomes dirty.

- The method of application is important as is the time of immersion or application because all sanitizers and concentrations take different times to work properly. Again, your supplier can set up the best program for a particular job and facility.

Many factors have an important bearing on whether the job is done correctly and cost-efficiently. Effective cleaning and sanitizing helps assure product safety and increases shelf life, so the effort is not only worthwhile, but necessary.

The Major Types of Sanitizers

The three most popular sanitizers for use in a retail food store are

- chlorine compounds
- iodine compounds
- quaternary ammonium compounds (quats)

There are many other approved sanitizers that are designed for specific problems encountered in food-processing operations. Local suppliers can supply information regarding specific sanitizers.

As you read the following sections, note that some disadvantages of sanitizers can actually be considered advantages, depending on the job to be done. For example, while some sanitizers may require rinsing from food-contact surfaces after application (on tables, slicers, saws, and so on), they need not be rinsed from walls, ceilings, and floors where the residue provides excellent, long-lasting protection against mold growth in coolers and processing rooms. Whenever chemical suppliers state that certain products need not be rinsed, ask these suppliers to provide an authorization letter from a regulatory agency.

Chlorine Compounds

Chlorine is one of the most effective and most cost-efficient sanitizers. There are several types of chlorine sanitizers, but one of the most popular is the liquid hypochlorite, commonly known as household bleach. If used in the right amounts, chlorine can meet the needs of a retail food store.

The main *advantages* of chlorine sanitizers are

- not affected by water hardness
- kills most types of bacteria
- relatively inexpensive to use
- concentration easily measured by convenient field test kit
- easy to apply by various methods
- versatile, may be used for many different applications

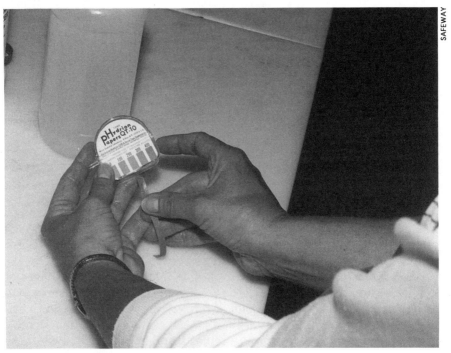

The strength of sanitizing solutions should be taken frequently using the appropriate test kit.

The main *disadvantages* of chlorine sanitizers are

- affected by the presence of organic matter (soils)
- corrosive to many metals if left in contact in strong solutions for extended periods
- irritating to the eyes, skin, and body tissues if not used in recommended concentrations
- reduced effectiveness in highly alkaline solutions
- offensive odor
- hazardous at high temperatures or under acid conditions
- carryover of chlorine taste and odors into food products
- environmentally unfriendly

A 50 ppm (parts per million) solution of 5.25 percent chlorine sanitizer provides an excellent sanitizing hand dip following hand washing with soap. Hands need not be rinsed or dried after using this hand dip.

The major drawback in using chlorine, especially household bleach, as a sanitizer is the chance of human error in mixing. Improper use of hypochlorites, particularly overuse, can cause problems such as eye and skin irritation, and off-flavors in foods. For this reason, it is better to let the chemical supplier set up a program in which the chemical is metered automatically from a faucet. Chlorine, as well as other sanitizers, can be dispensed this way. A simple metering valve attached to the water line will save money and reduce the chance of safety problems.

The sanitizer can also be sprayed onto equipment and surfaces with a pressurized spray pump. These pumps can be purchased at reasonable prices.

Iodine and Iodine-containing Compounds

Iodine is most often used in food stores when combined with a detergent or as a one-step germicidal detergent called an iodophor. Although these compounds are quite effective as sanitizers, they are not used as frequently because they may cause staining, odors, and off-flavors if they are used incorrectly. Because iodine compounds are so concentrated, not more than a 25 ppm solution can be used. Any human error in mixing can cause serious problems.

The main *advantages* of iodine solutions are

- relatively noncorrosive to metal surfaces
- nonirritating to skin

- not affected by hard water
- kill most types of bacteria
- active at low concentrations
- may be applied by a variety of means
- relatively inexpensive to use

The *disadvantages* of iodine compounds are

- reduced effectiveness in highly alkaline solutions
- may stain, give off odors, and create off-flavors if used in incorrect concentrations
- somewhat affected by the presence of organic matter
- dissipate quickly in hot water (above 120°F, 48.9°C)
- less effective than chlorine in killing bacterial spores

Quaternary Ammonium Compounds (Quats)

Quats are among the most widely used sanitizers. They are less versatile than chlorine because their antibacterial qualities are often reduced considerably when in contact with hard water or commercial-type cleaners. In fact, the FDA's proposed *Unicode* (6) specifies that quats (at 200 ppm) must be used in waters up to 500 ppm hardness. They are very effective as sanitizers when used according to the instructions on the label and as recommended by a supplier under the correct conditions.

The main *advantages* of quats are

- highly stable
- nonirritating and noncorrosive
- active against many microorganisms
- remain active in mild alkaline solutions
- most need not be rinsed at 200 ppm (see manufacturer's instructions)
- form a bacteriostatic film
- excellent wetting and penetration
- efficient in presence of organic soils
- no carryover of taste or smell

The major *disadvantages* of quats are

- may not destroy certain types of organisms (depending on the compound)
- reduced effectiveness of some quats in hard water or acid conditions

- may leave a film on treated surfaces
- moderately expensive
- moderately toxic

Recommended Concentrations, Contact Times, and Exposures

Concentration of the sanitizer and time of exposure are critical to effective sanitizing. The minimum concentrations of chlorine, iodine, and quaternary ammonium sanitizers, along with their contact times at the proper temperatures, are provided in Table 8.1.

Sanitizing with Heat

Sanitizing with heat is used extensively in dish and glassware washing. Large institutional dishwashers for the most part sanitize in the final rinse through the use of hot water (180°F, 82.2°C) on the surface of the dishes for a fixed period of time to destroy harmful microorganisms. The surface of the dishes must reach 165°F (73.9°C) or higher to be sanitized effectively. Sanitizing with heat is rarely used in food retail units due to the impracticality of getting enough hot water for extended periods over massive equipment surfaces.

Table 8.1   Minimum Concentrations and Contact Times for Sanitizers*

Sanitizer	Temperature	Sanitizing Method	Concentration (ppm)	Contact Time (minutes)
Chlorine	At least 75°F (23.9°C)	Immersion	50–100	1
		Circulation	100–200	2
		Spray or fog	200–300	2
Iodine	At least 75°F (23.9°C)	Immersion	12.5	1
		Circulation	12.5	2
		Spray or fog	25	2
Quaternary Ammonium Compounds (Quats)	At least 75°F (23.9°C)	Immersion	200	1
		Circulation	200**	**
		Spray or fog	200	2–3

* Local regulatory agencies may have slightly different requirements.
**Tends to foam on circulation. Check with your supplier for specific information to meet your needs.

The Development of Uniform Procedures

To assure maximum efficiency when carrying out sanitizing procedures, the following basic questions must first be considered:

- What is to be cleaned?
- When is the cleaning to be done?
- How often is the cleaning to be done?
- Who is to do the cleaning?
- How is the cleaning to be done—step by step?
- Who is responsible for control and follow-up?

The answers to these questions can then be used to develop cleaning and sanitizing procedures. Consider, for example, a program for cleaning and sanitizing a meat department. First, everything to be cleaned must be listed (see the left-hand column in Table 8.2, for example). Next, the schedule should show how often cleaning is needed. Some items will need cleaning every four hours, some will require daily, weekly, or monthly cleaning.

The next three columns should indicate who is responsible for each cleaning job, who checked that the job was completed, and how much time it takes to clean each piece of equipment. These times are very important to the scheduling of cleanup personnel. Last, and very important to the effective completion of daily cleaning and sanitizing, are step-by-step procedures on how to clean each piece of equipment or surface. Once this is done for each piece of equipment, effective follow-up is all that is needed to see that the job is accomplished according to the written procedure.

Since writing a procedure for cleaning and sanitizing every piece of equipment can be a time-consuming job, it might be wise to contact equipment manufacturers for cleaning instructions. Several trade associations and companies have also developed sanitation manuals designed for use in cleaning and sanitizing programs.

Standards and procedures are the backbone of an effective cleaning and sanitizing program. Once they are committed to paper, managers will be able to measure the effectiveness of a sanitation program.

Scheduling Personnel

Each department, depending on its specific needs, should schedule cleaning and sanitizing procedures into its daily routine. Sanitizing is too important a job to be left to chance. If cleaning and sanitizing tasks are left

Table 8.2   Sample Cleaning and Sanitizing Schedule

Store # ___**S6**___   Date ___**Week ending 5/22/93**___   Dept. ___**Meat**___

Item to Be Cleaned	Cleaning Frequency	Responsibility Do	Audit	Time Allowed (Minutes)	S	M	T	W	T	F	S
Saw #1	4 hours	Joe	Bob	15	✓	✓	✓	✓			
Saw #2	4 hours	"	"	15	✓	✓	✓	O			
Table #1	4 hours	"	"	10	✓	O	✓	O			
Table #2	4 hours	"	"	10	O	✓	✓	O			
Cuber	4 hours	"	"	15	✓	✓	✓	✓			
Grinder—Lg.	4 hours	"	"	30	✓	✓	O	✓			
Grinder—Sm.	4 hours	"	"	15	✓	✓	O	✓			
Lugs	As needed	"	"	30	✓	✓	✓	O			
Pans	As needed	"	"	15	✓	✓	✓	✓			
Pkg. Machine	Daily	Sue	"	30	O	✓	✓	✓			
Scale	Daily	"	"	10	✓	✓	✓	✓			
Walls	Weekly	"	"	90	✓	✓	✓	✓			
Ceiling	Monthly	"	"	45	✓	✓	✓	✓			
Floors	Daily	Joe	"	60	✓	O	✓	O			
Utensils	4 hours	"	"	10	✓	✓	O	✓			
Cooler Fans	Monthly	Sam	"	30	✓	✓	✓	✓			

Auditor will rate department   Legend: ✓ = Satisfactory
daily according to legend   O = Unsatisfactory

undone, spoilage or pathogenic microorganisms can grow to dangerous levels on work surfaces, equipment, and utensils.

Table 8.2 indicates the amount of time needed to fulfill each cleaning and sanitizing task in the example meat department. Since every store is different, however, this schedule should be considered only as a guideline.

Cleaning should be an ongoing process throughout the day. It is important to remember that each department has different cleaning and sanitizing requirements. While end-of-the-day cleaning may be suitable in one department, hourly cleaning of equipment may be necessary in another.

Training Personnel

Modern training techniques must be used to educate employees in cleaning and sanitizing procedures. All personnel, not just the cleaning and sanitizing crew, must be educated to understand *why* strict procedures must be carried out.

They must learn about the effect bacteria have on food products as a result of unclean and unsanitary equipment and facilities, as well as the impact on safety, shelf life, and profitability. If employees fully understand how important the jobs of cleaning and sanitizing are to product safety and quality, customer satisfaction, and the total profit picture of the company, they will be more likely to put their lessons into practice.

Follow-up and Control

Follow-up and control are the final, and most important, stages in a comprehensive cleaning and sanitizing program. One way of following up on cleaning and sanitizing protocols is for management to make sure that each task has been effectively accomplished through visual inspection. The results of the inspection should then be recorded on a permanent record for future monitoring (see Table 8.2).

Visual cleanliness is not the only aim of a cleaning and sanitizing program. All equipment, utensils, and surfaces must be as sanitary, or as free from harmful microorganisms, as possible. A microbiological examination of all equipment that has been cleaned and sanitized will quickly reveal the levels of microorganisms that still exist and whether these levels are within an acceptable range.

To perform a microbiological examination, a petri dish or culture plate (a clear-plastic saucer-like dish with an overlapping lid) should be filled with agar, a sterile gelatin-like substance. When kept at the recommended temperature, the agar forms a perfect environment for the growth of bacteria. The dish, therefore, provides an excellent monitoring mechanism to detect and enumerate microorganisms left on clean and sanitized equipment and dry surfaces.

The plates often easiest and least expensive to use are the type with a raised agar that can be applied directly to the surface to be tested. These are called RODAC® plates (7).

The following care should be taken when using the plates:

- The plates should be kept covered until used to preserve the sterile environment.
- The plates should be refrigerated until used to keep the agar from drying out.

- Many plates will have expiration dates that should be adhered to. If they are refrigerated, however, they can last much longer than when stored at room temperature.
- The plates must be incubated (i.e., used to grow bacteria) at the same temperature each time for continuity and consistency (24 hours at 98.6°F or 37.0°C is recommended).

Bacteria Sampling Procedure

A sampling procedure for determining the level of bacterial contamination on equipment and surfaces is shown in Figure 8.2. The steps in the procedure are as follows:

1. Remove the lid from the RODAC® plate, being careful not to contaminate the agar.
2. While holding the lid in one hand (also to avoid contamination), use moderate pressure to apply the plate's agar to the surface being tested.

Figure 8.2   Bacteria Sampling Procedure

Remove the lid from the RODAC® plate, being careful not to contaminate the agar.

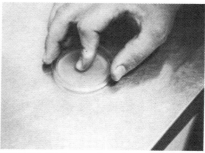

Hold the lid in one hand and apply the plate's agar to the surface being tested.

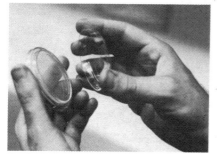

Replace the lid on the plate.

Number the plates used with a grease pencil or felt-tip pen.

Use of RODAC® plates courtesy of Bioquest Division of Becton, Dickinson and Company.

3. Replace the lid on the plate.
4. Number the plates used with a grease pencil or permanent felt-tip pen.
5. Note the number on a bacteria monitoring report. A completed monitoring report is shown in Table 8.3.
6. Repeat this procedure for all equipment being tested.
7. When sample testing is completed, incubate plates for 24 hours at 98.6°F (37.0°C).
8. Upon completion of the incubation period, remove plates from the incubator, count colonies (each dot on the plate surface), and note the count on the monitoring report.

Interpretation of Results

Because each facility and situation is different, interpretations on the bacteria readings will be relative. As a start, the following guidelines are suggested:

- Acceptable: 0–50 bacteria colonies
- Conditional: 50–150 bacteria colonies
- Unacceptable: over 150 colonies or too numerous to count (TNTC)

Table 8.3 Bacteria Monitoring Report

Store # **56**   Dept. **Meat**   Date **5/22/93**   Time **7 AM**

Sample Number	Surface Tested	Colony Count	Rating	Remarks
1	Cutting Table 1	36	Acceptable	
2	Band Saw	25	Acceptable	
3	Knife	TNTC*	Unacceptable	
	Code:	0–50	Acceptable	
		50–150	Conditional	
		Over 150	Unacceptable	
		TNTC*	Unacceptable	

*Too numerous to count

On surfaces used for ready-to-eat foods, the general standard might be

- Acceptable: 0–10 colonies
- Conditional: 10–25 colonies
- Unacceptable: over 25 colonies

The monitoring method described above will provide a way to measure a store's level of bacterial contamination at a particular point in time and will demonstrate how effective a store's cleaning and sanitizing program really is. A combination of monitoring and using cleaning checklists should net excellent results.

Conclusions

Cleaning and sanitizing are the building blocks for an effective food store sanitation program, which is vital for the success of your HACCP program. As such, the jobs of cleaning and sanitizing should be familiar to all employees, from top management down.

The store employees responsible for these important tasks must be aware of the necessity of following established protocols for keeping all surfaces, utensils, and pieces of equipment in as sanitary a condition as possible. The ultimate responsibility for the condition of each department, however, rests in the hands of its manager. By explaining to employees the importance of proper cleaning and sanitizing, by following through with inspection, and by providing encouragement, every department manager can boast a clean, sanitized, and safe environment for preparing and marketing food products.

References

1. National Restaurant Association. Educational Foundation. *Applied Food Service Sanitation*. New York: John Wiley and Sons, Inc., 1992.
2. Stone, L. S., and E. A. Zottola. "Scanning Electron Microscopy Study of Stainless Steel Finishes Used in Food Processing Equipment." *Food Technology* 39, no. 5 (1985): 110, 112–114.
3. Stone, L. S., and E. A. Zottola. "Effect of Cleaning and Sanitizing on the Attachment of *Pseudomonas fragi* to Stainless Steel." *Journal of Food Science* 50, no. 4 (1985): 951–56.

4. The *List of Proprietary Substances and Nonfood Compounds* is available from the Superintendent of Documents, U.S. Government Printing Office, Washington, DC 20401.
5. Banner, Mark J. "Principles of Sanitation." Unpublished manuscript, 1991.
6. U.S. Food and Drug Administration. Center for Food Safety and Applied Nutrition. *Proposed Food Protection Unicode.* 1988.
7. RODAC® is a registered trademark of Becton, Dickinson and Company.

9

Personal Hygiene and Employee Practices

The image of a clean and sanitary food store is reflected not only in the look and organization of each department, but also in the appearance, personal habits, and work habits of its associates. Customers cannot have faith in the quality and safety of the products they buy if supermarket personnel look untidy or unhealthy and handle foods in an unsanitary manner. One important aspect of any comprehensive sanitation program, and an important part of the HACCP food safety assurance pyramid, is a set of guidelines mandating the appearance, hygiene, and personal cleanliness of all food store employees, as well as the sanitary handling of food products.

When the shopping public was asked about perceived threats to food safety, it rated unsanitary handling by supermarket employees as one of the ten most important threats to the food they eat, according to a recent Food Marketing Institute survey (1). This is far ahead of unsanitary handling by shoppers and processors or rodent and insect infestations. As you know, bacteria are transported from place to place throughout a food-preparation area by hands, dirty aprons, utensils, and equipment, a cough, a sneeze, or hundreds of other people-related ways. Bacteria consequently get into food where they can cause spoilage and sometimes illness. The control of harmful microorganisms therefore depends on people and the care they take with their health, personal hygiene, and work habits.

Employee Health

Food store employees' health has a direct effect on the health of the store's customers. Employees who handle fresh-prepared food should not be permitted to report to work if they are ill. Most government agencies that inspect food stores have regulations in their ordinances and codes to this effect, but for many years the rules were not strictly followed. In the past, employees were not allowed sick days, and out of necessity, many of them would report for work even if they were ill. Today, however, more companies have policies that allow employees to remain at home if they are sick. These company rules benefit not only the employees and the stores they work in, but they protect the customers as well.

Educating employees about the effect of illness on the store's customers is an important first step in implementing a viable employee health and hygiene program. Many people simply do not realize that their minor sore throats or respiratory-tract infections can be potentially harmful starting points in transferring microorganisms from employees to food products and then to store customers.

The symptoms of the so-called common cold—from sore throat to sinus pain—are signs that microorganisms are taking over, with possibly dangerous consequences not only for the cold sufferer, but for whomever he or she may come into contact with. The same is true for the first signs of gastrointestinal discomfort—nausea, vomiting, diarrhea, or stomach cramps.

Even when the ailment ends, some of the microorganisms that caused it may remain with the person after recovery and serve as a source of potential recontamination (2, 3). For example, *Salmonella enteritidis* and the hepatitis A virus can remain in the system for a long time after a person recovers from these illnesses (3).

Respiratory-tract infections can be spread very easily to large groups of people through sneezing or coughing. "Strep throat" can be passed from one person to the next in this manner, as can influenza, tuberculosis, and other respiratory diseases.

Healthy individuals also harbor sizable numbers of bacteria. Staphylococci are found on the hair and skin, and in a person's mouth, throat, and nose (2, 3). The lower intestinal tract is a common habitat for many bacteria. It has been estimated that up to 50 percent of healthy people who work with food are carriers of disease agents transmitted by food (3). Figure 9.1 shows the bacteria that are present on the lips, nose, and hair, and clearly illustrates how bacteria are transmitted during a sneeze.

One of the easiest ways to spread bacteria is by hand contact. A person's skin provides an excellent site on which a variety of bacteria can live. The temperature, skin secretions, and tiny folds and wrinkles provide a perfect place for bacteria to reside. Careless contact transfers the bacteria onto utensils, work surfaces, equipment, and food. Staphylococci are also present in infected cuts, burns and sores, and pimples, as well as the other places mentioned previously. Careless touching of these areas transfers bacteria to the employee's hands, then to food and on to the customer.

Diseases can be spread rapidly by hand contact. In 1990, an outbreak of over 100 confirmed cases of hepatitis A virus was linked to the deli department of a major retail food chain. Company executives voluntarily closed the store, temporarily replaced the entire deli staff, cleaned and sanitized all areas of the operation, and disposed of all in-store prepared, ready-to-eat foods. The supermarket chain also made arrangements for several area hospitals to screen 2,500 customers for the virus.

Although the store acted very responsibly and handled this situation in a professional manner, the adverse publicity and monetary losses related to discarded products, extra salaries, investigation costs, and medical screenings were very costly. It is the responsibility of management to take the proper steps to ensure that workers who have health problems are not allowed to work near or to handle food products. Of course, the manager who always seems to be short of personnel may tend to look the other way if an employee is brave enough to work despite an illness. Although such a cavalier attitude may save a few hours up front, it will in the long run damage the store's image, as the above case study demonstrates.

To ensure that employees are able to follow good personal habits, management must provide not only leadership and motivation, but also adequate facilities to encourage good personal hygiene and proper work

Figure 9.1   Bacteria and People

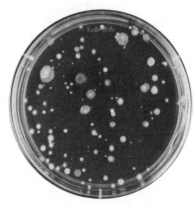

In the laboratory, bacteria grow on gelatin-like food (agar) in covered, sterile, plastic plates (petri dishes).

The bacteria grow rapidly by keeping them at a warm temperature (98.6°F, 37.0°C). Twenty-four to 48 hours later, small colonies or clumps of bacteria approximately the size of a pinhead or larger can be seen in the agar. Each of these colonies contains millions of bacteria.

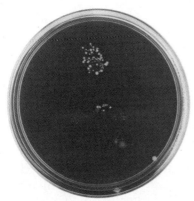

The lips and nose play an important role in harboring bacteria. This plate shows what happens when the lips and nose are pressed against agar in a petri dish.

Hair is also a source of bacteria and has no place in food. It is unappetizing, unappealing, and adds bacteria to food. Effective hair restraints should be worn whenever a person works with food. This picture shows the bacteria associated with human hair.

Figure 9.1   (continued)

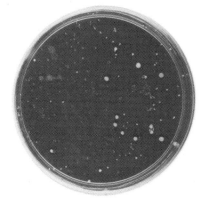

Bacteria can also find their way into food through coughs, sneezes, and vigorous nose blowing. This picture shows that a single sneeze produces a mist of small droplets containing bacteria.

Each sneeze contains between 10,000 and 100,000 bacteria, and they are moved through the air at more than 200 mph.

Source: Robert B. Gravani, "Safe Food Preparation: It's In Your Hands," Cornell Cooperative Extension Miscellaneous Bulletin 128 (Ithaca, NY: Cornell University, 1982).

habits. This includes such items as adequate toilet facilities with hand-washing sinks, hot water, soap, and single-service towels in dispensers or hot-air dryers; dressing facilities; designated places for eating and smoking; and most importantly, hand-washing facilities in preparation areas. Although these are required by law in most states, there are still many food stores in which facilities are grossly inadequate.

Hygiene and Personal Cleanliness

Many of the rules for personal hygiene may seem elementary to some people since they have been following these rules since childhood (3, 4, 5). It is, however, important to understand that not everyone comes from the same background and understands the importance of personal cleanliness. As well, many of the rules bear repeating, even for the well informed, because the personal cleanliness of food store personnel can *never* be overemphasized.

Good hygiene begins at home, before the start of the workday. A checklist of procedures to be followed before reporting to the food store includes the following:

- bathing or showering daily
- keeping hair clean and neatly combed
- wearing a minimum amount of makeup (fingernail polish is not allowed)
- having clean hands and clean, well-trimmed nails
- wearing clean clothes—socks, undergarments, and the like
- having clean teeth and fresh-smelling breath
- using deodorant
- having a clean, shaven face (although some stores allow beards if they are neatly trimmed)
- wearing clean shoes

Food store workers who do not practice the rules of good personal hygiene can transfer millions of bacteria into and around the department and store. They are also a poor advertisement for the store. A dirty or unkempt worker can offend customers and influence their opinion about the quality and safety of products in the entire store.

Management must make perfectly clear the personal-hygiene principles it expects its personnel to follow from each employee's first day on the job. Guidelines should be presented in employee handbooks and pamphlets, and practical reminders should be posted in washrooms, locker rooms, and break areas to reinforce their importance to all employees. The rules should also be clearly explained to each employee by a supervisor so that there is never any misunderstanding. It is especially important to fully explain the rules when an employee first begins work in the deli or one of the other fresh-prepared food departments. Personal hygiene and employee cleanliness is a number *one* priority.

Upon arrival at work, the employee should

- put on a clean uniform (if required by the store)
- remove any excess jewelry (wedding bands are acceptable)
- cover the hair with an effective hair restraint—hat or hair net (in food-processing, food-preparation, and food-serving departments)
- follow other company policies regarding personal hygiene and cleanliness

Hand Washing

The final step that all employees must take before they begin work is to *wash their hands*. The main purpose of proper hand washing is to protect public health by preventing the transfer of disease-causing bacteria to foods. Although hand washing is a simple and easy task, you would be surprised how many people avoid washing their hands or do it improperly. In several informal studies, it was estimated that nearly 60 percent of the people did not wash their hands after using the toilet. Disease-causing bacteria associated with human wastes can easily be transmitted to foods if hands are not thoroughly and properly washed. Hand washing is one of the most effective ways to limit the spread of bacteria from people to food. Hands should be washed thoroughly—this includes between the fingers, the back of the hands, and exposed portions of the arms.

A proper hand-washing technique for people working with food is as follows (3, 4):

1. Allow enough time to wash hands properly. Use water as hot as the hands can comfortably stand—105° to 120°F (40.6° to 48.9°C).
2. Moisten hands, soap thoroughly with a self-foaming soap, detergent, or disinfectant soap, and wash to forearms.
3. Scrub hands thoroughly, using a brush for the nails.
4. Rub hands together, using friction for 20 to 60 seconds.
5. Pay particular attention to the areas between the fingers and to the exposed areas of the wrist and forearm.
6. Rinse thoroughly under running water.
7. Dry hands using single-service towels or a hot-air dryer.

Figure 9.2 shows the technique for effective hand washing.

Washing hands is an activity that should be repeated frequently throughout the day and is especially critical after performing any of the following activities (3, 4):

- using the toilet
- sneezing into the hand or using a tissue or handkerchief
- handling raw foods, particularly meat and poultry
- touching areas of the body such as the mouth, nose, hair, ears, or scratching anywhere on the body
- touching infected or otherwise unsanitary areas of the body
- touching or handling soiled materials, equipment, or work surfaces
- handling garbage
- eating foods or drinking beverages
- smoking or using chewing tobacco
- leaving and returning to the department for lunch, break, etc.

Figure 9.2   Proper Hand-washing Technique

1. Allow enough time to wash hands properly. Use water as hot as the hands can comfortably stand—about 105°F (or 40.6°C) or higher.

2. Moisten hands, soap thoroughly with a self-foaming soap, detergent, or disinfectant soap, and wash to forearms.

3. Scrub hands thoroughly, using a brush for the nails.

4. Rub hands together, using friction for 20 to 60 seconds.

Hand washing is also critical between different tasks in a food-preparation area. An employee should *always* wash his or her hands when switching from working with a raw product to working with a cooked, ready-to-eat product.

If hands are not washed after any of these activities are performed, bacteria can hitchhike from one area to another. Hand-sanitizer liquids that lower the number of microorganisms on the surface of the skin are frequently being used by people who prepare foods. These sanitizers are used after the hands are thoroughly washed and should not be used as a substitute for hand washing (3).

Figure 9.3 shows how bacteria on hands can be reduced by effective hand washing.

As a general rule, *hands should not be used any more than absolutely necessary when handling food products.* Employees should always use tongs,

Figure 9.2 (continued)

5. Pay particular attention to the areas between the fingers and to the exposed areas of the wrist and forearm.

6. Rinse thoroughly under running water.

7. Dry hands using single-service towels or a hot-air dryer.

Photographs by Cornell University Photography.

spatulas, clean disposable gloves, paper wrappings, spoons, or any other utensils or aids that prevent hands from coming into direct contact with ready-to-eat food. Hands are among the primary causes of contamination in the processing and handling of food. Habits like picking the nose, scratching the ears, sneezing, touching the face, and similar activities involve the hands—the same hands that touch foods in processing, preparing, and packaging foods.

In some municipalities, laws require that employees who handle foods must wear *clean*, disposable gloves. Gloves should be changed frequently, especially when they become dirty and certainly between handling raw and ready-to-eat foods. Remember, to be effective, gloves must be changed frequently!

Figure 9.3 Effective Hand Washing Reduces the Number of Bacteria Present

An unwashed hand that looks clean is touched to the agar.

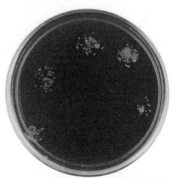

The plate is incubated at 98.6°F (37.0°C) for 24 hours. The heavy growth of white colonies indicates that this hand was not very clean and that millions of bacteria were present.

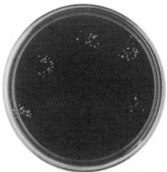

After washing the hands for 15 seconds with hot water and soap, bacteria are reduced in number.

Washing the hands with soap and water for another 15 seconds reduces the bacteria even more.

After washing, the hands are not sterile because bacteria are hidden in the folds of the skin, but proper hand washing will significantly reduce the numbers of bacteria present.

Fingernails should be kept neatly trimmed and clean. Dirt harbors bacteria and gets under long or ragged nails. The plate at right shows bacteria present in fingernail scrapings.

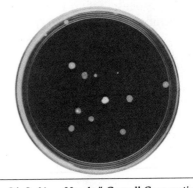

Source: Robert B. Gravani, "Safe Food Preparation: It's In Your Hands," Cornell Cooperative Extension Miscellaneous Bulletin 128 (Ithaca, NY: Cornell University, 1982).

Bad Habits Can Cause Sanitation Problems

There are a number of other ways an employee can inadvertently spread bacteria in a food store department besides not observing personal-hygiene rules (5). A good department manager should be aware of the potential harm some sloppy work habits can cause. The following practices are some of the main ways in which the good sanitation practices of a department can be compromised:

- using wiping cloths to remove perspiration
- washing hands in sinks used to prepare foods
- spitting on the floor or into sinks
- coughing or sneezing in a food-preparation area
- picking up ready-to-eat food products with bare hands
- leaving food products uncovered or covering them carelessly
- chewing gum or tobacco
- smoking

Many of these actions may seem harmless, and employees may easily become lax in their personal-hygiene practices and work habits. The harried deli employee, left to serve a number of anxious customers, may not remember to practice good sanitation habits. Problems will arise especially when the store is busy or a department is short-staffed. It is primarily the department manager's job to remind employees that the health of the customers and the reputation of the store rests literally in their hands.

Conclusions

Foods can be contaminated by poor personal hygiene and careless work habits. First, employees should report to work only when they are healthy. They should also be clean and neat when they are working in a food store. Personal-hygiene habits should begin at home. Employees should never report to work unless they have bathed and attended to the other aspects of their personal appearance.

Once in the food store, employees should comply with all of the guidelines mandated by their supervisors to guarantee that the food products they handle and sell are not compromised in any way. Hand washing should be practiced on a regular basis, and other adequate precautions should be taken to prevent the spread of bacteria.

The onus for cleanliness cannot be placed only on the employee, however. Management must provide *clear* guidelines and adequate facilities to ensure that the employees can keep themselves clean and tidy. Washrooms, lockers or changing areas, and designated eating and smoking zones must be available. Disposable gloves and any other accessories that will make food handling safer should also be provided. These gloves should be changed frequently and especially after they become soiled.

Finally, management should teach employees to respect the food products they prepare, handle, and sell. Food items should be treated with caution and care at every level of the store. The high regard with which products are handled is one of the best advertisements for the store's commitment to quality, service, and safety. The appearance of store employees, their work habits, and the care with which they do their jobs all help to maintain this image.

Three simple rules for controlling bacteria can be used as a quick reminder for employees:

1. Limit or prevent contamination.
2. Don't let microorganisms "hitchhike."
3. Always practice good personal hygiene.

Remember, safe food preparation is in your hands!

References

1. *1993 Trends: Consumer Attitudes and the Supermarket.* Washington, DC: Food Marketing Institute, 1993.
2. Marriott, N. G. *Principles of Food Sanitation.* 2d ed. New York: Van Nostrand Reinhold/AVI, 1989.
3. National Restaurant Association. Educational Foundation. *Foodservice Sanitation.* 4th ed. New York: John Wiley & Sons, Inc., 1992.
4. Gravani, Robert B. *Safe Food Preparation: It's In Your Hands!* Cornell Cooperative Extension Publication, Miscellaneous Bulletin 128. Ithaca, NY: Cornell University, 1982.
5. *Food Handler's Pocket Guide for Food Safety & Quality.* Washington, DC: Food Marketing Institute, 1989.

10

Effective Pest Control: Rodents and Birds

Rodent and insect damage to food products and food store equipment cost supermarkets millions of dollars annually. Rats, mice, and insects are also the worst public-relations representatives a food store can have—they are easily spotted in any part of the store and are offensive to almost everyone. Insects and rodents, however, can be controlled and eliminated. A well-planned, comprehensive pest-control program provides a strong foundation for a store-wide HACCP-based food safety assurance program.

For easy reference, the material on pest control has been divided into two chapters. This chapter provides a general introduction to the control and elimination of food store pests, and then focuses specifically on rodents and birds. The following chapter provides details on insect control and discusses the role of professional pest-management services in controlling and eliminating rodents and insects in the food store.

147

An Essential Complement to a Comprehensive HACCP Program

Rodents and insects can affect five vital areas of a retail food store operation:

- *Economics*: spoilage, damage, and loss of product.
- *Health*: pest-borne disease.
- *Safety*: rodents can start fires by chewing on wires, and insects (cockroaches) can short-out computers.
- *Aesthetics*: customer rejection of product or service, or even the whole store as a viable place to shop.
- *Workplace environment*: pest infestations can affect employee morale.

The economic losses due to rodents and insects are enormous. Every time insects are found in food, the entire package must be discarded. The same holds true when there is evidence that rodents have chewed open a food package or birds have contaminated products with their fecal matter. If food inspectors find widespread evidence of pest infestation, they may order a great deal or all of the suspect food product seized and destroyed. Many times this leads to court action, resulting in fines, closures, adverse publicity, loss of sales, and sometimes even legal action.

Rodents, insects, and birds can also cause foodborne illness by contaminating food, equipment, and utensils. Rats and mice, which feed in garbage and sewers, may carry disease-causing organisms in their fur or intestinal tract and on their feet. Flies, cockroaches, and other insects are found not only in places where food is stored, prepared, and sold, but also in toilets, sewers, garbage, and other sources of pathogens. As these insects move from one area of the food store to another, they can carry harmful microorganisms with them.

The first phase of good pest control is to list the ways in which rodents and insects can flourish in the food store. Do rodents and insects have access to stored raw food products in the bakery department? Can they gain access to prepared foods that are kept overnight? Do product spills and food wastes remain for long periods of time in food-preparation areas?

Once these problem areas are identified, steps to control the pests must be undertaken (1, 2, 3). There are three important aspects to pest control:

- Prevent the entry of rodents, insects, and birds (pest-proofing).
- Restrict the availability of shelter and food.
- Destroy them if they do gain access to the food store.

Preventing the Entry of Rodents and Insects

Food store operators must reduce and try to eliminate all possible sources of entry by rodents and insects by making certain there are no openings around all outside doors, especially at the bottom. This is a common problem with receiving doors. Seal all cracks in walls, doors, or openings ¼ inch (0.6 cm) or less in size, which may provide an entrance to pests. Make sure windows and screens fit tightly and are in good repair, and that air curtains are working properly. Openings around pipes should be permanently sealed with an adequate protective material, such as concrete, caulking, or a variety of other permanent products. Rodents can also gain entry by climbing pipes or wires; therefore, metal shields or guards should be placed over these. In addition, be certain that vents or exhaust fans—ideal sources of entry for pests—have suitable covering to keep out rodents and insects (3, 4).

Vendors' boxes and bottles returned by customers can introduce pests to the supermarket. Employees can also bring pests from home in purses, lunch boxes, gym bags, and other personal items (2). Stores should have procedures for inspecting all incoming products and should refuse to accept any items that are infested with pests. Procedures should also be in place to isolate and remove infested products from the premises to prevent the rapid dispersion of pests to other parts of the store.

Restricting the Availability of Shelter and Food

It is inevitable that some pests will gain entry to a food store, no matter how vigorous the control efforts (1, 2, 3). Once they do get in, however, their survival depends on how quickly they can seek out and gain shelter. Rodents and insects can easily make permanent homes in cardboard boxes, lumber, rags, trash, or any other rubbish kept inside or outside of the store. The junction of a floor and a wall is also a favored place of residence, as are any places that are dark or seldom visited by store personnel—equipment and supply rooms, locker facilities, and similar locations. Other good nesting spots include janitorial rooms, heating and cooling equipment rooms, spaces behind large walk-in coolers and freezers, switch boxes, and the motors of display cases, water fountains, and ice machines. Empty spaces in equipment, gondolas, suspended ceilings, cabinets, walls, and floors are the most common sources of shelter for pests in food stores (2).

Making it difficult for rodents and insects to find food and water is another important part of pest control—necessary, but an often difficult one to accomplish in a food store. Since many pests can survive on small crumbs and scraps of food, thorough cleaning and good sanitation practices are of the utmost importance.

Certain practices in retail food stores will provide rodents and insects with ideal conditions to breed and proliferate:

- poor storage practices
- product spillage
- improperly cleaned equipment
- improperly cleaned facilities
- improper containers for garbage
- garbage containers not closed tightly
- trash and garbage left to accumulate outside the store

If the grocery store provides pests with a good food source, they will settle in, breed, and continue to cost the store money, time, and the goodwill of customers. Food store personnel must be vigilant in reducing the food sources that pests need to survive.

Controlling Pests

Despite the best of efforts, pests still manage to gain entry into food stores and must be eliminated as quickly as possible (2). Every store operator should have a well-structured and ongoing pest-management program as part of a store-wide HACCP program. While the services of a professional company can be of great help in controlling pest infestations, the success of the program rests primarily with the retailer. Cleanliness, good sanitation, good building maintenance, and attention to details are the most important steps in preventing pest entry and survival in the food store (1, 2, 3).

To isolate the points at which pests gain access to food stores and find food sources to sustain them, retailers should know some basic facts about the creatures they are trying to eliminate. The remainder of this chapter focuses on rodents and birds.

Rats and Mice

Rodents, which have plagued humans since prehistoric times, are a major problem to the food industry today. Rodents are somewhat elusive adversaries because of their keen senses of smell, touch, and hearing, as well as their ability to adapt to a wide range of living conditions.

Although there are many kinds of rodents—including squirrels, woodchucks, muskrats, porcupines, and beavers—those that are most troublesome to the food industry are Norway rats, roof rats, and house mice.

These rodents have been responsible for more human illness and death, as well as destruction of food, than any group of mammals. They can carry about 35 diseases that affect humans and livestock.

No one knows for certain, but it is safe to say that there are millions of rats living in the United States today. It is estimated that each of these rats eats more than 25 pounds (11 kg) of food a year. These rodents also damage and contaminate far greater amounts of food and materials through gnawing, chewing, body contact, and the discharge of their body wastes (1, 4, 5, 6). Food store employees need to be familiar with rodents and their habits in order to understand how to control them.

Rodent Types

The *Norway rat* is the most widely distributed rat species in the United States and is found in every state. The *roof rat* is confined primarily to the coastal portions of Washington, Oregon, and California, as well as to a large part of the Southeast, from Texas to Maryland. They are common in gulf seaports and frequently board ships in ports. *House mice*, like Norway rats, are prevalent throughout the country. It is important to be able to

RODENT CONTROL LABORATORY, NEW YORK STATE DEPARTMENT OF HEALTH

Norway rats are burrowers. They often establish their burrows around dumps, sewers, and buildings, and under trash close to food and water. Indoors, they will commonly build nests in wall voids, underneath equipment, and within neglected storage areas, false ceilings, and floors.

distinguish between the different species since each one requires a different method of control.

Norway Rat

The Norway rat is also called the barn rat, brown rat, gray rat, sewer rat, water rat, wharf rat, and house rat (5, 6, 7). It is a burrowing rat, harboring in burrows about 2 to 3 inches (5 to 8 cm) in diameter in the ground. Rats often establish their burrows around dumps, sewers, and buildings, and under trash close to food and water. Indoors, they will commonly build nests in wall voids, underneath equipment, within neglected storage areas, false ceilings, and floors, and in other areas that provide the rats with an undisturbed place to build a nest.

The Norway rat will eat almost any food (about 1 ounce or 28 grams per day), but it prefers garbage, meat, fish, cereal, nuts, fruits, vegetables, and pastry. Rats usually move within a limited area to find food, water, shelter, and a mate. This distance is called the "home range" and extends for a radius of about 100 to 150 feet (30 to 46 m) from the nest.

The Norway rat has a stocky body and weighs 7 to 18 ounces (198 to 511 g) when fully grown. The Norway rat has between 8 and 12 young per litter and about four to seven litters per year. Its body fur is coarse and ranges from reddish to grayish brown with buff-white underparts, but there are many color variations, including all-black Norway rats. The nose is blunt, and the ears are small, close set, and do not reach the eyes when pulled down. The tail is scaly, seminaked, and shorter than the head and body combined.

Roof Rat

The roof rat is also known as the black rat, ship rat, grey-bellied rat, Alexandrine rat, and white-bellied rat (1, 5, 6, 7). The roof rat is an excellent climber and commonly lives above the ground, building its nest in trees, in clinging vines, on the sides of buildings and fences, or inside buildings in attic areas, ceiling voids, or wall voids in roofline areas. These rodents prefer to eat seeds and fresh fruits and vegetables, but they will eat almost anything that is available, when necessary. Their home range extends for a radius of about 100 to 150 feet (30 to 46 m) from the nest. Roof rats are smaller and sleeker in appearance than the Norway rat. Adults weigh 5 to 9 ounces (141 to 256 g). The color of the fur is usually grayish black to a solid black, and the belly varies from buff white to dull gray. The snout is pointed; the ears are large and reach the eyes when pulled down. The tail is long and reaches the snout when pulled over the body. The roof rat has four to eight young per litter and about four to six litters per year.

STEPHEN C. FRANTZ

Norway Rat

It is important to be able to distinguish between the different rodent species since each one requires a different method of control. The Norway rat (*Rattus norvegicus*), shown above, has a stocky body, a blunt nose, small ears, and a scaly, relatively short tail. The roof rat (*Rattus rattus*), at right, is smaller than the Norway rat and has a pointed snout, large ears, and a long tail. The house mouse (*Mus musculus*), below, is much smaller than the roof rat and has large ears and a long tail.

Photos courtesy of University of California, Statewide IPM Project.

STEPHEN C. FRANTZ

Roof Rat

JACK KELLY CLARK

House Mouse

House Mouse

The house mouse is the smallest of the rodents and is widely distributed throughout the United States (*1, 5, 6, 7*). It is, in fact, the most numerous and widespread mammal on earth, with the exception of humans. The house mouse is usually found in and around buildings, nesting in walls, cabinets, furniture, and stored food products. It eats a variety of foods, including cereals, grains, nuts, seeds, lard, butter, meat, bacon, pastry, candy, and insects. This highly inquisitive rodent typically has a limited home-range radius of about 10 to 30 feet (3 to 9 m). Sometimes, however, the mouse may move into stored pallets of groceries and only move a couple of feet in any direction from its nest.

The house mouse is identified by a small, slender body weighing about ½ to 1 ounce (14 to 29 g) as an adult. The ears are large, and the tail is seminaked and as long as the head and body together. The fur is usually dark gray on the back and light gray on the belly, but many color variations are possible. Albino (white), black, and mixtures of black and white have been bred in the laboratory. The house mouse has four to seven young per litter and approximately eight litters per year.

Rodent Identification

Rodents involved in an infestation must be properly identified before an effective control program is undertaken. Materials, equipment, and methods to control one type of rodent may not be effective against another. The diagrams in Figure 10.1 provide a simple way to distinguish between a Norway rat, a roof rat, a young rat, and a house mouse.

Young rats can be distinguished from mice by their differences in body build. Young rats have larger hind feet and their tails are much thicker than the tails of house mice. The heads of young rats are much larger and their fur is much fuzzier when compared to mice. In general, the house mouse is much smaller and has finer fur than the young rat.

Senses, Agility, and Reactions of Rodents (*1, 5, 6, 7*)

Touch: well developed in highly sensitive whiskers, or *vibrissae,* and certain guard (tactile) hairs. Rats and mice prefer to run along walls or between objects where they can keep their whiskers in contact with side surfaces.

Vision: relatively poor. Rodents are nearsighted. They are also color-blind, so any distinctive coloring of poison baits does not reduce the bait's acceptance.

Smell: keen. Rodents apparently like the odors of most foods eaten by people. They are accustomed to the smell of people, so the odor of people on baits and traps does not repel them.

Figure 10.1   Field Identification of Domestic Rodents

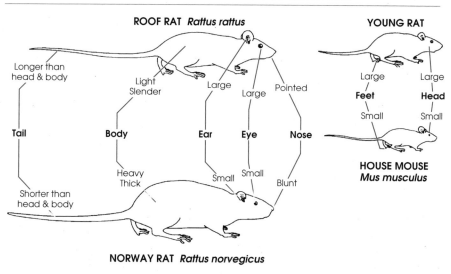

Source: H. D. Pratt and R. Z. Brown, *Biological Factors in Domestic Rodent Control*, HDEW
Publication no. (CDC) 77-8144 (Atlanta, GA: Centers for Disease Control, 1977).

Taste: highly developed. Rodents prefer fresh food to decayed food.

Hearing: a keen sense of hearing. They can locate the source of a noise within 6 inches (15 cm). Unusual noises cause rodents to attempt to escape.

Balance: excellent. A falling rodent always lands on its feet. The roof rat even maintains its balance while walking on suspended wires.

Reaction to strange objects: rats may avoid a new sound or a strange object in their environment for up to several days, particularly if other rats are also alarmed by it. Other objects—food or garbage—are readily accepted by them. As rodent-population pressures build, rats frequently exhibit "chain-fright" reaction to disturbances. Most mice tend to explore new objects and to be caught in newly set traps. Some mice, however, can also develop new object reactions and be as elusive as rats.

Climbing: roof rats and house mice are good climbers, while the Norway rat can climb quite well when necessary.

Jumping and reaching: rats can jump nearly 2 feet (0.6 m) vertically, 3 feet (0.9 m) with a running start; they can jump 4 feet (1.2 m) horizontally and 8 feet (2.4 m) from an elevation that is 15 feet (4.6 m) above the finish point. Rats can reach upward about 18 inches (46 cm). House mice can jump 13 inches (33 cm) vertically.

Table 10.1   Characteristics of Common Rodents*

Characteristic	Norway Rat	Roof Rat	House Mouse
General appearance	Large, robust	Sleek, graceful	Small, slender
Adult size			
Weight: oz./grams	7–18 oz./198–511 g	5–9 oz./141–256 g	0.4–1.0 oz./11–29 g
Length			
Head & body	7–9½ in./18–25 cm	6–8 in./15–20 cm	2–3½ in./5–9 cm
Tail	6–8 in./15–21 cm	7–10 in./18–25 cm	3–4 in./7–10 cm
Snout	Blunt	Pointed	Pointed
Ears	Small, covered with short hairs; do not reach eyes	Large, nearly naked; can be pulled over eyes	Large, some hair
Eyes	Small	Large, prominent	Small
Tail	Dark above; pale beneath	Uniformly dark	Uniformly dark
Fur	Brown with scattered black (agouti); venter gray to yellow/white; shaggy	Agouti to gray to black; venter white, gray, or black; smooth spindle	Light brown, light gray; smooth
Droppings	Capsule-shaped, ½–1 in./1–3 cm	Spindle-shaped, ½ in./1 cm	Rod-shaped, ⅛–¼ in./0.3–0.6 cm
Senses			
Sight	Poor, color-blind	Poor, color-blind	Poor, color-blind
Smell, taste, touch, hearing	Excellent	Excellent	Excellent
Food	Omnivorous, often prefers meats (0.8–1.0 oz./22–30 g per day)	Omnivorous, especially fruits, nuts, grains, vegetables (0.5–1.0 oz./15–30 g per day)	Omnivorous, prefers cereal grains (0.1 oz./3 g per day)
Water	0.45–0.9 fl. oz./13–27 ml per day	0.45–0.9 fl. oz./13–27 ml per day	0.09–0.27 fl. oz./3–8 ml per day; can subsist without free water
Feeding habits	Shy (new object reaction); steady eater	Shy (new object reaction); steady eater	Inquisitive; nibbler
Climbing	Readily climbs; limited agility	Very agile; active climber	Good climber
Nests	Usually burrows	Walls, attics, vines, trees; sometimes burrows	Within structures, stored food; burrows

Table 10.1   (continued)

Characteristic	Norway Rat	Roof Rat	House Mouse
Swimming	Excellent swimmer	Can swim	Can swim
Home-range radius	100–150 ft./30–45 m	100–150 ft./30–45 m	10–30 ft./3–9 m
Age at mating (months)	2–3	2–3	1½–2
Breeding season	Spring and fall peaks	Spring and fall peaks	Yearlong
Gestation period (days)	22	22	19
Young per litter	8–12	4–8	4–7
Litters per year	4–7	4–6	8
Young weaned per female each year	20	20	30–35
Length of life	1 year	1 year	1 year

*Data are averages and not representative of extremes.
Source: Adapted from Gary W. Bennett et al., *Truman's Scientific Guide to Pest Control Operations*, 4th ed. (Duluth, MN: Edgell Communications, 1988).

Swimming: good swimmers. They are able to swim up through floor drains and toilet-bowl traps.

Table 10.1 compares the characteristics of the Norway rat, roof rat, and house mouse.

Rats and mice are nocturnal creatures, tending to stay in the shadows of some shelter. If rodents cannot get around an object, they will go through it. Rodents are capable of gnawing through a variety of materials, including lead sheathing, cinder block, aluminum siding, glass, and improperly cured concrete. Rodents can also squeeze through very small openings—½ inch (1.3 cm) for rats, and ¼ inch (0.6 cm) for mice. A mouse or a baby rat can therefore squeeze through an opening about the size of a nickel or larger, and the full-grown rat can go through an opening about the size of a quarter (1, 4, 5, 6). Some experts say an opening larger than the width of a pencil will permit rodent entry and should be properly sealed.

Identifying the Presence of Rodents

There are ten rodent signs to look, smell, or listen for during a rodent-control inspection (1, 3, 4, 5, 6, 7):

Droppings (feces). Droppings are the most commonly encountered signs of rodent activity. The house mouse may produce between 50 and

100 droppings daily, while the rat may excrete as many as 150 droppings daily. Mouse droppings measure ⅛ to ¼ inch (0.3 to 0.6 cm), with at least one—and sometimes both—ends pointed. The droppings of the Norway rat measure ½ to 1 inch (1 to 3 cm) in length and have blunt ends. Rodent droppings are usually soft, moist, and shiny black, but the color may vary according to what the rodent has been eating. Older droppings are hard, dry, and gray in color. The older droppings are actually the more dangerous, for as they dry up and become powdery, they will blow around and get into foodstuffs. Each rat dropping contains more than 300 hair fragments that can eventually find their way into food.

Tracks. Tracks are easily seen when there is dust or soft, moist, or wet soil. The rodent's hind foot usually leaves the most visible track. The hind foot of a rat measures about ¾ to 1 inch (1.9 to 2.5 cm) in length, whereas the mouse's hind-foot track measures only about ⅜ inch (1.0 cm) or less. Rats and some mice also leave "tail drag" marks that appear between their footprints.

Gnawing damage. Rodents gnaw on a variety of objects. Look for signs around doors, windows, utility lines, and packaged goods, especially in food storage. Mice frequently gnaw small, clean-cut holes about 1.5 inch (4 cm) in diameter. Gnawed holes from rats are about 2 inches (5 cm) or more in diameter and often contain rough, torn edges. Rats commonly gnaw on wooden structural members, such as door corners, edges of pallets, and wall studs.

Burrows. Holes and fresh diggings around foundations and under floors, sidewalks, platforms, embankments, and similar places can all indicate the presence of rats. Roof rats may construct globular nests within bushes, vines, or trees, although their nests are most commonly found in woodpiles or other locations off the ground.

Runways. Runways are evident in rodent infestations because the creatures repeatedly and routinely use the same pathways between their nests and food sources. Runways are easiest to detect with Norway rats. Runways along floors or rafters usually show an absence of dirt or dust.

Grease marks/smears/rub marks. Look for darkened areas along walls adjacent to pipes, beams, and openings where rodents travel. These marks are made by the oil and dirt of rats and mice as they rub along the walls. Grease marks may also appear on the bottom of joists, where rodents have been traveling along beams or sill plates, on stairways, or around burrow openings in walls, floors, or ceilings. Grease marks are difficult to find in dirty areas.

Urine stains. Urine stains may be found on runways and areas that rodents frequent. Rodent urine will fluoresce blue-white under ultraviolet light. Regulatory-agency inspectors often carry ultraviolet lights to detect the presence of rodent urine and then confirm their findings with a chemical test.

Live or dead rodents. An inspection during the rodent's high-activity period (at dusk or after dark) often can provide information as to the severity of the rodent infestation, as well as the activity area of the rodents.

Rodent sounds. High-pitched squeaks, gnawing sounds, scratching, digging, and sounds of rodents fighting can be heard if one carefully listens and conducts the inspection quietly.

Rodent odors (especially mice). Both rats and mice produce characteristic odors from urine and various body glands. Rodent odors may be particularly pronounced in large mouse infestations and may persist for a considerable length of time after the mice have been eliminated from a building.

Where to Look for the Evidence

In food stores, rodents will usually attempt to establish themselves in quiet areas that are *warm* and also close to food (1, 2, 4, 5, 6). In addition to these areas, other typical places where rodents can be found are

- along walls and in corners
- under piles of rubbish or trash
- around or between pallets
- around or under old boxes
- around or under discarded equipment
- any place that is dark, quiet, and secluded—including motors, locker rooms, storage rooms, and equipment rooms

Rodents use walls, pipes, rafters, and steps as runways to food, water, and shelter. Being creatures of habit, they continually use the same runways. In locating runways, it is important to remember that rodents like to keep in contact with at least one vertical surface, such as a wall.

Control of Rats and Mice

The best way to control a rodent population is to prevent one from getting started (1, 2). Sanitation is the backbone of a successful rodent-control program, and this fact cannot be stressed enough. A well-designed and well-executed sanitation program is the most important tool that store management can use to prevent rat and mouse infestations. If these creatures have established a foothold in the food store, their source of food and water must be reduced or eliminated, and any rodents that are on the premises must be destroyed.

Sanitation, including good housekeeping practices, proper storage practices, and facility maintenance, is the first step to creating a rodent-free environment. Rodent-proofing a facility must also be accomplished. All doors, windows, and other openings must be tight-fitting. Openings around pipes must be sealed with concrete, caulking, or other suitable materials. Wires, pipes, and any other items that provide access to air vents should be removed, and all vents should be screened properly. All outside doors, especially receiving doors, should be closed when not in use. Any possible entryway for rodents, either on, above, or below the floor, must be blocked. The initial expenses involved in these steps may be high, but in the long term, the savings will more than compensate for them.

Trash, both inside and outside the building, must be removed to eliminate any possible nesting and hiding places. The areas around garbage dumpsters should be cleared of foods scraps that can attract pests. The dumpsters should have securely fitting lids and should be manufactured and maintained in such a way as to prevent rodent entry. Any cluttered areas within the store should be attended to as well.

Proper storage practices are very important in rodent control. Boxes of food, supplies, and other articles should be stored at least 6 inches (15 cm) off the floor and about 18 to 24 inches (45 to 61 cm) away from walls. This practice creates aisles that permit inspection and cleaning, and reduces rodent harborage areas.

Rodent problems in food stores usually result when sanitation is poor and improper food-storage practices exist. As part of a store-wide pest-control program, enough time should be built into the system for thorough cleaning and disposal of foodstuffs and refuse throughout the day (or at the end of the working day). Even a few crumbs overlooked near the bread slicer or a broken bag of pet food can nourish a mouse or rat family for quite a while. Garbage or food discards must be in suitable heavy-duty containers that are kept tightly covered. These containers should be easy to clean, rust-resistant, and watertight. Garbage should not accumulate for long periods, but should be removed frequently.

A program to destroy the rodents that do make it into the store is necessary. A competent, reputable pest-control company should be contacted to assist in any rodent-control program (see chapter 11 for more information). The pest-management professional will use a number of methods to eliminate rodents from the store. The use of a variety of mechanical traps and glue boards makes it possible to capture the rodent and dispose of it.

With poison baits, the rodents may die in inaccessible places, causing disagreeable odors in the store or warehouse. There is also the danger of the rodents contaminating food products with poison baits.

Whenever possible, the control of pests should be accomplished without the use of pesticides. For example, when controlling mice, spring traps, mechanical traps, and glue traps are preferable to poison-bait boxes for the following reasons:

- Spring, glue, and mechanical traps are effective and relatively inexpensive.
- Rodents are easily found and removed when caught.
- No odor remains; this may not be the case when a rodent eats poison and dies in an inaccessible corner.
- There is no danger of accidental poisoning to humans.

Spring traps should be placed perpendicular to the wall, with the bait or trigger part of the trap closest to the wall. Peanut butter makes an excellent bait, but rodents also like dry dog food, fried bacon, apples, and raisins. Glue boards should be placed in rodent runways and where rodent activity has been observed.

For mice, there are multiple-catch "curiosity" traps that are readily available and very effective (1, 2). They work without the use of bait. The mice walk into a small opening in the trap similar to a mouse hole. This sets off the trap, which literally spanks the mice or leads them into another

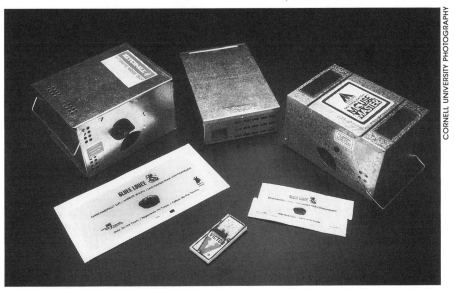

Although the best way to control rodents is to use an effective sanitation program to prevent rodent infestations, if a rodent population does get established in a food store, it may be necessary to use some of the above rodent-control devices. (Devices provided by Acme Pest Control, Inc.)

chamber that is escape-proof. They then usually die from stress and deprivation or can be drowned and disposed of. These traps work on a windup principle and can capture up to a dozen or more mice. The traps should be checked frequently to remove mice or their carcasses. There are also nonwindup traps available.

Birds

Unlike rodents and insects, birds are considered by most people to be desirable animals (1). Unfortunately, certain birds, such as pigeons, house sparrows, and European starlings (as well as others), can be considered pests that are capable of transmitting diseases, contaminating foods, and damaging structures. In addition to the potential for disease transmission, birds in retail food stores can also contaminate food products with fecal matter, feathers, nesting materials, dirt, and ectoparasites (such as lice, mites, bedbugs, fleas, and ticks) that they may harbor (1).

Bird-management professionals recommend using the following five basic approaches to effectively manage bird problems in and around food stores (1):

- *Conduct a bird-management survey.* Identify the pest bird species, their numbers, activity patterns, and note what problems or potential problems are created.
- *Eliminate food and water.* Use effective sanitation practices to remove food and water.
- *Eliminate shelter by altering habitats to exclude birds.* Deny birds access to the building for use as a nesting, roosting, or loafing site.
- *Use repellents.* Mechanical and chemical repellents that are designed to affect one or more of the bird's senses, to scare them away, or to make roosting uncomfortable have been effective.
- *Use population reduction.* Reduce pest bird populations through carefully designed programs.

A bird-management professional should be consulted *before* attempting to control any bird problem because there are a variety of laws that protect birds. Careful attention to details is very important in dealing with bird pests because of the adverse publicity that could be generated.

The most important consideration in managing any food store pest is *proper sanitation practices* and an *emphasis on prevention!*

References

1. Bennett, G. W., J. M. Owens, and R. M. Corrigan. *Truman's Scientific Guide to Pest Control Operations.* 4th ed. Duluth, MN: Edgell Communications, 1988.

2. Corrigan, R. M. Personal communication, Purdue University, 1992.

3. Gravani, R. B. "Food Deterioration and Spoilage by Rodents." In *Food Science Facts.* Fact Sheet no. 117 and Fact Sheet no. 118. Ithaca, NY: Cornell University Institute of Food Science, 1983.

4. Caslick, J. W., and D. J. Decker. *Rat and Mouse Control.* Information Bulletin no. 163. Ithaca, NY: Cornell University Division of Biological Sciences and Department of Natural Resources, 1980.

5. Pratt, H. D., B. F. Bjornson, and K. S. Littig. *Control of Domestic Rats and Mice.* Atlanta, GA: U.S. Department of Health, Education, and Welfare, 1977.

6. Pratt, H. D., and R. Z. Brown. *Biological Factors in Domestic Rodent Control.* Atlanta, GA: U.S. Department of Health, Education, and Welfare, 1977.

7. Frantz, S. C., and D. E. Davis. "Ecology and Management of Food-Industry Pests." In *FDA Technical Bulletin 4,* edited by J. R. Gorham, 243–313. Arlington, VA: AOAC International, 1991.

11

Effective Pest Control: Insects

Throughout history, insects have competed with humans for food and shelter, and have affected the health and peace of mind of many people. It is estimated that there are over 800,000 species of insects in the world (1) and, as with bacteria, some are beneficial while others are harmful. Some insect species can be particularly troublesome to the food industry by contaminating food and causing deterioration and spoilage of products. Some species can also transmit diseases.

Insects are particularly destructive to cereal grains, dried foods, fruits, and vegetables. It has been estimated that insects destroy 5 to 10 percent of the U.S. grain crop annually. Insects do not destroy food by consuming great quantities of it, but once they damage the integrity of a product, further deterioration may result from invasion by bacteria, yeasts, or molds. A small insect hole in a fruit or vegetable may not be a severe problem, but it can lead to bacterial or mold contamination that can spoil the entire product.

164

There are several insects that can cause real problems in food stores, including flies, cockroaches, and stored-product pests such as moths, weevils, and beetles. These insects can enter retail stores in a variety of ways because they are usually attracted to

- food
- shelter
- water
- odors
- light
- color

It is important for food store employees to know more about the characteristics of certain insects so appropriate preventive and control measures can be implemented. Some characteristics of insect pests that frequently infest retail stores are discussed in this chapter.

Flies

Although there are many types of flies, houseflies are the most common insects to infest retail food stores. These insects breed in garbage, human and animal wastes, sewage, and almost any kind of warm, moist organic material (1, 2, 3, 4). With their hairy bodies and sticky feet, flies can transmit disease-causing bacteria and filth to clean food, equipment, and utensils. Because flies have no teeth, they cannot chew food and can only ingest liquid materials. To get solid foods in liquid form, the fly vomits on the product and the liquified food is then "sponged up" by the insect and passed into its digestive tract. In the process of vomiting, bacteria from a previous meal are spread over the food. Bacteria are also spread by their mouth parts, on their body hairs, on the sticky pads of their feet, and in their feces.

Flies can enter a facility through small openings and, like any other insect, must have food, warmth, and moisture to survive. The female housefly normally will lay her eggs in filth, garbage, food residues, or other decaying organic matter. The eggs do not hatch into flies, but first appear as small white worms commonly known as maggots. The maggots then go through the pupal stage and evolve into flies (1, 2, 5). The life cycle of the housefly takes from 7 to 45 days and is shown in Figure 11.1.

A female fly and succeeding generations can produce a large number of flies in a very short period of time. For example, during warm weather,

Figure 11.1   Life Cycle of the Housefly

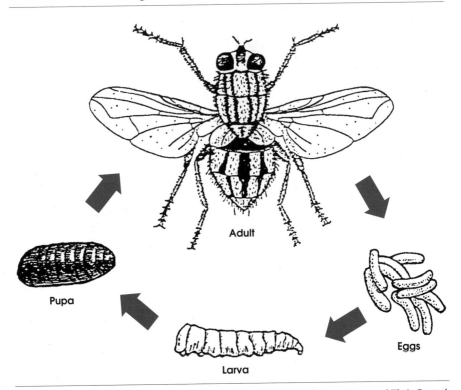

Adult

Pupa

Eggs

Larva

Source: H. D. Pratt, K. S. Littig, and H. G. Scott, *Flies of Public Health Importance and Their Control*, CDC 76-8218 (The Centers for Disease Control, 1976).

two or more generations of flies may be completed in a month. Houseflies are most abundant in late summer and early fall.

The first step in a successful fly-management program is to reduce the number of flies in and around the building. The key to this is maintaining an effective sanitation program both inside and outside the store (*1, 2, 3*).

Preventing Entry

All possible sources of fly entry must be eliminated or tightly controlled. Doors and windows should be tight-fitting, and screens, if used, should be in good repair. Screens should be 12-mesh for houseflies and 18-mesh for smaller flies (*3*). Exhaust fans or vents should have tight-fitting, self-closing louvers or screens.

EFFECTIVE PEST CONTROL: INSECTS

Receiving doors should be open only as long as necessary to receive incoming supplies. An excellent way to keep out flies is to use an air curtain or air blower over the receiving door, since flies have a hard time flying through a high velocity of air. The air curtain or blower should be wired to go on when the door is opened. It should be noted that the most effective fly-control measures are the elimination of breeding sources, appropriate screening of all openings, and proper door-use management (2, 3). Air curtains will not provide a high level of control if other measures are not successfully implemented.

Restricting Shelter and Food

Garbage management in and around retail stores is the most critical aspect of fly management (2, 3). By properly handling and managing food wastes, debris, and other garbage, the reproductive cycle of the insect can be broken and serious fly infestations can be prevented. Since flies like to lay eggs in warm and moist decaying organic matter, it is necessary to make sure that such a medium does not exist. Food spills, garbage, and other debris should be cleaned up at once. Dirty aprons, rags, and other soiled or dirty materials must not be allowed to accumulate and should be removed from the premises on a regular basis. Thorough cleaning and sanitizing are essential in preventing fly infestations.

Garbage cans should be cleaned daily and always kept tightly covered. All food scraps and garbage should be placed in securely sealed plastic bags before being put in dumpsters. Since garbage dumpsters are a major breeding ground for flies and also are attractants for new flies, they *must* be kept clean (3). The areas under and around the dumpster should be free of food debris and decaying matter, and must be cleaned regularly as part of the store's sanitation program. To break the fly reproductive cycle, garbage pickup should occur twice weekly. Dumpsters should also be kept as far away from the store as possible. The flies will be attracted to the receptacles away from the building and fewer flies will be found near the structure. Potential sources of fly infestations must be carefully monitored, and precautions should be taken to avoid conditions that would allow fly populations to increase.

Fly Control

Because it is virtually impossible to eliminate the entry of all flies, measures must be taken to destroy those that do manage to enter. It is illegal to use fly strips or flypaper in food-processing areas because flies or fly parts may drop into the food or onto equipment after they touch the poison on the strips or are caught on the paper. Flypaper can, however, be used in loading-dock and warehousing areas, and may help reduce the number of flies in the store. Regulatory agencies are also very strict about the chemicals used to kill flies in food areas. Those chemicals that are approved must be used under very strict, controlled conditions. It is very important that only personnel who are properly trained and certified be involved in applying pesticides in stores.

An effective method of controlling those flies that do get into a store is the placement of a fly electrocuter in or around the loading-dock area. The flying-insect electrocuter works on the principle that flies are attracted to low-frequency ultraviolet light. When flying into the lights, the insects touch a low-voltage electrical grid that electrocutes them. They then drop down into a tray or drawer in the device. A new continuous fly-control system is also now available. It uses an ultraviolet light to attract flies and a low-voltage electrical pulse that causes them to become disoriented and fly onto an adhesive board on the bottom of the unit, where they become trapped and die. Federal authorities allow this fly-control system to be used in food-preparation areas because it does not cause contamination from insect body parts. Careful placement of any of these units is important and should be done in consultation with insect-control experts. Insect light traps are extremely effective in controlling flies, but they must be properly installed (3). For example, correct height of the trap is critical to its success, as is the correct location. A trap should not be visible to flies from outside the store because it could serve as an attractant. Installing these devices should be left to a professional. Most of these devices have been approved by the Food and Drug Administration (FDA) and the U. S. Department of Agriculture (USDA), and comply with Occupational Safety and Health Act (OSHA) standards. To be sure, retailers should ask the

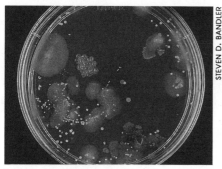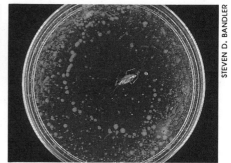

Insects can easily spread bacteria to all items that they come in contact with. The petri dish on the left shows the bacterial contamination from a live fly; the dish on the right shows contamination from a live cockroach.

manufacturer to provide proof of acceptance or compliance with these agencies and seek advice from the regulatory agencies that inspect the store.

Cockroaches

Another insect that frequently causes problems in food stores is the cockroach. This troublesome, unpleasant insect is found in almost every habitable land throughout the world (1, 4).

Research has shown that cockroaches can transport many types of pathogenic bacteria. They are also objectionable because of their odor, which is very unpleasant and noticeable when cockroach populations reach high levels. The odor results from a combination of their excrement, fluids from their scent glands, and the fluid regurgitated from their mouths while feeding.

Cockroaches will actively seek out warm, dark, and humid areas. They try to avoid light and prefer to hide in cracks and crevices. Cockroaches hide in these areas during the day and then come out to seek food at night. In fact, cockroaches spend about 75 percent of their time resting in cracks and crevices (3). When disturbed, they run rapidly for shelter and disappear through openings to their hiding places.

Cockroaches need little moisture and very small amounts of food to survive. They are not capable of biting, but rather scrape and chew a variety of products. They are natural scavengers and will eat almost anything. Although cockroaches prefer starchy foods like bread, potatoes, and beer, they will consume other foods, including sweet beverages, vegetables, pet foods, cereals, tobacco, grease, soiled clothing, paper, and

CORNELL UNIVERSITY PHOTOGRAPHY

Cockroaches will eat almost anything. The glue from this envelope has been scraped off and chewed by cockroaches.

the glue at the base of paper grocery bags and in book bindings (*1, 4*). Cockroaches damage more food and materials than they consume. They contaminate products through body contact, chewing, and with their feces. It is virtually impossible to starve these insects in areas where food is processed, stored, or prepared; even the smallest crumb can provide a meal for a cockroach.

Cockroaches are very hardy insects. They can survive the loss of legs or antennae, withstand great temperature variations, endure depressurization, and go for long periods without food or water.

The cockroach lives and breeds in areas close to its food supply, but it will wander great distances and even migrate to new areas in search of food. Although there are some 55 species of cockroaches found in the U.S., four species commonly cause problems in retail stores. These insects are the

- American cockroach
- German cockroach
- brown-banded cockroach
- oriental cockroach

A typical American cockroach. Note the broad, flattened shape and six long legs.

American Cockroach

Adult American cockroaches are reddish brown to dark brown and are 1.5 to 2.0 inches (3.8 to 5.1 cm) long. They are among the largest cockroaches found and are also known as the water bug or Palmetto bug (1, 4). Adults of both sexes have fully developed wings but rarely fly. Under ideal conditions, an adult female can live up to 14 or 15 months, males for a somewhat shorter period.

Egg case. The egg case, or capsule, of the American cockroach is ⅜ inch long (1 cm) and is reddish brown or black. The female cockroach deposits her egg case that contains about 14 to 16 eggs within a day after it is formed. The eggs hatch approximately 55 days later. During the adult life span, a female will produce about 15 to 90 egg cases.

Habitat. American cockroaches prefer dark, moist areas of basements and furnace rooms. They are also found in sewers and are often located around pipes, plumbing fixtures, floor drains, manholes of sewers, and on the underside of metal covers of large sump pumps in boiler rooms.

German Cockroach

The German cockroach is the most active and most common of all the cockroaches (1, 4). In some areas they are referred to as Croton bugs. They

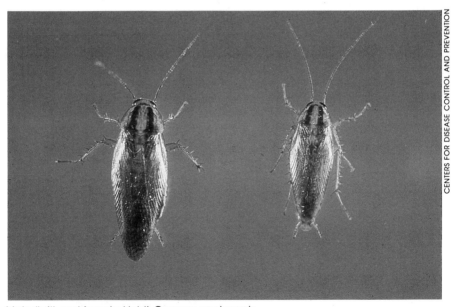

CENTERS FOR DISEASE CONTROL AND PREVENTION

Male (left) and female (right) German cockroach.

are usually light brown, but can be very dark. Adults are ½ to ⅝ inch long (1.3 to 1.6 cm) and are more slender than other cockroaches. German cockroaches can be easily identified by the two dark stripes running lengthwise behind the head. Their wings are well developed and folded over, giving them a pointed appearance at the rear end. They rarely fly and do not move far away from their resting place.

Egg case. The egg capsule of the German cockroach is tan in color, and the female carries the capsule for about a month until the eggs are ready to hatch. Adult females will usually produce 4 to 8 egg capsules in their lifetime. Each capsule contains about 30 to 48 eggs—more than the other cockroaches. Adult German cockroaches usually live up to one year, and three or more generations can occur during this time.

Habitat. German cockroaches are often found in kitchens and cooking areas because they like moisture and food. They live around sinks, water pipes, and cupboards, in stoves, and under refrigerators, water fountains, and other appliances. They are particularly attracted to fermented foods and beverage residues, such as beer spills.

Brown-banded Cockroach

The brown-banded cockroach resembles the German cockroach but is slightly smaller and lacks the two dark stripes (1, 4, 5). The adults are ⅜ to

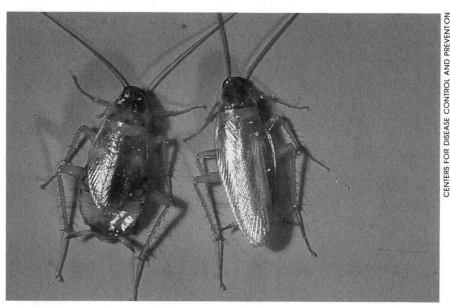

CENTERS FOR DISEASE CONTROL AND PREVENTION

Male (left) and female (right) brown-banded cockroach.

½ inch long (1.0 to 1.3 cm) and are light brown to pale gold in color. These cockroaches have two brownish yellow bands that traverse the back. The male has fully developed wings, will fly when disturbed, and is lighter in color than the female, whose wings are short and nonfunctional. The female has a broader body than the male.

Egg case. The egg case of the brown-banded cockroach is light brown in color. The female carries her egg capsules for one to two days and then attaches it to a protected surface. Usually this is in an out-of-the-way place, like the sides or under surfaces of infested objects such as shelves, the bottoms of drawers, and tables. There are about 18 eggs in each case, and females produce about 14 egg capsules in their adult life. The adult life span is about ten months and there may be two generations annually.

Habitat. The brown-banded cockroach prefers high locations in heated rooms and is often found on ceilings or high on walls. They are also found behind light fixtures and in switches, closets, and furniture, or near the motors of refrigerators and other appliances. They are frequently transported in furniture. Brown-banded cockroaches prefer feeding on starchy materials, but can be found feeding on almost anything. They are more often found in homes, apartments, hotels, and hospital rooms than in stores, restaurants, and kitchens.

Oriental Cockroaches

The oriental cockroach is often referred to as the black beetle or shad roach (1, 4). It is dark brown to shiny black with a greasy sheen and is 1 to 1¼ inches long (2.5 to 3.2 cm). The male has fully developed, short wings, while the female has underdeveloped wings. Females are broader and heavier-looking than males. Neither the male nor the female can fly.

Egg case. The egg case of the oriental cockroach is dark brown to nearly black in color and usually contains 16 eggs. The female carries the egg capsule about 30 hours and either drops it or attaches it to a protected surface near a food supply. Females produce an average of eight capsules.

Habitat. Oriental cockroaches are found in damp, dark areas at or below ground level, such as basements, sewers, drains, and crawl spaces. They enter buildings through sewer drains. Oriental cockroaches feed on all kinds of filth, rubbish, and other decaying organic matter.

Preventing Their Entry

Cockroaches enter food stores in a variety of ways. Cockroach egg cases, nymphs, or adults can be brought into the building with raw materials, supplies, returnable bottles, or food. They can also be brought in on nonfood supplies, such as packaging materials, office supplies, and laundry, and on hand trucks, carts, and pallets.

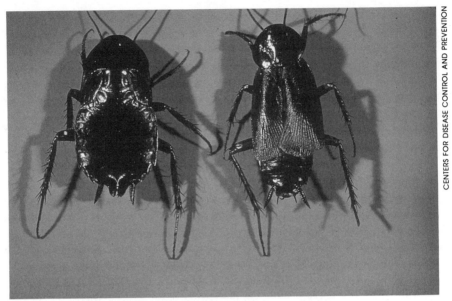

CENTERS FOR DISEASE CONTROL AND PREVENTION

Male (left) and female (right) oriental cockroach.

All incoming materials should be carefully inspected on arrival for the presence of insects. The telltale signs of cockroach activity include egg cases, droppings, or live insects. Products that are infested should be refused and sent back to the supplier. Records should be kept of products that were received infested to ensure a thorough inspection of any future shipments from those suppliers. It may be difficult to refuse a shipment of products, but it is more difficult to repair the damage done by accepting an infested order.

In addition to being brought in on regular deliveries, cockroaches can be attracted to an area by spilled product, garbage, and other sources of food outside the building. Once close by, they can enter the building through cracks, crevices, openings, door junctions, sewers, and a variety of other places. They can come from nearby infested buildings, homes, or apartments.

Sometimes employees, vendors, salespeople, and customers can bring cockroaches into a facility. Cockroaches can be carried in lunch boxes and clothes, or in sacks, cartons, shopping bags, handbags, or other personal items. It is important to inspect all vending machines periodically for the presence of cockroaches and to inquire about what precautions vendors are taking to prevent a cockroach infestation (3).

Restricting Shelter and Food

Since cockroaches require very little in the way of shelter and food, it is very difficult to control their access to these life-sustaining items. Good housekeeping and thorough cleaning, however, will help suppress their populations as well as allow control efforts to be more successful. Good housekeeping both inside and outside the building is the key to restricting shelter and food (1).

Outside the Building

The exterior of the building should be kept neat and clean. Trash, including old equipment, old cartons, rags, pallets, boards, and any unwanted material that might provide a breeding ground or shelter for cockroaches (as well as other insects and rodents) must be eliminated.

Spilled product around shipping and receiving areas must be picked up quickly. For cockroach control, it is critical that dumpsters, compactors, and trash bins be emptied on a regular basis and the areas around them kept free of litter and food debris.

It is vital that the loading dock be kept clean and free of old materials, equipment, and nonessential items. Any voids behind dock leveling mechanisms must be routinely checked for debris and cleaned. All cracks, crevices, and openings around pipes, wires, doors, and windows leading into the building must be properly sealed so that insects cannot enter.

Inside the Building

The maintenance of all interior floors, walls, and ceilings is very important in cockroach control. Just as with the exterior of the building, all cracks and holes passing through walls or floors and crevices behind baseboards, door frames, electrical outlets, sinks, and the like must be properly sealed. Depending on the repair, concrete, epoxy, grout, or durable caulking materials should be used to seal these openings. Cracks in mortar or wall joints should not be neglected. Avoid hanging shelves, cabinets, or other items on the walls unless they are sealed securely to prevent insect infestation.

Ingredients must be stored in tightly closed containers. Spilled products and food debris on floors, around equipment, and on food-contact surfaces should be cleaned up quickly. Industrial vacuum cleaners should be used to minimize dry-product accumulation and then emptied promptly. Food supplies should be stored off the floor in an orderly fashion. Remember that cockroaches like to hide in dark, warm areas, so check motor housings, switch boxes, electrical outlets, and mechanical, compressor, and other utility rooms for signs of insect activity.

Water leaks and dampness, found in the areas around sinks, water fountains, water coolers, hoses, toilets, break rooms, janitorial closets, and mop rooms, provide the kind of environment that cockroaches thrive in. Be sure to check these areas frequently for the presence of insects and repair any leaks and eliminate dampness.

When looking for cockroaches, always use a flashlight and look in "hard-to-get-to" places such as the junctions of equipment, in cracks and crevices, behind and under machinery, equipment, and materials, under ledges, in hollow tubular equipment such as carts and dollies, and in many other areas where one would not normally expect a cockroach problem. The offices, employee lunchrooms, and locker rooms are areas that must be kept clean and checked regularly for signs of insect activity. Empty boxes must be managed properly because cockroaches utilize the folds in the boxes for harborage (3). Do not allow boxes to remain around the store for long periods of time. Dispose of them quickly.

Frequent cleaning, rearrangement of supplies, and attention to detail will help restrict the shelter and food that cockroaches need to survive.

Cockroach Control

Chemical control of cockroaches is recommended only in combination with other nonchemical control procedures and not as the primary method. Chemical control should be done by pest-management professionals who are well trained, competent, and knowledgeable in the safe use of pesticides. Professional pest-control operators should be consulted when considering the chemical control of a cockroach problem (or any insect or rodent problem) in a food store. These technicians have usually received the proper training in the use of insecticides and will have the necessary state certification for applying pesticides.

To determine which areas of a food facility are infested, roach traps can be used. The better traps are made of paper and contain a sticky substance similar to the glue used on traps for rodent control. Since cockroaches like to crawl in dark cracks and crevices, they are attracted to the traps and get caught in the sticky material. It should be noted that cockroach traps are effective in determining the area and level of infestation, and for monitoring the effectiveness of a control program, but they are not designed to provide any degree of control (3).

The key to cockroach control is frequent cleaning of the facility, especially around corners, in cabinets, under pallets, and near other potential nesting and breeding places. Remember, a good sanitation program can help prevent serious insect problems.

Other Insects

There are many other insects that can cause problems in food stores. Insects such as moths, weevils, and beetles infest a variety of stored food products such as grains, flour, milled cereal products, beans, dried fruits and vegetables, spices, nuts, pet food, and similar products (1, 5). Most stored-food-product insects are small and can enter the establishment in a variety of ways. After entering, they can hide in cracks and crevices, and attack foods. It is important for store employees to be observant for any insect (as well as rodent) activity. Follow your company's procedures for reporting the sighting of insect and rodent activity in and around the store. Also be aware of consumer complaints regarding the insect infestation of foods. When customers return foods and complain about insects, be sure to follow up and carefully inspect those products in your store. Some brief information on several important stored-food-product insects is given below. Figure 11.2 shows a number of these insects.

Moths

There are three common moths that attack stored food products (1, 4, 5).

The *Indian-meal moth* is about ⅜ inch long (1 cm) and is tan and reddish brown, with a copper luster. The moth larvae seldom attack sound kernels, but feed on all kinds of grain and grain-based products, flour, seeds, powdered milk, crackers, candy, nuts, dried fruits, chocolate, dog food, and virtually all dried food products. The larva of the Indian-meal moth spins a web as it grows.

The *Mediterranean flour moth* is ⅜ inch long (1 cm), pale gray, and prefers flour and meal, but also attacks grain, bran, cereal products, nuts, chocolate, beans, dried fruits, and many other foodstuffs. The larva spins silken threads wherever it goes, and webs and mats together particles of food on which it is feeding.

The *Angoumois grain moth* is a small (⅔ inch long or 1.7 cm), buff or yellowish white moth that attacks only whole, unbroken kernels of corn, wheat, and other grains and seeds. Larvae enter whole kernels of grain and, as they develop into moths, destroy the kernels. This moth is frequently found in stores and warehouses.

Weevils

Most weevils have elongated beaks or snouts and can be easily differentiated from other beetles (1, 4, 5).

The *granary weevil* is blackish or chestnut brown and is 3/16 inch long (0.5 cm) or smaller. It is primarily found in the northern states and feeds

Figure 11.2   Common Stored-Food-Product Insects*

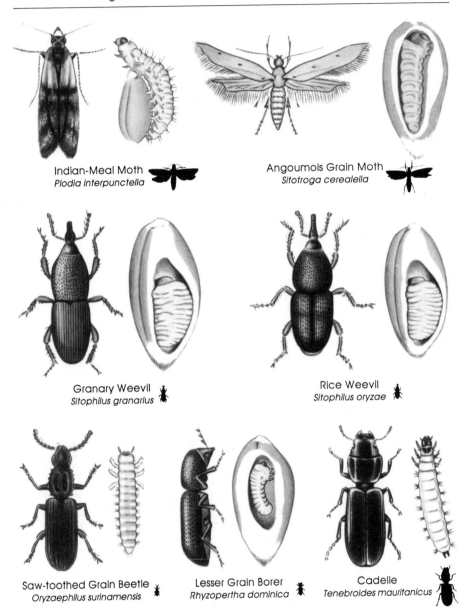

Indian-Meal Moth
Plodia interpunctella

Angoumois Grain Moth
Sitotroga cerealella

Granary Weevil
Sitophilus granarius

Rice Weevil
Sitophilus oryzae

Saw-toothed Grain Beetle
Oryzaephilus surinamensis

Lesser Grain Borer
Rhyzopertha dominica

Cadelle
Tenebroides mauritanicus

*The black silhouette adjacent to each insect's name shows the insect's actual size.

Source: Adapted from "Principal Stored Grain Insects," Picture Sheet no. 1 (Washington, DC: Food and Drug Administration, U.S. Department of Health, Education, and Welfare).

on a variety of whole grains, including oats, wheat, rye, and barley. It does not fly.

The *rice weevil* is 3/32 inch long (0.2 cm) and is reddish brown to black. It feeds on a wide variety of grains, and it can fly. The rice weevil is probably the most destructive pest of stored grain.

Beetles

A variety of beetles attack stored foods, and many of these insects are capable of penetrating packaged foods. They usually enter through cracks, tears, rips, or poorly sealed packages. Most common stored-product beetles are about 1/8 inch (0.3 cm) long and have a reddish brown, brown, or black hard shell. Some of these pests include the saw-toothed grain beetle, confused flour beetle, drug store beetle, dried fruit beetle, lesser grain borer, and the cadelle. These insects feed on a wide variety of foods such as cereals, grains, macaroni, dried fruit, spices, and nuts (1, 4, 5).

Sanitation and Pest Control

A key rule is that most beetles and moths become a problem in areas where dried foods, especially grains, are stored for extended periods of time (3). Grain spills on shelves, under gondolas, and in storage areas, unless cleaned quickly, can be a source of infestation. Store employees should be on the lookout for insect (and rodent) activity in the store. If spotted, the location of the insect (or rodent) should be immediately reported to a supervisor so appropriate inspection, identification, and control measures can be taken. Figure 11.3 is an example of a checklist that can be used in a store sanitation and pest-control inspection (1).

An effective store-wide sanitation program is of primary importance in controlling insects in food stores. Insects can be controlled by

- preventing infested materials from entering a food establishment
- thoroughly inspecting all food products, ingredients, packaging materials, and so on, when they are received
- rotating stock and keeping materials that furnish food or harborage moving through the store
- regularly checking and inspecting food-storage areas
- repairing structural deficiencies that allow insects to enter (broken screens, open windows, and so on)

Figure 11.3   Sanitation and Pest-Control Inspection Checklist

---

Store: _____

Date: _____

Time: _____

Inspected by: _____

Particular attention should be paid to these pest "hot spots," including the deli, bakery, meat, seafood, bulk-food, and produce departments, restaurant and salad-bar areas, and pet-food aisles.

	Yes	No	Action Required
A. EXTERIOR AREAS			
1. Pest harborage	___	___	_____
2. Pest breeding	___	___	_____
3. Garbage-handling systems	___	___	_____
4. Garbage storage area	___	___	_____
5. Garbage containers	___	___	_____
6. Garbage-container cleaning	___	___	_____
7. Trash disposal	___	___	_____
8. Paving and drainage	___	___	_____
9. Weed control	___	___	_____
10. Perimeter rodent control	___	___	_____
11. Perimeter insect control	___	___	_____
B. BUILDING EXTERIOR			
1. Rodent-proofing	___	___	_____
2. Insect-proofing	___	___	_____
3. Bird-proofing	___	___	_____
4. Roofs	___	___	_____
5. Other surfaces	___	___	_____
6. Lighting	___	___	_____
C. BUILDING INTERIOR			
1 Walls	___	___	_____
2. Floors	___	___	_____
3. Ceilings	___	___	_____
4. Cleanability	___	___	_____
5. Pits	___	___	_____
6. Floor drains	___	___	_____
7. Plumbing	___	___	_____
8. Ventilation	___	___	_____
9. Condensation	___	___	_____
10. Lighting	___	___	_____
D. FOOD STORAGE			
Packaged and Dry-Food Storage			
1. Pest evidence	___	___	_____
2. Proper storage practices	___	___	_____
3. Good housekeeping practices	___	___	_____
4. Empty-container storage	___	___	_____

Figure 11.3 (continued)

	Yes	No	Action Required
D. FOOD STORAGE (cont.)			
Damaged-Goods Storage			
5. Segregation	___	___	_____
6. Repackaging	___	___	_____
7. Proper housekeeping	___	___	_____
Returned Goods			
8. Adequate handling program	___	___	_____
Refrigerated Areas			
9. Pest evidence	___	___	_____
10. Condensation	___	___	_____
11. Cleaning satisfactory	___	___	_____
12. Other	___	___	_____
E. FOOD-HANDLING PREPARATION AREAS			
1. Enclosed areas easily opened	___	___	_____
2. Spaces under and behind equipment clean	___	___	_____
3. Counter and surface areas clean	___	___	_____
4. No permanent food storage in preparation areas	___	___	_____
F. GARBAGE AND TRASH AREA (INDOOR)			
1. Storage areas for receptacles adequate	___	___	_____
2. Storage area clean	___	___	_____
3. Containers of proper type	___	___	_____
4. Garbage containers regularly covered	___	___	_____
5. Shows evidence of regular cleaning	___	___	_____
G. BOTTLE RETURN AND STORAGE AREA			
1. Proper management	___	___	_____
2. Clean	___	___	_____
3. Regular pick up	___	___	_____
H. TOILET AND LOCKER FACILITIES			
Toilet and Locker-Room Facilities			
1. Adequate for current number of employees	___	___	_____
2. Sanitary and in good repair	___	___	_____
3. Door self-closing and does not open into food area	___	___	_____
4. Adequate ventilation and no offensive odors	___	___	_____
5. Lockers regularly emptied and cleaned	___	___	_____
6. Area free of old clothes and trash	___	___	_____

Figure 11.3 Sanitation and Pest-Control Inspection Checklist (continued)

	Yes	No	Action Required
H. TOILET AND LOCKER FACILITIES (cont.)			
Hand-washing Facilities			
7. Adequate and convenient	___	___	_____
8. Appropriate trash receptacles	___	___	_____
I. LUNCHROOM			
1. Accessible for cleaning	___	___	_____
2. Clean	___	___	_____
J. VENDING MACHINES			
1. Easily cleaned	___	___	_____
2. Pest harborage	___	___	_____
K. OFFICE AREAS			
1. Clean	___	___	_____
2. Regular trash removal	___	___	_____
L. FRONT-END			
1. Checkout aisles clean	___	___	_____
2. Area below checkout counter clean and free of debris and clutter	___	___	_____
3. Pest evidence	___	___	_____
M. OTHER AREAS			
1. Floor areas clean	___	___	_____
2. Equipment, counters, and displays easily cleaned	___	___	_____
3. Pest harborage	___	___	_____
N. INFESTATION			
1. Rodents	___	___	_____
2. Insects	___	___	_____
3. Other	___	___	_____
O. EVIDENCE OF PESTS			
1. Rodents	___	___	_____
2. Insects	___	___	_____
3. Other	___	___	_____

Report reviewed on (date): _____

By (inspector): _____

With: _____

Source: Adapted from G. W. Bennett, J. M. Owens, and R. M. Corrigan, *Truman's Scientific Guide to Pest Control Operations*, 4th ed. (Duluth, MN: Edgell Communications, 1988).

- avoiding spills, and cleaning and disposing of spilled product quickly and properly
- regularly and thoroughly cleaning machinery (inside and out), equipment, utensils, bins, and shelves, as well as areas under sacks, bags, and other containers where food is stored
- storing foods at the proper temperature

Professional Extermination Services

Again, it must be stressed that cleanliness and good sanitary practices are the keys to controlling rodents and insects. Without these, no professional pest-control service can solve a pest problem.

Any pest-management professional hired to help control pests should be certified by the state and have full knowledge of all pest-management practices and all pesticide applications permissible under the law. Insist that the pest-control professionals provide you with a thorough description of services rendered for each store visit. For example, request that the professionals number each mouse or insect trap, and ask for a drawing indicating the location of traps in the store. Have them also provide a report of areas where you, as the department or store manager, must improve for the program to be effective.

At the beginning of the contract with a pest-management professional, service may be required weekly or even more frequently until adequate control is obtained. The frequency of inspection and service will vary according to the problems of each store. However, the very minimum amount of service is usually once a month after control has been achieved. In some cases, however, biweekly service is required (3). More infrequent visits can be scheduled depending on the season and condition of the store.

It is important for the food store management to understand that with professional pest-control services, like any other service, "you get what you pay for." Not all pest-control companies are the same. Some companies may have more highly trained staff, others may use the most up-to-date pest-control technology, while still others use only the cheapest control measures available. When selecting a good pest-control company, store managers must shop around and research the situation thoroughly. They should check to see how long the business has been in operation, whether it belongs to the State Pest Control Association, and whether it has well-trained technicians to service the food store. Good pest-control service is often provided by those professionals who have had good training and at least one year of on-the-job experience (3).

Do-It-Yourself Programs

The first step in any do-it-yourself pest-control program is the *thorough training* of all store employees. It is not sufficient simply for a store sanitation supervisor to walk around with a spray can of insecticide "taking care of problems." This could lead to greater problems.

Each state has its own regulations concerning the application of pesticides. Regulatory agencies are actively enforcing laws on the indiscriminate use of pesticides in the food industry. Care must be taken by anyone applying pesticides because the pesticides can cause as much or more damage as the pests they are trying to eliminate.

In the long run, making the store environment unsuitable to pests is the cheapest, safest, and most effective way of controlling them. A well-designed sanitation program is the key to accomplishing this task. A well-planned and effective pest-control program will provide a strong foundation for your HACCP program.

References

1. Bennett, G. W., J. M. Owens, and R. M. Corrigan. *Truman's Scientific Guide to Pest Control Operations.* 4th ed. Duluth, MN: Edgell Communications, 1988.
2. Hedges, S. "Biology and Control of Houseflies." *Pest Control Technology,* June 1991.
3. Corrigan, R. M. Personal communication, Purdue University, 1992.
4. Pratt, H. D., K. S. Littig, and H. G. Scott. *Household and Stored-Food Insects of Public Health Importance and Their Control.* Publication no. CDC-77-8122. Washington, DC: The Centers for Disease Control, 1977.
5. U.S. Department of Agriculture. "Stored Grain Insects." In *Agriculture Handbook,* no. 500. Washington, DC: 1979.

12

Construction and Maintenance of Facilities and Equipment

An effective sanitation program is composed of the proper cleaning and sanitizing of equipment and utensils, good personal hygiene and employee practices, and a well-designed and implemented pest-control program. These components provide the foundation for a store-wide HACCP program. Another important area that directly influences a store's sanitary environment is the construction and maintenance of facilities and equipment.

Store associates will find it difficult to maintain a sanitary environment in the time available if the facilities and equipment are not *easily cleanable*. The type of materials used, the design, and the age and condition of the equipment and facilities determine how much time and effort will be required to accomplish the cleaning and sanitizing tasks. Facilities and equipment that are old, in disrepair, and are difficult to clean and maintain may eventually cause many associates to ask, "Why should we work hard cleaning a place that management does not care about or will not invest any money in maintaining?"

If a company is committed to a strong sanitation and food safety assurance program, it should begin by making necessary improvements to the facilities and equipment, and by creating a positive attitude toward the importance of sanitation to customer satisfaction.

Benefits

Several benefits of well-designed and well-maintained facilities and equipment are

- compliance with the law
- long-range cost savings
- better employee attitude and motivation

Let's look closer at these benefits.

Compliance with the Law

When building or remodeling a store, management must check the state, county, or local health codes and regulations before proceeding. In fact, in some jurisdictions it is against the law to change the store without first getting the approval of regulatory agencies.

These codes and regulations are designed to protect the health and welfare of people. They also will usually save the retailer money in the long run, since the facility and equipment will be much easier to clean and maintain if designed and installed according to the regulations.

Long-Range Cost Savings

With adequately designed, installed, and maintained facilities and equipment, costs will be reduced in the following ways:

- reduced labor-hours used to clean and sanitize
- reduced equipment breakdowns and maintenance
- extended equipment life
- reduced facility repairs

Implied savings might be realized as follows:

- lower utility costs, especially in the area of refrigeration, where dirty equipment makes the internal parts work harder
- less chance of customer foodborne illness that could possibly come from unsanitary or faulty equipment

- reduction of product loss and labor due to rewraps caused by dirty equipment, inadequate refrigeration, or contaminated facilities
- reduction of employee accidents and safety-related problems
- increased sales due to improved product quality and store image

By spending a little more money to create a well-designed and well-maintained store, management will save many dollars in the long run on the above benefits.

Employee Attitude and Motivation

If you have ever worked in an older store with obsolete equipment, you can readily empathize with the problems of cleaning and maintaining that equipment. In addition, the negative attitude and lack of motivation that goes along with having to work with such equipment can lead employees to put off cleaning as long as possible, which, of course, compounds an already bad situation. Some examples are

- the old frozen-food case with a buildup of ice that must be chipped and scraped as well as thawed for many hours in order to be cleaned
- the refrigerated display case that when being cleaned and flushed with water has drains which either stop up or back up all over the floor
- the product sink of galvanized metal that is so pitted with age it cannot be properly cleaned
- lack of floor drains or inadequate floor drains that cannot take the amount of water necessary for cleaning
- uncleanable or rough and porous surfaces of walls and floors, including such materials as cinder block for walls and bare cement for floors
- pieces of equipment constructed in such a way that cleaning is virtually impossible
- rusty equipment—dollies, tables, shelves, etc.
- lack of or inadequate hand-washing facilities
- inadequate hot-water supply

Employee attitude and motivation should not be taken lightly. Poor worker motivation can cost a store thousands of dollars each year in lost productivity. Inadequate employee facilities in the lunchroom or rest rooms can create a negative attitude that will carry over into the work habits of employees. Take a look around your store or stores and see what kind of attitude might be created by the condition of the work and employee rest areas. If you cannot objectively say that this is the kind of store you would enjoy working in daily, then how do you think your employees feel? And how is this attitude reflected to the customers?

Obviously, the construction and maintenance of facilities and equipment is very important to the total success of any food safety assurance program. In this chapter, some guidelines for store operators to consider seriously when constructing a new store or remodeling an existing facility will be listed. As stated earlier, doing it the right way may cost a little more initially but will save untold dollars in the long run.

The two principal factors that must be considered concerning equipment and facilities are

- design and construction
- materials to be used

As a general guideline, let us keep in mind throughout this chapter that the objective is *to facilitate cleaning and sanitizing of the equipment and surroundings as an important means of assuring the safety of foods that are processed and prepared in the store.* If we hold steadfastly to this principle, the task will be relatively simple and straightforward.

Many of the requirements mentioned in this chapter are found in the *Food Protection Unicode* proposed by the U.S. Food and Drug Administration (1).

The Facility

Design and construction of the store includes such items as walls, floors, ceilings, and permanent fixtures (e.g., lighting, vents, and windows). Smooth materials impervious to dirt and moisture should be used as much as possible to facilitate cleaning and sanitizing. In the sales areas this is not always possible due to decor requirements that complement the store's particular image, but in all food-preparation areas, such materials are required, both from a regulatory standpoint and to enhance the effectiveness of the sanitation program.

Walls

Walls of coolers, product processing rooms, and food-preparation areas should be smooth, nonabsorbent, and easily cleanable. Since these areas require frequent cleaning, walls and wall coverings should be constructed of materials such as fiberglass, porcelainized steel, stainless steel, or ceramic tile. New materials are also always coming on the market.

Materials to avoid as wall coverings in processing areas or storage coolers because of their absorbency and difficulty in cleaning are brick, wood, cement block, plastic boards, acoustic-type boards, and rough-finish cement. Painted surfaces are not recommended due to the possibility of peeling and flaking that could introduce foreign materials into food during preparation. (If surfaces must be painted, an epoxy-type paint should be used.)

Additions to existing walls of such unauthorized, difficult-to-clean materials as plywood boards for holding labels, hooks for cleaning equipment, or pegboards tend to defeat the good accomplished in using the correct wall materials in the first place.

Floors

Many different types of floors are found in the processing rooms and coolers of retail food stores. Much of this flooring is not conducive to cleaning and sanitizing. Floors in these areas should be constructed of waterproof, acid-resistant materials and should be free of cracks, holes, or other indentations that may harbor bacteria, insects, or other contaminants (2).

Preferred materials for such floors include quarry tile, sealed concrete, ceramic tile, terrazzo, epoxy resin, or vitrified brick. Although a floor of quarry tile is relatively expensive to install, it often lasts well over ten years, with little or no repairs. Some of the epoxy-type floors also provide an easily cleanable base.

Floor materials that should be avoided if possible in processing areas are wood, vinyl or asphalt tile, bare concrete, carpeting, or any other material which is not easily cleanable or may not be impervious to dirt, water, or other contaminants.

One of the biggest problems with floors today is that to make them safe, they must be somewhat abrasive. Unfortunately, the more abrasive they become, the harder they are to clean properly. In fact, some floors that are finished like fine sandpaper for safety's sake become even more dangerous when grease gets spilled on the floor.

Most regulatory agencies no longer allow the use of sawdust, wood shavings, granular salt, baked clay, or similar materials as covering on processing-room floors due to their high contamination factor (1). Some stores put cardboard on the floor to prevent slipping and change it twice a day to satisfy certain regulatory agencies that accept it in the interest of safety. Others use mats and duckboards that are nonabsorbent, grease resistant, and easily cleanable.

Still other stores, in addition to frequent floor cleaning, give each worker a pair of rubber boots with nonslip soles and heels. The boots are left at work and used on the job.

The choice of floor material is of great importance to a sanitation program as it can, in the long run, save many hours of cleaning time as well as provide a more sanitary and safe environment for the processing of products. It is an investment that should not be taken lightly.

Floor Drains

The lack of floor drains in product processing areas makes cleaning time-consuming and makes it difficult to accomplish the level of sanitation desired by many regulatory agencies.

Most operators who are building new facilities or are remodeling existing ones try to put drains in the processing rooms and coolers (although some local health authorities prohibit drains in coolers, even though they comply with approved guidelines of not connecting with sanitary drainage lines within the store). Stores with drains are able to take advantage of the latest in power-cleaning equipment and other cleaning programs that require liberal amounts of water. The only options available to the operator without floor drains is to use a mop and bucket or to obtain a water vacuum to take up water left on the floor. These options are grossly inadequate solutions to the problem.

If at all possible, store operators should have properly installed trapped drains of at least 4 inches (10 cm) in diameter (may vary with local health codes) in all processing rooms and preferably all coolers. The floor should be sloped or pitched to the drain for easy runoff. It is recommended that a large processing room be provided with more than one drain. Some health agencies request a drain for each 400 square feet (37.2 m²) of floor space in processing rooms. In addition, floor drains should be provided with rodent-proof screens and covers.

Before leaving the subject of floors, it must be emphasized that to best facilitate cleaning, the point at which the floor and the wall meet (floor/wall junction) should be curved whenever possible.

Ceilings

Like walls, ceilings should be smooth, impervious to dirt, moisture, or other contaminants, and easily cleanable. There should be no exposed studs, joists, or rafters. Painted or plastered ceilings should be avoided due to the obvious possibility of flaking or peeling that could introduce dangerous foreign materials into fresh products destined for the consumer. Materials such as plastic or fiberglass would be desirable for processing-area ceilings. When choosing new materials, always ask yourself the question, "Is it easily cleanable?"

Lighting

Spotting the dirt and grime is much harder in a dimly lit facility than in an adequately illuminated facility. Good lighting makes dirt more conspicuous. It is therefore recommended that a minimum of 50 footcandles be planned for working areas and 30 footcandles for other areas where cleaning is necessary. At least 10 footcandles of light should also be provided in walk-in refrigeration units, dry-food storage, and all other areas.

Some of the areas where good lighting is especially necessary are

- sales areas
- food-processing areas (to make sure that food is always prepared in a sanitary manner)
- dry and refrigerated storage areas (to be able to inspect the quality of the food as well as detect any unsanitary conditions that could lead to contamination)
- hand-washing stations
- ware-washing areas
- utensil and equipment storage areas
- toilets (to facilitate cleaning and monitoring)
- waste-disposal or trash-storage areas (to check for possible pest infestation)

When engineering a store for sanitation, remember that proper lighting levels must be part of the plan (2).

Lights located over or within food-storage, food-preparation, and food-display facilities and areas where utensils and equipment are cleaned and stored should be shielded, coated, or shatter resistant to prevent breakage. Properly shielded lights will protect employees, food, and equipment from glass fragments if breakage does occur.

Plumbing Requirements

Most cities, towns, and counties have specified plumbing requirements that must be followed when building a new store or remodeling an existing one. A permit to build or remodel will usually not be issued until the plumbing requirements have been satisfied. So, before following the plumbing requirements listed below, make sure that they conform with your local requirements. The following are universal guidelines that apply almost everywhere (2).

Among the most important aspects of store plumbing are sewage disposal and sanitary drainage lines. Improper disposal of sewage can cause serious contamination, which can and has led to food-poisoning cases. For this reason, many regulatory agencies require a periodic microbiological test of the water supply (usually annually).

Health authorities mainly check to make sure that the sewage drains into a public sewage system and that your sewage system is constructed according to local health-code requirements. Health inspectors will look for the location of sanitary drainage lines to make sure that they do not run overhead where food is prepared. For example, you may have a toilet located upstairs in your store and the drainage lines might be running across the ceiling of the deli department and then down. Any difficulty with the plumbing could therefore cause severe contamination problems. If these lines are already there, a catch-trough should be installed under them to help prevent any possible problems.

Additional items health inspectors most often look for include the following:

- Sanitary drainage lines from toilet facilities and sinks must not connect with drainage lines from floor drains and equipment-cleaning sinks within the store. Any backflow could cause serious contamination problems.

- Overhead leakage from drainage lines or any water line could cause contamination problems. For this reason, all plumbing lines that may produce condensation must be insulated to prevent dripping.

- Grease traps or catch basins should be placed away from the food-processing areas and the sales area to prevent product contamination and also to keep customers and employees from becoming nauseous from the smell when the trap is being cleaned. Try to have the trap cleaned during hours when customer traffic is light, preferably early in the morning or late at night. Many times, in spite of all precautions taken, the awful smell gets into the sales area. One special trick shared by an experienced maintenance man might be valuable to you. Try dumping a box of cinnamon in the trap during the cleaning operation and this should all but eliminate any odor problems during cleaning operations.

- Backflow, which is the flow of contaminated liquids and materials back into the approved water supply, is a constant threat that must be prevented. It can occur with equipment that has a direct water-supply connection, such as commercial dishwashers and coffee machines in stores with snack bars and coffee shops. Much of this equipment either comes with backflow-prevention devices or can be equipped with them. In any event, a backflow-prevention device should be in place before the equipment is used (2, 3).

- Backsiphonage, which is similar to backflow, can occur when the water level in a sink, for example, reaches a higher point than the water source or faucet, and an accompanying drop in water pressure causes the contaminated water or liquid to flow backward into the line (2, 3). Care should be taken to prevent backsiphonage from occurring.

- The water supply should be tested at least annually, but it is equally important that the water come from an approved source in the first place. Remember that water can be a chief source of contamination if not properly checked and handled. To do an adequate cleaning and sanitizing job, enough hot water must be available in all areas of the store on a continual basis. The temperature of the water should be between 140°F and 150°F (60.0°C and 65.6°C) for cleaning. If hot-water sanitizing is used (mostly with dishwashers), then 180°F (82.2°C) water should be available. Remember that water that is too hot for cleaning operations (above 160°F or 71.1°C) will tend to bake protein particles right onto the equipment, making for an inadequate cleaning job.

- Mixing valves should be located at all sinks to produce desired water temperatures for the jobs to be accomplished.

- Water outlets (both hot and cold) should be available in all areas where frequent cleaning and sanitizing take place. This is particulary true for display cases, which must be cleaned at least weekly. It might also be beneficial to put some floor drains in the sales area to facilitate cleaning.

Hand-washing Facilities

As you know, a serious source of contamination in processing and preparation areas is the hands. To help ensure that "people contamination" is kept at the lowest possible level, hand-washing stations should be located in or adjacent to all work areas where the processing or preparation of food takes place. In addition to placing hand-washing stations in processing areas, washing sinks, of course, must also be available in rest rooms.

Hand-washing facilities should have

- an adequate sink of stainless steel, porcelain, or other smooth, cleanable material
- hot and cold water, preferably with a mixing valve available to temper the water
- dispensers containing liquid or powdered soap (bar soap is not acceptable)
- hand-drying facilities, such as hot-air dryers or single-service paper towels

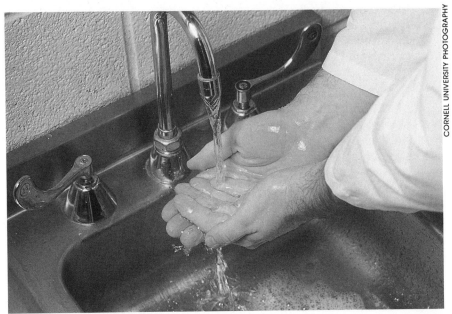

Hand-washing facilities should be located in or adjacent to all food-processing and food-preparation work areas.

The problem most often found when checking hand-washing facilities or rest rooms is the unavailability of soap and towels. In a store where soap is used frequently, the soap dispensers always seem too small to hold more than a day's supply and therefore are usually empty. Several soap and chemical companies offer ready-mixed soap that fits right on the wall dispenser. With this kind of dispensing system, there are few empties, despite constant use.

Locker Rooms and Toilet Facilities

Since street clothes and personal belongings can contaminate food, food-preparation surfaces, and equipment, it is important that employees have lockers or suitable facilities to store these items (1, 3). These dressing rooms and locker areas should be kept clean and orderly. Work clothes should be stored in a clean place until used. After they are used and soiled, they can easily be kept in a container or laundry bag until laundered.

If work clothes are washed and dried at the store, adequate laundry facilities, including a washer and dryer, should be available. These appliances can be operated in storage rooms that contain packaged foods or packaged single-service articles.

Toilets in retail stores can sometimes become real problems. Sloppy housekeeping in this important area can result in the spread of disease. The cleanliness of toilet facilities can also affect the attitudes, work habits, and motivation of store employees. Toilet facilities should be kept clean, in good repair, and properly supplied with hot water, soap, and hand-drying facilities. Food should never be stored in these rooms!

Ventilation

Many regulatory agencies are placing more emphasis on proper ventilation in retail food stores, especially where food is processed and prepared (delis, snack bars, bakeries, etc.). An adequate ventilation system within a controlled store environment will produce the following benefits (3):

- reduce objectionable, stale odors
- reduce airborne bacteria
- reduce moisture and vapors that can cause condensation and growth of mold and bacteria
- reduce the amount of other contaminants in the air, such as smoke, dust, and dirt

A proper ventilation system for a retail store would consist of the following equipment:

- a central heating, cooling, and filtration system
- exhaust fans
- a hooded overhead exhaust unit vented through the ceiling
- special air filtration and purifying units

Consult your local health authority before installing a ventilation system.

NEW YORK STATE DEPARTMENT OF AGRICULTURE AND MARKETS

To prevent contamination from street clothes and personal belongings, employees should store these items in suitable lockers.

General Storage

When planning to build or remodel a store, don't forget to include some general storage space for equipment, utensils, and single-service articles. These items cannot be stored in locker rooms, toilets, garbage rooms, or mechanical closets. They must be kept in a clean and dry area.

Equipment and utensils that have been properly cleaned and sanitized should be stored off the floor. This will help prevent contamination from splashes, dust, and the like. Equipment and utensils should be air-dried and then stored covered or inverted whenever practical.

Single-service items, such as utensils, cups, trays, and containers, can easily become contaminated if care is not taken during storage. These articles should be stored off the floor in closed cartons, and employees should handle them properly.

Cleaning Supplies and Equipment Room

One of the most neglected areas in the store—and the one that should be among the most important—is the cleaning supplies and equipment room. This room should ideally have enough space for storage of

- power cleaning equipment, such as floor scrubbers, buffers, and high-pressure sprayers
- cleaning supplies (see chapter 8)
- a sink for washing and cleaning mops, with adequate counter and floor space
- adequate hooks for brooms, mops, and brushes to dry, with special areas designated for wax mops
- a receptacle for dirty dust-mop heads

The room should be kept clean and orderly, and have proper ventilation and lighting. Cleaning and maintenance supplies, particularly poisonous or toxic materials, must be properly labeled and kept in an orderly fashion in the supply room. To avoid product contamination, these detergents, sanitizers, caustics, acids, polishes, and other chemicals should never be stored with food, equipment, or utensils.

One person should be responsible for the maintenance of the room and keeping it locked at all times. Because control is absolutely necessary in the supply room, only the person responsible for its maintenance and the manager should have keys to this room.

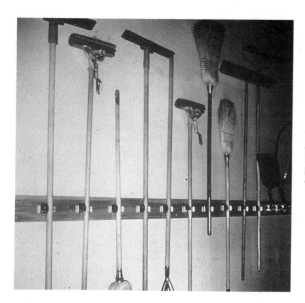

The cleaning supplies and equipment room should be kept clean and orderly, and have proper lighting and ventilation.

Disposal of Garbage and Trash

Without adequate disposal of garbage and trash, there is not only a danger of contamination from discarded products, but also the threat of infestation by rodents, insects, and other pests (see chapters 10 and 11). Effective engineering of trash and garbage disposal can be accomplished through the following methods:

- Provide garbage containers of durable materials with tight-fitting lids; these containers should not leak and they should be impervious to moisture.
- Sufficient numbers of containers should be on hand to hold all garbage and trash between pickups from your hauler.
- Containers or receptacles should be washed after each pickup if they have contained foodstuffs.
- Garbage disposals in produce departments help reduce the total load of garbage to be handled and the possibility of contamination.
- Discourage scavengers from rooting through discarded foodstuffs in trash cans; they are responsible for much of the contamination around trash areas when they leave lids off dumpsters, trash cans, etc.

NEW YORK STATE DEPARTMENT OF AGRICULTURE AND MARKETS

Garbage management is a key element of rodent and insect control.

- Mechanical compactors can help reduce the size of the trash load to a smaller area in an enclosed dumpster that is picked up periodically by a trash hauler.
- Mechanical cardboard balers are also useful in handling the heavy load of boxes left after daily stocking of the grocery shelves. Cardboard that is packed into neat bales for resale or recycling reduces the clutter in the back room and leaves more room for other types of trash in the dumpster or compactors.
- In the meat department, trimmings should be placed in bone barrels, preferably lined with plastic bags, that can be closed after use to prevent foul odors and possible contamination of fresh product. Some renderers will not take trimmings in plastic bags since they are said to interfere with the operation of rendering machines. If this is the case, tight-fitting lids should be provided for those cans that are full or not being used. Meat trimmings should be refrigerated whenever possible to reduce odors and further buildup of bacteria counts. Operators contemplating new or remodeled facilities should consider a small room or cage within the cooler where trimmings and scraps can be kept separate from fresh product.

Garbage management cannot be overemphasized because it can mean the difference between an effective sanitation program and a store having overwhelming problems with insect and rodent infestations.

General Facility Design

Other general facility-design recommendations include the following:

- All outside openings must be protected to block the entry not only of rodents and insects, but also of other pests such as birds, dogs, cats, and even an occasional muskrat or raccoon.
- No gaps should be allowed on the bottoms, tops, or sides of windows and doors.
- Construction defects, such as holes in cement blocks, broken drains, large cracks at floor/wall junctions, and other possible sources of entry to pests, must be repaired immediately.
- Exhaust fans and ventilation ducts to the outside must be protected by self-closing louvers or fine-mesh screens.
- Windows must have tightly fitting screens without holes.
- Receiving doors should be equipped with air curtains that help to prevent the entry of flying insects and other contaminants.
- Equipment or fixtures, unless easily movable, should either be sealed to the floor or elevated on casters or legs at least 6 inches (15 cm) off the floor (1).

A sanitation program can be totally effective only if the entire facility is designed with sanitation in mind.

Equipment Design, Construction, and Maintenance

An effective sanitation program relies not only on employees and the job they do of cleaning and sanitizing, but also on the cleanability of equipment and fixtures. If equipment is difficult or almost impossible to clean properly, the ultimate effect will be an ineffective sanitation program. Equipment that is not easily cleanable could cause

- shortened product shelf life
- product contamination
- abnormal maintenance problems and costs
- reduced equipment life

If you are a store operator or have the responsibility for equipment purchasing, you must realize that the time to think of the store sanitation

When purchasing equipment, an important sanitation criterion is to make sure it is easily cleanable.

program is when purchasing the equipment, not after it is in the store. The first and most important criterion in purchasing equipment with sanitation in mind is that it be *easily cleanable*. This means that all parts, especially those coming in contact with food, must be easily disassembled for cleaning without special tools. Other important criteria for equipment are

- Corners and edges should be rounded.
- Metal surfaces should have smooth, easily cleaned seams.
- Food-contact surfaces should be smooth and free of crevices, inside threads, ledges, bolts, and rivet heads.
- Food-contact surfaces must be capable of resisting pitting, cracking, or peeling. Surfaces must also be nontoxic and they must not transfer any odor, color, or taste to food products. Food-contact surfaces should be nonabsorbent.
- Gaskets and packing and sealing materials should also be easily cleanable, nontoxic, and nonabsorbent.
- Whenever possible, non-food-contact surfaces should be resistant to peeling, cracking, or pitting.

These criteria suggest that when purchasing equipment

- Stainless steel is preferable to painted or coated surfaces.
- Galvanized metal should be replaced with stainless steel or other acceptable materials on equipment or fixtures.
- Knives should have one-piece handles molded to the blades.

Refrigerated display cases must be judged on the maintenance of product temperature as well as the ease of cleaning and durability of construction materials. Size and capacity of drains are also important considerations. Manufacturers are considering ease of sanitation in designing new cases.

When purchasing equipment, it is wise to look at equipment that meets the criteria mentioned above.

One organization, NSF *International*, develops and publishes widely accepted standards for equipment design, construction, and installation (3). Equipment manufacturers who think that their products meet NSF *International* standards can request an evaluation against these standards. If the equipment meets the standards, the manufacturers can then display the NSF *International* seal or mark. Many regulatory agencies specify that equipment used in food stores and foodservice facilities meet NSF *International* or similar standards.

The information provided in this chapter can help store owners/ operators and managers save literally thousands of dollars through adequately designed and maintained facilities and equipment. Remember, it will be difficult and more costly for store associates to maintain a sanitary store environment if the facilities and equipment are not easily cleanable.

References

1. U.S. Food and Drug Administration. Center for Food Safety and Applied Nutrition. *Proposed Food Protection Unicode.* 1988.
2. Imholte, T. J. *Engineering for Food Safety and Sanitation.* Crystal, MN: Technical Institute of Food Safety, 1984.
3. National Restaurant Association. Educational Foundation. *Applied Foodservice Sanitation.* New York: John Wiley and Sons, Inc., 1992.

13

Food Laws, Regulatory Agencies, and Inspections

In the early 1900s, the retail food store was for all practical purposes ignored by federal, state, and local regulatory agencies. While inspectors made their presence known in slaughterhouses and canneries, they were a rare sight in the supermarket.

As recently as 30 years ago, most of the product sold in the food store had been processed and packaged somewhere else or sold in a raw state—and it was generally assumed that the customer would cook it to a high enough temperature to destroy most of the harmful bacteria that might be present. During this period, there were still store operators who had never seen a state, county, or local food inspector. Today, however, as in-store food preparation and processing becomes more sophisticated and as the potential health hazards are increasing, government agencies are taking a closer look.

Historical Review

Early in the twentieth century, the American author Upton Sinclair wrote a novel called *The Jungle*, which focused on the life of a Lithuanian immigrant working in the meat-packing industry in Chicago. Sinclair took a look at the unhealthy and unsanitary conditions that existed in meat-packing houses during that period. The book was probably responsible for prompting President Theodore Roosevelt's administration to pass the first federal food laws pertaining to the meat-packing industry. The Federal Meat Inspection Act and also the Food and Drugs Act were signed into law in 1906 (1).

In the 1930s, many states had inspectors who went into food stores to collect food samples to test for compliance with standards of identity regulations. This led to the situation in which regulatory agencies began inspecting stores using the regulations that were also used for food-processing plants. These "general" food laws were not specifically designed for retail stores and had to be interpreted by the agency doing the inspection.

Another major step in guarding the wholesomeness of the food we buy occurred in 1934, when the U.S. Public Health Service undertook the development of an ordinance for the sanitary control of food prepared and served in public eating establishments (2). In 1935, a tentative draft of this ordinance was published to help state and local health regulatory agencies maintain adequate sanitation levels in their jurisdictions. Based on field trials, the ordinance was revised and published in 1940 under the title *Ordinance and Code Regulating Eating and Drinking Establishments* (2). Although not a federal regulation, this code has in reality become partially official since many state, county, and municipal regulatory agencies have adopted it. The U.S. Public Health Service has given the ordinance credit for improving the level of sanitation and public health in restaurants and institutions throughout the country. It is significant to the retail food industry because so many food store inspectors have used it as their guideline in inspecting retail food stores. The ordinance has been revised a number of times since 1940.

As food stores expanded their offerings in the 1960s, there was a corresponding concern about the wholesomeness and safety of the products being sold. Some state regulatory-agency officials and retail food store trade associations and company executives decided to develop reasonable food store regulations.

A number of factors contributed to this working relationship. First, industry leaders realized that providing consumers with safe food products was in their best interest. These leading retailers worked hard to assure shoppers that everything possible was being done to protect the safety and welfare of everyone who shopped in their stores. Another factor was the growing strength and importance of consumer groups. These groups played a major role in putting pressure on regulatory agencies to develop stronger legislation relating to all aspects of the retail food trade.

In 1974 the Association of Food and Drug Officials (AFDO), an organization made up of regulatory officials and food-industry leaders, submitted a "Retail Food Market Document" to the Food and Drug Administration for review, revision, and publishing as a national standard. This document contained the sanitary requirements for the operation of retail food stores. The FDA reviewed the document, reviewed state laws, and developed the information into a model sanitation ordinance format (similar to the foodservice sanitation ordinance). The model ordinance was published in the *Federal Register* in 1977 and was substantially revised on the basis of comments that were received. A second version was published in 1978; the final draft appeared in 1982 under the title *Model Retail Food Store Sanitation Code (3)*.

The growth in popularity of self-service bulk foods in the 1980s also focused a great deal of attention on the retail food industry. With its open containers of product and self-service approach to marketing, the bulk-food department requires great care to preserve the wholesomeness and safety of the foods being sold. The FDA introduced its *Bulk Food Sanitation Guidelines* in 1984; food store operators throughout the country must comply with these regulations.

Another area of food store sanitation that is receiving careful scrutiny by the Occupational Safety and Health Administration (OSHA) and the Environmental Protection Agency (EPA) is the use of toxic materials for cleaning and sanitizing. OSHA established guidelines to protect workers in its 1970 OSHAct, which includes regulations that govern aspects of food store sanitation. In 1988, OSHA adopted further guidelines known as the Hazard Communication Standard (HCS or HAZCOM) to protect workers from the effects of potentially dangerous chemicals. The ways in which cleaners, solvents, and disinfectants are handled—including their disposal—are also regulated by the EPA. These agencies and regulations will be discussed in this chapter.

Regulatory Agencies

Government agencies enforce laws regulating nearly every aspect of the food industry, including the production, processing, handling, packaging, labeling, and advertising of foods. Regulations also exist that control the business practices used in buying and selling food and grocery products.

The agencies that regulate and enforce food, employee, and customer safety range from local boards of health to federal agencies. Some of the federal agencies and their responsibilities related to food safety and quality are described below (4, 5).

U.S. Department of Agriculture (USDA)

While there are many agencies within the USDA, only those that are involved in assuring the safety and quality of foods will be mentioned in this book.

Food Safety and Inspection Service (FSIS)

The Food Safety and Inspection Service of the USDA

- inspects domestic and imported meat, poultry, and processed meat and poultry products
- establishes ingredient standards and approves recipes and labels for meat and poultry products
- monitors the meat and poultry industries for violations of inspection laws
- conducts a food safety education program for institutional and home food handlers

FSIS carries out its meat and poultry inspection responsibilities under the federal Meat Inspection Act and the Poultry Products Inspection Act. These laws are aimed at ensuring that meat and poultry products sold for human consumption are safe, wholesome, and accurately packaged and labeled.

Agricultural Marketing Service (AMS)

The Agricultural Marketing Service carries out a wide variety of programs to facilitate the marketing of agricultural products. AMS is responsible for the development of quality grade standards and for providing voluntary grading services for meat, poultry, eggs, dairy products, and fruits and vegetables. It is also responsible for enforcing the Egg Products

Inspection Act that requires continuous USDA inspection of egg-products processing plants.

Animal and Plant Health Inspection Service (APHIS)

This USDA unit is responsible for regulatory programs to control or eliminate animal and plant pests and diseases. These programs are designed to protect the animal industry against pathogens and disease, and to also help reduce the risk of foodborne illness in humans.

Agricultural Research Service (ARS)

The mission of the Agricultural Research Service is to develop new knowledge and technology in all areas of agriculture. The ARS carries out research on the safety and quality of foods.

U.S. Department of Health and Human Services (HHS)

Two agencies in the U.S. Department of Health and Human Services play a direct role in assuring food safety: the Food and Drug Administration and the Centers for Disease Control and Prevention.

Food and Drug Administration (FDA)

The FDA is an agency within the Department of Health and Human Services that is responsible for assuring that both domestic and imported foods (except meat and poultry products) are safe and wholesome. The FDA also regulates food product labels and enforces the tolerance (maximum legal limits) for pesticide residues in foods. The federal Food, Drug,

The FDA operates in six regions that cover the entire nation.

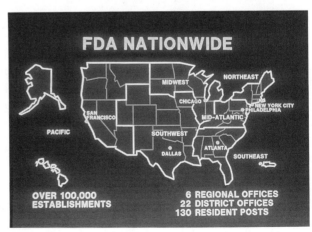

FDA NATIONWIDE

OVER 100,000 ESTABLISHMENTS

6 REGIONAL OFFICES
22 DISTRICT OFFICES
130 RESIDENT POSTS

and Cosmetic Act is the major law relating to the FDA's food-safety activities. Inspections of food-processing plants and warehouses are carried out by FDA investigators located in district offices throughout the United States.

Centers for Disease Control and Prevention (CDC)

The centers are responsible for protecting public health through disease surveillance and prevention programs, and by responding to public-health emergencies.

U.S. Environmental Protection Agency (EPA)

The Environmental Protection Agency was established in 1970 to protect and enhance the environment. The EPA is responsible for establishing, enforcing, and monitoring environmental standards. The EPA is also responsible for regulating all pesticide products sold or distributed in the U.S. and for establishing tolerances for pesticide residues in or on food commodities and animal feeds. The EPA enforces the Federal Insecticide, Fungicide, and Rodenticide Act (FIFRA). All pesticides used in the U.S. must be registered with the EPA and carry warning labels that have been approved by this agency.

The EPA also has jurisdiction over solid-waste management, including the disposal of hazardous or dangerous chemicals. Many chemicals used in the food store—like cleaners and sanitizers—are classified as *household hazardous wastes*. Although in many states there are no regulations that cover the disposal of these items, the EPA suggests that they be collected and treated as hazardous waste. Household hazardous wastes should not be poured into drains or storm sewers, or be included in the normal refuse dumpster for transportation to the landfill. Such regulations are in place in many communities around the country, and the store manager should check with local and state officials to be sure that his or her store is in compliance with the most up-to-date rulings (6).

U.S. Department of Commerce (USDC)

The **National Marine Fisheries Service** (NMFS), a unit of the National Oceanic and Atmospheric Administration (NOAA), is part of the U.S. Department of Commerce. The NMFS provides a voluntary fishery product inspection and grading program on a fee-for-service basis. This service complements the FDA, which has regulatory jurisdiction over the public-health aspects of seafood products.

U.S. Department of the Treasury

The **Bureau of Alcohol, Tobacco, and Firearms** (BATF), a unit of the U.S. Department of the Treasury, is responsible for administering and enforcing laws relating to the production, use, and distribution of alcohol and tobacco products.

Figure 13.1 provides an overview of the federal agencies mentioned above, along with their food safety and quality activities. The Occupational Safety and Health Administration (OSHA), another federal regulatory agency that has an impact on the retail food industry, is discussed later in this chapter.

Food Safety Regulations and Guidelines

Since the passage of the Food and Drugs Act of 1906, a number of regulations have been enacted for the protection of public health and safety (1). Some of the regulations and guidelines of particular interest to food store sanitation are listed below for easy reference.

- The **Food, Drug, and Cosmetic Act of 1938** is an extensive revision of the original Food and Drugs Act of 1906. It prohibits the shipment and receipt in interstate commerce of foods that are adulterated or misbranded.
  Under this section, the FDA has authority to look at the records of wholesale and retail operations, as well as manufacturing plants, and to inspect the facilities to determine whether sanitary conditions are being maintained.
- The **Meat Inspection Act of 1906** and the **Poultry Products Inspection Act of 1957** provided for the inspection of red meats and poultry products by the USDA prior to shipment in interstate or foreign commerce. Mandatory inspection of meat and poultry that does not enter into interstate or foreign commerce was later required under the **Wholesome Meat Act of 1967** and the **Wholesome Poultry Act of 1968**.
- The **Federal Insecticide, Fungicide, and Rodenticide Act** (FIFRA) specifies pesticide residue levels that can safely be present in or on foods.
- The **Model Retail Food Store Sanitation Code of 1982** defines practices and procedures to be followed by retailers to protect public

Figure 13.1   **Federal Agencies and Their Food Safety and Quality Responsibilities**

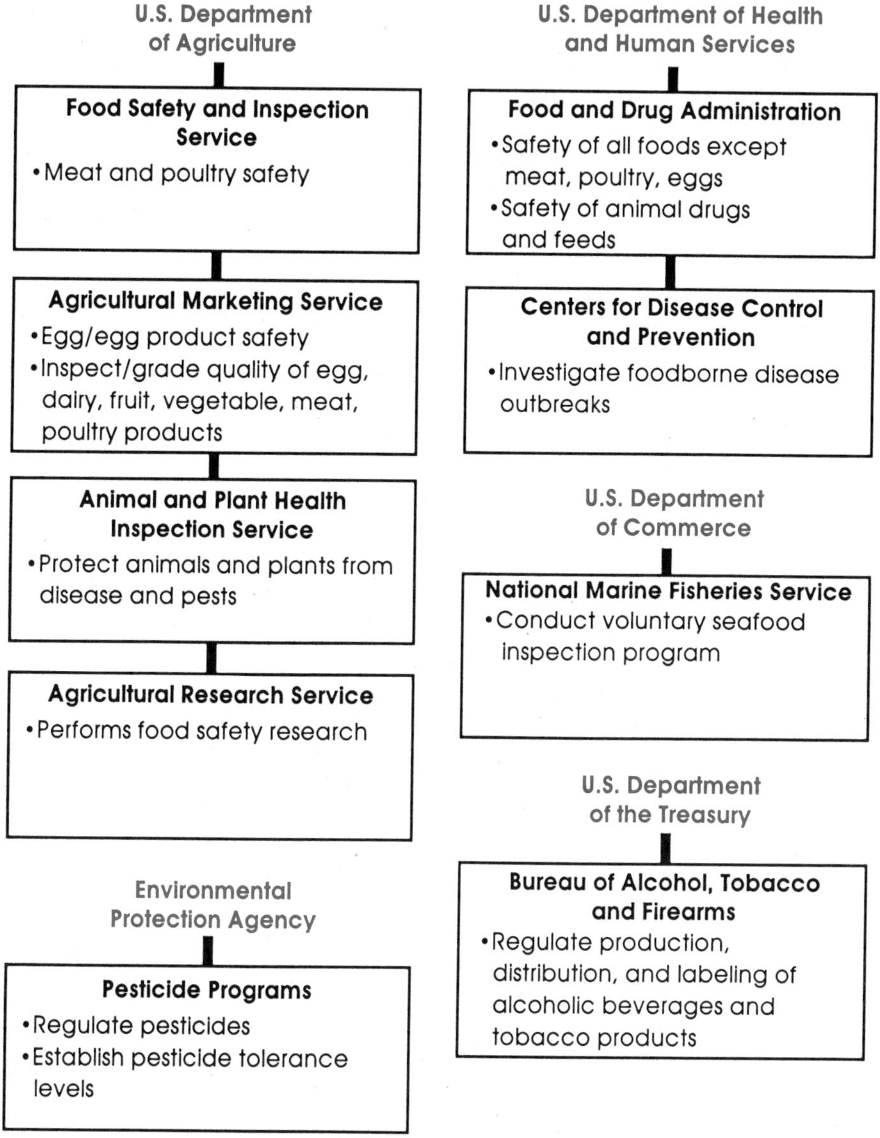

**U.S. Department
of Agriculture**

**Food Safety and Inspection
Service**
• Meat and poultry safety

Agricultural Marketing Service
• Egg/egg product safety
• Inspect/grade quality of egg,
dairy, fruit, vegetable, meat,
poultry products

**Animal and Plant Health
Inspection Service**
• Protect animals and plants from
disease and pests

Agricultural Research Service
• Performs food safety research

**Environmental
Protection Agency**

Pesticide Programs
• Regulate pesticides
• Establish pesticide tolerance
levels

**U.S. Department of Health
and Human Services**

Food and Drug Administration
• Safety of all foods except
meat, poultry, eggs
• Safety of animal drugs
and feeds

**Centers for Disease Control
and Prevention**
• Investigate foodborne disease
outbreaks

**U.S. Department
of Commerce**

National Marine Fisheries Service
• Conduct voluntary seafood
inspection program

**U.S. Department
of the Treasury**

**Bureau of Alcohol, Tobacco
and Firearms**
• Regulate production,
distribution, and labeling of
alcoholic beverages and
tobacco products

Source: D. C. Cress, K. P. Penner, and F. M. Aramouni, *Food Safety—Common Terms, Acronyms,
Abbreviations, Agencies and Laws* (Manhattan, KS: Kansas State University, 1993).

health. Several states adopted this code and many of its guidelines will, no doubt, be modified and incorporated in the new FDA *Food Code* that will be released in the fall of 1993.

- The **Bulk Food Sanitation Guidelines of 1984** specifies practices and procedures for customer self-service of bulk foods. These guidelines supplement the *Model Retail Food Store Sanitation Code of 1982* and take into consideration the potential public-health problems that arise when customers come into contact with bulk food and become part of the packaging process. The primary goal of this publication is to prevent the spread of communicable disease, outbreaks of foodborne illness, and unintentional and intentional contamination of food.

- The **Safe Food Transportation Act of 1990** guarantees that food products will not be transported in vehicles previously used to transport solid waste or hazardous materials. This act establishes specific safety requirements that must be met by all who are involved in the delivery of food.

While all of these laws and regulations may seem a bit detailed, it is important to remember that these laws were passed to protect public health and assure the safety, wholesomeness, and quality of foods that are processed, prepared, merchandised, and sold. It is helpful for store personnel to be informed about the laws and regulations pertaining to their jobs and the agencies that enforce them.

Occupational Safety and Health Administration

A division of the U.S. Department of Labor, OSHA's main purpose is to protect workers from dangers in the workplace. In 1970, the United States Congress enacted the Occupational Safety and Health Act (OSHAct). The law was designed "to assure safe and healthful working conditions for working men and women; by authorizing enforcement of the standards developed under the Act; by assisting and encouraging the States in their efforts to assure safe and healthful working conditions; by providing for research, information, education, and training in the field of occupational safety and health; and for other purposes" (7).

The OSHAct primarily covers safety factors in the workplace, but it also overlaps some other established laws and has some points directly related to sanitation and health. Retail food stores have seen an increased

UNITED STATES DEPARTMENT OF AGRICULTURE

Inspections are conducted by federal, state, and local agencies.

incidence of inspections by OSHA personnel, who examine, for example, the following sanitation-related situations:

- housekeeping practices
- waste disposal and waste-disposal containers
- vermin control
- water supply
- toilet facilities and toilet-room construction
- washing facilities
- changing (locker) rooms
- clothes-drying facilities
- eating and drinking areas (for employees)
- storage
- food handling

OSHA inspectors can operate separately from state and local inspectors. In fact, situations have arisen in which the local inspector passes a store, but it is cited by an OSHA inspector. Regardless of whether the local agency has approved the store, the manager is still responsible for responding to violations cited by the federal authority (and vice versa).

Preparing for an OSHA inspection is similar to preparing for a sanitary inspection—the store manager must be well-versed in the OSHA regulations and should conduct practice inspections on a frequent basis. The OSHA inspector should be treated with the same courtesy extended to state or local inspectors, and if any violations are noted, they should be resolved as soon as possible (8).

Hazard Communication Standard (HCS or HAZCOM)

OSHA's Hazard Communication Standard, which came into effect in 1988, emphasizes that all employees have both a need and a right to know the identities of the chemicals they work with, as well as the hazards such chemicals can pose. Employees must also be made aware of the measures available to protect them from these workplace chemicals (9).

OSHA mandates that all store employees be given training in the handling of potentially dangerous chemicals or other products. These include many of the cleansers and sanitizers used in food store sanitation. It is strongly recommended that store managers or head-office personnel establish a written hazard communication program for all store employees.

Food-Safety Inspections

In addition to the *federal* agencies discussed earlier in the chapter that are involved in food safety and quality, state, county, or local regulatory agencies, such as the department of agriculture or the department of health, enforce *state* food safety and quality laws. Inspectors or sanitarians from these state, county, or local agencies probably inspect your store on a regular basis. It is therefore necessary for a store manager to know all of the rules and regulations that apply to his or her store, from the federal level to the local level. If in doubt, be sure to contact the appropriate agency for the most up-to-date literature available, and make sure that you have read the current sanitation code in effect in your area. If you have specific questions about a regulation, it is important to ask regulatory-agency officials for their interpretation and then comply with the regulation.

Sanitary inspections, like other store inspections, can cause anxiety, even if a store manager feels he or she has the cleanest, most sanitary store and the best-educated employees possible. Store managers should keep a number of important points in mind:

- Be sure to meet the inspector promptly and be cordial and polite. Don't think of regulatory inspectors as enemies—they are working in partnership with you to keep the public safe.
- Be professional at all times. Don't try to become overly familiar with the inspector, thinking that if you act like a "pal" the inspector will overlook an infraction. Inspectors are professionals and should be treated as such.

- Do not be defensive or hostile. This won't help your case. Be polite and answer any questions as completely and as directly as possible.
- Do not try to bribe the inspector. Offering free food products or money is illegal and could result in stiff fines or penalties.
- Make it a point to accompany the inspector on the tour of the store. If the store manager is unable to accompany the inspector, he or she should designate some other manager to accompany the inspector—the store safety manager or a department manager, for example. The person who accompanies the inspector should take careful notes and make sure to verify any problems that may arise. In some instances it may be possible to correct a deficit even while the inspector is still on the premises. For example, a deli department employee who is not wearing gloves can be directed to do so immediately.
- If you feel that the inspector has made an error, it is appropriate to challenge the point *politely*. If the inspector does not agree with you and you think you are right, you may have the option to appeal to those higher up in the regulatory agency. You should know the workings of the regulatory agency responsible for food store sanitation in your jurisdiction and how an appeals process works.
- Prevention is the best cure, as the old saying goes. Your store should have an effective sanitation program in place, with its own inspection checklist. Each department manager, and all employees, should be aware of this policy. The store manager, in association with department managers, should self-inspect on a regular basis. It is also helpful to the state or local inspector if you make the store sanitation policy known to him or her. Let the inspector see your store's sanitation inspection forms, sanitation procedures, and cleaning schedules, and ask for suggestions to improve them. If you have a HACCP program in place, you should also share it with the inspector.
- Be sure to report the findings from the inspection to your superiors so appropriate action can be taken to correct the violative conditions.
- If you have many violations, or a few significant violations, expect to be inspected again. Be ready for the reinspection and take care of the violations as soon as possible. If the violation involves a piece of equipment that will have a future delivery date, have the purchase order handy to show the inspector so that he or she can verify that you have acted in a timely manner.

The Future

As the supermarket industry continues to grow and diversify its offerings—many stores now offer everything from freshly smoked meats to take-out pizzas and salads made to order—regulatory agencies have had to reconsider laws regarding the preparation, storage, and handling of more and more products. In order to keep up-to-date, the FDA is working on a new sanitation code, the *Food Code*, that will be released in the fall of 1993. This code will cover more diverse health-related situations than could even be anticipated when the earlier regulations were drawn up, and will prompt many states to reevaluate their regulations and guidelines for food stores.

The public has been made increasingly aware of the risks involved in handling, storing, and serving certain food products through such publicized incidents as *Salmonella*, hepatitis A, and *E. coli* outbreaks. It is therefore incumbent upon food store executives to keep abreast of new rules and regulations that impact their stores' products and implement strategies to prevent foodborne illnesses.

References

1. Schultz, H. E. *Food Law Handbook*. Westport, CT: AVI Publishing Company, 1981.
2. U.S. Department of Health, Education and Welfare. Public Health Service. Food and Drug Administration. *Food Service Sanitation Manual*. DHEW Publication no. (FDA) 78-2081. 1976.
3. Association of Food and Drug Officials and the U.S. Department of Health and Human Services. *Retail Food Store Sanitation Code*. 1982.
4. Cress, D. C., K. P. Penner, and F. M. Aramouni. *Food Safety—Common Terms, Acronyms, Abbreviations, Agencies and Laws*. Manhattan, KS: Kansas State University, 1993.
5. Van Wagner, L. R. "Government Agencies." *Food Processing* 52, no. 9 (September 1991).
6. *Decision-Makers Guide to Solid Waste Management*. United States Environmental Protection Agency. Washington, DC: 1989. Also see Note 6, chapter 4.
7. *Public Law 91-596*. 91st Congress, S. 2193, December 29, 1970.
8. Tuohey, S. M., and G. S. Hayward. *Managers' Guide to Safety and the Retail Environment*. Ithaca, NY: Cornell University Home Study Program, 1993.
9. U.S. Department of Labor. Occupational Safety and Health Administration. *All About OSHA*. Washington, DC: 1991.

14

Departmental Sanitation

Each food store department plays a different role in a total food store safety assurance program. This chapter provides sanitation guidelines for eight major departments: meat, produce, deli, seafood, bakery, dairy, frozen food, and grocery and the front end. All of these department sanitation guidelines reinforce concepts already discussed in previous chapters of the book and provide a review of important areas of concern. Much of the information presented is from *A Total Food Store Sanitation Program,* which was developed by a joint committee of the U.S. Department of Agriculture (USDA) and the National Association of Retail Grocers of the United States (NARGUS) (1). Remember, the principles of food sanitation are the foundation of the HACCP food safety assurance pyramid and should be an integral part of your food safety assurance program.

The Meat Department

The meat department contributes greatly to a store's sales and profits. Meat is also one of the most perishable products in the store. Therefore, sanitation in this department is of paramount importance.

Some of the major factors that spell the difference between success and failure in meat department sanitation are

- handling of product in receiving, storage, processing, and display
- personal hygiene of employees
- cleanliness and sanitation of equipment and facilities

Handling of Meat Products

The quality and safety of meat products are directly related to the supplier of the product *and* the way it is handled from the time it is processed until the time it is consumed. One of the best ways to ensure that the product received at the store is relatively sound is to buy meat only from approved and government-inspected suppliers who are using the HACCP system in their facilities.

Receiving

It is important to accept meat products that have been shipped in clean trucks where care has been taken to protect the product from contamination. The temperature of incoming meat products should never exceed 40°F (4.4°C). Incoming meat should be moved at once to the storage cooler by store personnel. Delivery personnel should be discouraged from entering the store since their outer clothes are in many cases dirty and contaminated.

Meat should *never* be accepted (no matter who the supplier) if there is any suspicion of contamination, too high temperatures, or other signs that the meat is in "poor" condition. In addition, boxes containing product should never be put on clean surfaces where processing or preparation will take place. These boxes can be dirty and may be contaminated with microorganisms.

After good-quality product has been received, it is then the responsibility of the retail meat department to handle it with the greatest of care during storage, processing, and display.

Storage

Meat products should be held in coolers at temperatures of 28° to 32°F (−2.2° to 0.0°C) (2). Product should be stored off the floor, whether in containers or in bulk, and away from the wall for proper air circulation.

Poultry and fish should be in coolers separate from fresh red meat and separate from each other. If this is not feasible, poultry and fish should be strictly segregated, with a drain convenient for melting ice. Raw foods should be stored on the bottom shelves of the cooler to prevent cross contamination of other foods. Ready-to-eat foods, such as luncheon meat and delicatessen items, *must never* be stored close to raw products because of possible cross contamination.

Barrels or containers used for meat scraps must be leakproof and tightly covered, and made of noncorrosive materials such as plastic or stainless steel that are easily cleanable. Since scrap barrels are normally stored in the meat processing room or cooler, it is important that none of this discarded meat touch fresh product or equipment that is used in the processing and storage of fresh product. One more word of caution— under no circumstances should drivers collecting meat scraps, bone barrels, or trash be allowed in the meat back room or cooler since most of these people have been handling old and sometimes contaminated product.

Processing

Many of the same rules apply to processing as to storage. First and foremost, there must be strict separation of raw and ready-to-eat products, as well as separation of product classes such as beef, poultry, pork, and fish. This is necessary because poultry and fish can carry higher levels of contamination than beef. Pork must be separated for another reason, that being the remote possibility of transferring a parasite of pork that causes the disease trichinosis to other products, especially beef.

Separation of raw and ready-to-eat products is absolutely necessary since ready-to-eat foods are not normally reprocessed to a high enough temperature to kill bacteria. Also, ready-to-eat foods usually contain fewer bacteria than raw products. Slicing cooked chicken on the same table where raw-product processing or preparation has taken place without first cleaning and sanitizing will result in product contamination and the possibility of foodborne illness.

Employees working in the meat room must therefore be trained in proper food-handling procedures. Cleaning and sanitizing must take place before switching from raw to cooked meat. This applies to all areas, whether it be employees' hands, cutting boards, containers, utensils, knives, or grinders.

What, then, should be done if in the middle of a poultry production run a customer wants a smoked ham cut in half? Assuming that the department has only one electric band saw, the most obvious answer is to keep a hand saw available for those special requests.

Some of the items often forgotten in the separation of products in production are aprons, coats, and gloves. These items can just as easily contaminate products as the actual production equipment. They must be changed, especially if switching to red meat after preparing fish or poultry.

As has been stressed throughout this book, temperature control is one of the most important aspects of an effective food safety assurance program. Products must not be kept within the temperature danger zone for long periods of time. Since most meat processing rooms are seldom kept below 50°F (10.0°C), time is of the essence in preparing and packing the product and moving it to the display case or holding cooler. Product should not be left in the processing room during coffee or lunch breaks, and only the quantity of meat that can be processed immediately should be taken from the storage cooler.

Display

Inadequate display-case refrigeration causes meat products to deteriorate before their time, which causes customer rejection. Meat department employees must then rewrap the product, which increases labor costs, retrims, throw-outs, and the use of packaging materials. As a result, department profits are significantly reduced.

To maintain maximum freshness and safety of meat products in the display case, the temperature of the products should be kept between 28°F and 32°F (–2.2°C and 0.0°C) (2). Because the thermometer in the case may be connected to the incoming air duct, the temperature may have to read as low as 20°F (–6.7°C) to give the desired product temperature. Meat department personnel must therefore check the display-case and product temperature with supplementary thermometers.

Incorrect display-case refrigeration is not always due to mechanical problems. One possible cause of poor refrigeration of product is stocking over the load line, either by clerks or by customers looking for a fresher package at the bottom of the case. Inadequate display-case refrigeration also occurs when a clerk covers the air intake and return ducts with product, thus blocking the air flow to the display case.

Figure 14.1   "Nosediving" in Refrigerated Display Cases

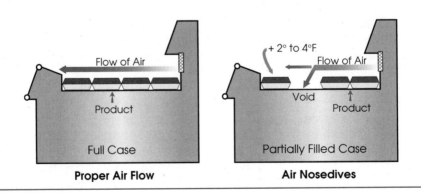

Another cause is voids, especially in the middle of the case. In a properly filled display case, air flows across the top of the case and adequately cools the product. When product voids are present in the middle of a case, some of the air will "nosedive" to the void (see Figure 14.1). Product at the front of the case therefore does not receive the proper amount of refrigeration needed to keep it at maximum freshness. Nosediving can raise the temperature of the front packages from two to four degrees Fahrenheit (one to two degrees Celsius).

Poor display-case refrigeration can also arise from improper maintenance or lack of cleaning. If accumulated dirt is blocking the outlets, the correct amount of cool air cannot get to the product.

Personal Hygiene

Most government-agency regulations require that personnel working in food-processing areas wear a hair restraint. Depending on the agency, this can mean anything from a cap to a hair net. Eating or smoking must not be allowed in any food-processing area. Aprons, coats, and gloves should be clean and changed frequently during heavy production, when changing product classes, when they become dirty, or when an associate leaves the department. All employees should be required to leave their work aprons or coats in the processing room before going to the rest room. This helps to keep contamination from being brought back from the rest rooms on work clothes. Also, meat personnel should not hang their potentially contaminated street clothes in the production area. Finally, do not allow employees with open sores, cuts, or respiratory problems to work in perishable areas.

ROBERT B. GRAVANI

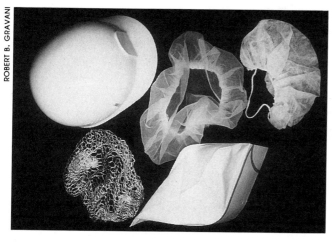

Personnel working in food-processing areas must wear a hair restraint.

Facilities and Equipment

If your facility is several years old, the meat department may lack a drain, adequate hot water, adequate water pressure, and other features necessary to take advantage of modern cleaning and sanitation equipment and methods. In this case, the only way to get the job done would be with the traditional bucket and brush method, followed by floor mopping. A good job can still be accomplished, but allow approximately 50 percent more time to accomplish the task.

If you have a modern facility with adequate drainage, smooth walls, waterproofed electrical outlets, and other modern features, you may be able to take advantage of power equipment that will save time in cleaning and sanitizing operations.

High-pressure cleaning equipment delivers water at about 500 psi (pounds per square inch), roughly ten times the pressure of water coming directly from the tap. This can provide exceptional cleaning, but it also can ruin the bearings on equipment if not used correctly by personnel. When cleaning meat display cases, make sure that the drains of the cases can take as many gallons of water per minute as the power cleaning equipment can pour out. Some display-case manufacturers will not guarantee their equipment if cleaned with high-pressure washers of certain specifications. Also, make sure that the pump of the high-pressure washer can withstand water temperatures as hot as are coming from the tap. Some of the smaller pumps cannot take water over 140°F (60.0°C). One additional point, for safety's sake, make sure all wiring and connections are waterproof.

Frequency of Cleaning

The frequency of cleaning in the meat department depends on many factors, including the

- size of the facility
- size compared to sales (overcrowding)
- sales volume
- number of meat items handled (pork, beef, poultry, fish)
- design of the facility
- regulatory-agency requirements

Traditionally, the meat department has been cleaned at the end of the production day by the remaining meat cutters or a cleanup clerk. In light of microbiological research, we now know that due to the lag phase of bacterial growth, meat departments can benefit from cleanups every four hours—the time it takes bacteria to adjust to a new environment before the maximum growth rate is achieved on a new surface. Cleanups every four hours will therefore reduce the number of bacteria transferred to products from processing or wrapping equipment. Cleaning and sanitizing should also occur between changes in product classes (e.g., from beef to pork).

As a general guideline, a regular cleaning schedule might be as follows:

1. Assemble all equipment first thing in the morning (all equipment is cleaned and sanitized properly the night before).

2. Begin production.

3. Clean as you work.

4. At the end of production runs, when changing product classes, or at four-hour intervals
   - Return unused meat to the cooler.
   - Cover or put away packaging materials.
   - Disassemble equipment to be cleaned.
   - Place equipment parts in sink of detergent solution.
   - Rough-clean in-place equipment.
   - Sweep and scrape floor.
   - Clean, rinse, sanitize, and air-dry equipment in the sink.
   - Clean, rinse, sanitize, and air-dry in-place equipment.
   - Assemble equipment.

5. End-of-the-day cleaning includes the above plus
   - Clean and sanitize floors.
   - Clean walls (weekly).
   - Clean ceiling tiles (quarterly).
   - Clean storage-cooler floors.
   - Clean all equipment not cleaned earlier. (Some of the following equipment would be cleaned as needed, such as when changing product classes, and would also be included as an end-of-the-day job: windows and display-case glass, scales, hooks and trees, knife holders, shelves and racks, trays and tubs.)

6. Place disassembled equipment on clean tables to air dry over night.

7. As needed, clean the following items that are often neglected: refrigeration fan guards (cooler, processing room), tray holders, dollies, product carts, light fixtures, cleaning equipment, trash containers, floor skids, plugs and electrical lines, overhead coils, and condensation drip trays.

To evaluate your current meat department sanitation program, check the guidelines listed in Table 14.1 against what is being done in your meat department. The meat department guidelines and the guidelines for each subsequent department discussed in this chapter are from the NARGUS/ USDA *A Total Food Store Sanitation Program* (1).

Table 14.1   Meat Department Sanitation Guidelines (1)

Meat Display

- Display cases will be washed and sanitized once a week. Blood and water from meat and poultry packages in the cases will be cleaned and sanitized as observed.
- Scales, wrapping stations, and exterior surfaces of service cases should be cleaned and sanitized daily (or more frequently, as needed). Service meat trays will be cleaned and sanitized daily. Glass areas and price tags will be cleaned and sanitized daily.
- Backup supply of retail cuts of meat will be trayed and be fully protected by film or paper. Containers used for packaging product for customer will be kept in a clean area.
- Product taken from display to be weighed and packaged for a customer will be protected by handling with waxed-paper guard. A sanitized wax paper or container will be used on the scales.
- Temperatures of the cases will be kept between 28°F and 32°F (–2.2°C and 0.0°C). The meat case will be policed and temperatures checked each morning and evening.
- Meats will not be displayed above specified fill lines. Air ducts will be kept open.
- Canned meats requiring refrigeration will be displayed at temperatures below 40°F (4.4°C).
- Centrally packaged processed meat will be removed on or before the expiration date. No packaged fresh meat will be displayed without a packaging date.
- Store-processed ground meat will be processed for each day's sale. All ground meat will be removed from sale after 48 hours.

- Floors will be cleaned and sanitized daily, walls monthly; ceilings will be vacuumed quarterly.

Meat Receiving

- Meat and meat products will be delivered to the store in clean trucks with indications that meat has been protected from in-transit contamination. Meat should be loaded on pallets or racks off the floor of the truck.
- Meat received at the store should not have a product temperature above 40°F (4.4°C), as measured by a thermometer inserted in the meat.
- Sides and quarters of meat will be moved directly from the truck to the breaking area or cooler on rails or, if carried, will be protected by a disposable sanitary cover. Delivery people will be restricted to receiving areas.
- Boxed meat will be moved directly to the cooler. Meat in boxes will be inspected and all leakers removed. Boxed meat will be stored on racks or shelves off the floor and away from the walls.

Meat Cooler

- Floors and walls will be cleaned and sanitized once a week. Drains will be clean and workable.
- Rails will be cleaned and treated with edible oil once a month.
- Blower, grills, ducts, condensation drip trays, overhead coils, and ceilings will be cleaned and sanitized quarterly or more often, if needed.
- Defrost cycles (set for nonworking hours, if possible) will be regulated so that condensation trays will adequately remove condensation from coils without spillover on stored meat products.

Table 14.1   (continued)

- Temperatures in coolers will be checked at the opening and closing of the store daily. Temperatures above 32°F (0.0°C) will be reported to maintenance. Thermometers will be located in the center of the cooler above stored products. Records will be maintained of daily temperatures (mechanical recorders are recommended for recording daily temperatures).
- All products will be stored away from walls to permit circulation of refrigerated air.
- Poultry and fish will be stored in areas away from red meat, with a convenient drain for disposing of melting ice.
- Containers for scrap meat will be of easily cleaned materials, leakproof, and with a tightly fitting cover. Containers will be cleaned and sanitized each time they are emptied, or, if plastic liners are used, they will be cleaned and sanitized weekly.
- Shelves and racks will be cleaned and sanitized once a week. Unwrapped meat will not be placed on shelves or racks.
- Hooks and trees will be cleaned and sanitized as used.
- Trays and tubs not kept continually under refrigeration will be cleaned twice a day and when products are changed.
- Grinders, chippers, saws, and other equipment used in the cooler will be cleaned and sanitized each day.

Meat Preparation

- The meat preparation room should be cleaned and sanitized every four hours, at the end of production runs, or when changing product classes.
- Floors will be cleaned and sanitized daily or more often, if necessary; walls will be cleaned and sanitized weekly; the ceiling will be cleaned quarterly. Only USDA-approved absorbent compounds will be used on floors.

- Packaging materials will be stored in segregated areas away from surfaces that come in contact with raw products. Reserve supplies will be kept in covered or closed containers.
- When meat preparation room temperatures are above 55°F (12.8°C), all products will be processed and returned to refrigerated displays or holding cases so that internal meat temperatures will not exceed 40°F (4.4°C).
- Care will be taken in moving products from the cooler to and through the cutting room to avoid contact with all surfaces except those being sanitized every four hours. All meat exposed to floor surfaces will be placed in the scrap-material container.
- Segregated cutting areas and sinks will be utilized for poultry, red meat, and fish. When changing from poultry or fish to red meat, all exposed equipment and surfaces will be cleaned and sanitized.
- Hands will be washed with soap and hot water, and dried by hot air or paper towel following the change in processing of poultry or fish to red meat, or after contact with contaminated surfaces. Hand contact with meat surfaces should be avoided whenever possible; hands should not contact other skin surfaces, including the lips, hair, and face, when processing meat.
- Care will be taken to avoid contact with surfaces of containers and packaging materials that will be in contact with meat surfaces during processing and packaging.
- Hair guards, clean hats or hair nets, and aprons or coats will be worn when handling meat. Hair, fingernails, and hands will be clean.
- Employees with cuts, open sores, and respiratory problems will not work in the meat department.
- No smoking or eating will be allowed in the meat department.

The Produce Department

Produce department sanitation is important because so much of the product has come from the soil where contamination is the heaviest or has been subject to possible animal contamination. Care must be taken with certain produce items to make sure they do not contaminate other products, such as meat and especially deli and bakery products. Imagine how an unclean case of parsley used to decorate a ready-to-eat product might affect the shelf life of that product and increase the risk of foodborne illness. Produce used in these departments should be thoroughly washed before being used and then strictly segregated in storage until needed.

Even within the produce department, there are certain ready-to-eat items that must be kept away from unwashed, potentially contaminated products. For example, the same knife used to slice watermelon or cantaloupe should not be used to trim celery or lettuce.

Product in the produce display cases should be kept fresh and free of decay and diseases. To display the produce correctly, equipment, shelf tags, tables, racks, and other display devices must be clean at all times. Potato and onion bins should be checked daily for off-standard product, and any residue from the product should be cleaned out. Refrigerated display cases should hold product below 40°F (4.4°C).

Today there are modern aids to keep the produce back room more sanitary and generally neat. The compactor and the garbage disposal provide excellent methods for getting rid of waste product. Facilities without modern equipment can use large plastic bags for garbage, tied and placed in the dumpster outside the back door.

Each produce department should either have its own hand-washing sink or one handy to the department since inspectors frown on using product-washing sinks for washing hands. Neither hand soap nor a soap dispenser should be placed by the product-washing sink.

Since most produce coolers are used for both wet and dry product, it is especially important that coolers be cleaned and sanitized at least once a week to prevent such cold-loving organisms as mold from getting a foothold and adversely affecting product and profit conditions. Because water from melting ice is a factor in produce coolers, all product must be off the floor so that contaminated water cannot seep into containers and affect product cleanliness and quality. The cooler temperature should be held at between 34°F and 36°F (1.1°C and 2.2°C) if possible, but never over 40°F (4.4°C).

Produce department sanitation guidelines are listed in Table 14.2.

As mentioned earlier, with all the soil and potentially contaminated moisture in the produce department, it is vital that the department be

---

Table 14.2 Produce Department Sanitation Guidelines (1)

Produce Display

- All produce on display will be clean and free from decay and other contaminants, and will be checked and policed regularly during the day.
- Perishable produce will not be displayed above identifiable load lines. Most perishable items will be displayed at temperatures below 40°F (4.4°C). Produce cases will be policed and temperatures checked each morning and evening.
- Cases, price tags, racks, tables, floors, and holding areas will be cleaned and sanitized weekly. Ceilings and walls will be vacuumed quarterly.

Produce Preparation

- Produce work benches will be cleaned and sanitized daily.
- Walls, ceilings, and light fixtures will be vacuumed quarterly.
- Floors will be washed and sanitized daily. Drains will be kept open and clean.
- Leakproof, easily cleaned trim barrels will be used for produce waste. These barrels will be equipped with plastic liners that will be closed and moved to the trash area upon filling. Barrels will be washed and sanitized once a week. Garbage grinders are encouraged, where permitted.

- Knives, tools, and equipment whose surfaces will contact produce will be cleaned and sanitized on a daily schedule.
- Sinks of nonabsorbent materials will be washed and sanitized daily.
- Produce will be stored on racks off the floor and away from walls.
- Clean hair guards, aprons, jackets, or smocks will be worn; hands, hair, and fingernails will be clean.
- No smoking or eating will be allowed in the produce department.

Produce Cooler

- Walls, ceilings, shelves, and blowers will be cleaned and sanitized monthly.
- Floors will be cleaned and sanitized weekly. Drains will be kept clean and open.
- Condensation drip trays will be washed and sanitized monthly.
- Produce will be on racks off the floor and away from walls to allow for adequate circulation of refrigerated air.
- FIFO (first-in, first-out) rotation will be followed.
- The temperature in the cooler will be below 40°F (4.4°C), as measured by a thermometer located in the center of the cooler above stored products.

---

regularly and thoroughly cleaned. A regular cleaning schedule might be as follows:

1. Display Area
   - *Daily:* Wipe outside of cases, mirrors, scales, and other display equipment and floors; check case lights and temperature.
   - *Weekly:* Clean plastic price tags, moldings, and insides of display cases and racks.

2. Processing Area
   - *Daily:* Clean floor and all equipment used in processing, including knives, tables, packaging machines, sinks, and pans.
   - *Weekly:* Clean walls, lift floor skids or pallets, and clean soap and towel dispensers.
   - *Quarterly:* Clean ceiling and light fixtures.

3. Cooler Area
- *Daily:* Clean floor
- *Monthly:* Clean walls, ceilings, shelves, drains, cooling unit, fan guards, condensation trays, light fixtures, and under skids.

The Delicatessen Department

Sanitation in both the deli and the bakery departments is particularly vital because products in these two departments are sold ready-to-eat. In most other departments, such as fresh meat, the customer will take the product home and cook it to above 145°F or 62.7°C (ground beef to 155°F or 68.3°C), thereby killing any harmful bacteria (see temperature guidelines in chapter 7). Not so with products from the delicatessen and the bakery.

It is therefore imperative that deli foods be as low in bacteria as possible to avoid any problems. Deli products must come from approved sources and be handled by knowledgeable people on sanitary equipment. If all this is accomplished and the products are kept below 40°F (4.4°C) or above 140°F (60.0°C), there will be little chance that public-health problems will occur. Ignoring basic sanitary practices in the deli department has put some retailers virtually out of business.

Separation of Product

Separation of raw and ready-to-eat products during preparation, as well as in storage and display, is of utmost importance in the deli department. Raw products for sale in a bulk service case must be physically separated so they do not come in contact with each other at any time. In addition, some provisions should be made so that deli clerks serving customers do not handle both raw and ready-to-eat foods with their hands without

- washing hands before changing products
- using separate utensils
- wearing clean, disposable gloves
- using wrapping tissue

The scale platform is a source of contamination if a piece of counter wrap is not used under the products being weighed. Deli clerks should also remember to change aprons and gloves, wash and sanitize small utensils before reuse, and avoid using the same pan for ready-to-eat products that was used for raw foods.

Employees working in the deli department must practice the rules of good personal hygiene and proper product handling.

Personal Hygiene

Deli products being sold to customers are generally cooked and ready-to-eat, and should contain relatively low numbers of bacteria if they have been handled correctly. However, unclean employees or those not following the sanitary practices discussed in chapter 9 and throughout this textbook will destroy any advantage the deli department has gained through proper product handling.

Employees working in the deli department should be very carefully screened prior to hiring in order to maintain a high standard for the deli operation. An unclean, sloppy deli employee will not only destroy customer confidence, but will also leave the department open to potential contamination problems.

Temperature

In the deli department, employees handle not only cold foods, but they must also handle hot, ready-to-eat products like chicken, ribs, beans, cabbage rolls, and sausage. It is important that the critical control points such as cooking, hot-holding, cooling, and reheating be carefully monitored and that corrective actions are taken if deviations are observed. Follow the food temperature control guidelines provided in chapter 7, especially the cooking temperatures for products that are prepared in the deli. The *internal* temperature of cooked products must be kept above 145°F (62.7°C) (3).

To check product temperatures, a probe-type thermometer should be inserted into the center of the product. Temperatures should be taken several times daily and recorded to protect you and the customer. Documenting temperatures of products that are held hot (>140°F, >60.0°C) provides a permanent record.

It is a very good idea to let customers know that hot foods must be kept above 140°F (60.0°C) and cold foods below 40°F (4.4°C). Also, make it clear that leftovers should be reheated to a temperature of 165°F (73.9°C). Many barbecue bags, for example, already have this information printed on the bag, and many retailers inform customers through signs posted in the deli.

All display cases, storage coolers, and processing rooms should have thermometers that are checked daily. Temperature in display cases and coolers should be held between 36°F and 40°F (2.2°C and 4.4°C).

Cleaning and Sanitizing

Remember, the deli department does not have the built-in protection that raw-product departments have because deli products may not be cooked to "safe" temperatures in the customer's home. For this reason, appropriate HACCP plans for potentially hazardous deli foods must be in place, as well as an effective cleaning and sanitizing program.

It is highly recommended that culture plates be used in the deli department to determine the effectiveness of cleaning and sanitizing procedures (see chapter 8). By using the guidelines in Table 14.3 and making any adjustments necessary, you will be operating a "top-notch" deli where safe and wholesome foods will be enjoyed by your customers.

The Seafood Department

Seafood products deteriorate very rapidly when kept at temperatures above 40°F (4.4°C). Proper handling and temperature control are therefore essential from the time the seafood is caught to the time it is prepared. Care should be taken to store fish and other seafood products between 30°F and 34°F (between –1.1°C and 1.1°C) and to handle them properly (2). Careless handling at temperatures above 40°F will definitely affect the flavor, odor, and texture of these products.

The handling of seafood at store level is critical from a food-protection standpoint. Fish, like poultry, can carry higher levels of contamination than many other products. Strict separation of fish from other perishable products, as well as separation of noncooked and ready-to-eat fish in receiving, storage, preparation, and display, is vital.

Table 14.3 Deli Department (Prepared-Food) Sanitation Guidelines (1)

Deli (Prepared-Food) Display

- Delicatessen food items will be kept at temperatures below 40°F (4.4°C) or above 140°F (60.0°C). Permanent thermometers should be installed in cases.
- Cases will be policed and temperatures checked each morning and evening.
- Product display trays and pans will be cleaned and sanitized after use. The tops of service cases and scales, utensils, glass areas, price tags, service shelves, and steam-table areas will be cleaned and sanitized daily.
- Refrigerated display cases will be cleaned and sanitized weekly. Display cases for hot foods will be cleaned and sanitized daily.
- Containers for retail sale of products will be kept in an orderly fashion, with product surfaces not exposed to contamination. Backup supplies will be covered or in enclosed areas.
- Floors will be cleaned and sanitized daily. Walls will be cleaned and sanitized monthly. Ceilings will be vacuumed quarterly.
- Hands should not touch products when serving customers.

Deli (Prepared-Food) Processing

- Cooked items to be held as backup supply will be moved directly to a refrigerated area and will be covered after cooling to 40°F (4.4°C) in the holding area. Backup supply of products will be reheated in an oven to 165°F (73.9°C) before placing them on the steam table.
- All surfaces coming in contact with prepared foods will be nonporous, and cleaned and sanitized following each production activity and upon completion of activities for the day. Spilled product will be cleaned as observed.
- The meat slicer will be cleaned and sanitized on a twice-a-day cycle, and broken down and cleaned and sanitized daily. Cheese slicers will be broken down and cleaned and sanitized daily.
- Ovens will be cleaned at least weekly.

- Utensils, including pans, trays, knives, can openers, and blenders, will be cleaned and sanitized after use.
- Deep-fat fryers will be cleaned at least weekly when changing cooking oil. Surfaces on and around the fryer, including walls and the floor, will be cleaned and sanitized daily upon completion of frying activities. Hoods, filters, and vents will be cleaned and sanitized weekly.
- Space will be provided for all pans and utensils to be air dried following sanitizing. Sinks will be cleaned and sanitized at least daily.
- A nonporous workstation will be used for processing uncooked meat, poultry, and fish. This area will be cleaned and sanitized following the processing of each of these items, and these products will be segregated from prepared-food items. If porous workstations are used, a separate workstation will be used exclusively for uncooked meat, poultry, and fish products. Separate sinks will be used for fish and poultry.
- Containers for retail sale of products will be kept in an orderly fashion, with product surfaces not exposed to contamination. Backup supplies will be covered or in enclosed areas.
- Floors will be scraped, cleaned, and sanitized daily. Spillage will be cleaned as observed. Walls will be nonporous, and cleaned and sanitized monthly. Ceilings will be vacuumed quarterly.
- Employees with cuts, open sores, and respiratory problems will not work in this department.
- All employees will wash hands with soap and hot water, drying with hot air or paper towels following exposure to contamination. Hand contact with food should be avoided whenever possible. Hands should not contact other skin surfaces, including the lips, hair, and face, when processing and handling foods.
- Hair guards, clean hats or hair nets, aprons, coats, and smocks will be worn when handling food. Hair, fingernails, and hands will be clean.

Table 14.3 Deli Department (Prepared-Food) Sanitation Guidelines (continued)

- Only employees of the deli department should be in or passing through this area.
- Trash and garbage will be held in nonporous containers and emptied when full. Containers will be cleaned and sanitized daily. If plastic liners are used, they will be cleaned and sanitized weekly.
- No smoking or eating will be allowed in the deli department.

Deli (Prepared-Food) Refrigerated Box
- Temperature will be held at 40°F (4.4°C) or below and will be checked each morning and evening.
- Floor and walls will be cleaned and sanitized weekly, ceilings monthly. Drains will be clean and workable.
- All products will be stored on shelves or platforms constructed to permit circulation of refrigerated air.
- Uncooked meat, poultry, and fish will not be stored in the same cooler with cooked foods.

- Cooked foods and ingredients will be held in pans, trays, and other containers with tightly fitted covers.
- FIFO (first-in, first-out) product rotation will be practiced.

Deli (Prepared-Food) Freezer
- Temperature will be held at 0°F (−17.8°C) or below.
- Items will be rotated using the first-in, first-out (FIFO) method.
- The freezer will be cleaned and sanitized quarterly.

Deli (Prepared-Food) Storage
- All products will be stored off the floor on pallets or shelves.
- All products will be in tightly sealed packages or closed containers.
- Floors, walls, and ceilings will be cleaned monthly.
- FIFO (first-in, first-out) rotation will be practiced.

Because separation is not always easy to accomplish given the limited space in many food stores, the seafood department may end up in the deli area. Unfortunately, this is probably the worst place seafood could be—right in the middle of all that the ready-to-eat food. Depending on your locality and regulatory agency, you may not be allowed to combine seafood with another department. In areas where it is allowed, chances are that separate sinks, processing equipment, and utensils will be required, as well as separate display cases and storage coolers.

Seafood personnel must not handle other products without first changing their coats and aprons, and thoroughly cleaning and sanitizing their hands and arms. This presents a problem in display and service if fish is located in the deli department. A clerk who is asked to do both deli and seafood jobs can potentially create a cross-contamination problem, so this individual needs to pay special attention to his or her work habits.

The slightly modified NARGUS/USDA guidelines in Table 14.4 are what should be accomplished from a food-protection standpoint in seafood departments.

Table 14.4 Seafood Department Sanitation Guidelines (1)

Seafood Receiving

- Seafood will be delivered to the store in clean trucks and clean containers. Products will be stacked on racks or pallets off the floor of the truck.
- Temperatures of seafood delivered to the store will be 38°F (3.3°C) or below.
- All seafood will be inspected for signs of spoilage or damage.
- Seafood will be moved directly to coolers to maintain product temperature at 30° to 34°F (–1.1° to 1.1°C) or below.
- Rough handling of seafood will be avoided to prevent bruises and punctures.
- Cooked or ready-to-eat seafood will not be shipped on trucks with live or uncooked seafood.
- Dollies, tubs, or other containers used for moving fish will be cleaned and sanitized daily, or more often if needed, and will be kept in good repair.

Seafood Display

- Display cases will be cleaned and sanitized weekly. They will be constructed with an unrestricted wide drain that will be kept clean and workable.
- The top of the service case, the scale, and wrapping surfaces will be nonporous and cleaned and sanitized daily, or more frequently as needed.
- Service fish trays will be cleaned and sanitized after each use.
- Glass areas will be cleaned and sanitized daily.
- Temperatures will be 30° to 34°F (–1.1° to 1.1°C) or below in the refrigerated zone. The display case will be policed and temperatures checked each morning and evening.
- Whole fish will be displayed on a bed of ice and with ice sprinkled on the product. Unpackaged fresh cut fish will be displayed on trays on a bed of ice with ice sprinkled on the product.
- Cooked fish will be displayed in a separate case from uncooked fish.
- FIFO (first-in, first-out) rotation will be followed.

- Floors will be cleaned and sanitized daily, or more often if necessary. Walls will be cleaned and sanitized weekly. Ceilings will be cleaned quarterly.

Seafood Preparation Area

- No other operations will be permitted in the area where uncooked seafoods are processed.
- All surfaces coming in contact with seafood will be nonporous and will be cleaned and sanitized daily. If preparation-room temperatures are above 50°F (10.0°C), a twice-a-day cycle for cleaning and sanitizing will be followed.
- Knives, tubs, pans, and other utensils will be cleaned and sanitized after each production activity.
- Separate work areas and sinks will be used for the processing of uncooked and cooked seafood products.
- Packaging materials will be stored in segregated areas away from surfaces that come in contact with raw products; reserve supplies will be kept in covered or closed containers.
- Frozen fish will be held at temperatures of –20° to 0°F (–28.9° to –17.8°C) or below.
- The backup supply of unfrozen fish will be held at temperatures of 30°F to 34°F (–1.1°C to 1.1°C) or below and will be repacked with clean ice as needed.
- Floors will be cleaned and sanitized daily, or more often if necessary; walls will be cleaned and sanitized weekly; and ceilings will be cleaned quarterly.
- Separate covered trash and scrap containers will be utilized with plastic liners. Scrap containers will be emptied frequently and cleaned and sanitized daily. Trash containers will be emptied when filled and will be cleaned and sanitized weekly.
- Hair guards, clean hats or hair nets, and aprons or coats will be worn when handling seafood; hair, fingernails, and hands will be clean.
- No smoking or eating will be allowed in the seafood department.

Table 14.4 Seafood Department Sanitation Guidelines (continued)

- Hands will be washed with soap and hot water and dried by hot air or paper towels after the processing of uncooked fish. Hand contact with fish surfaces should be avoided; hands should not contact other skin surfaces, including the lips, hair, and face.

- Care will be taken to avoid contact with surfaces of containers and packaging materials that will be in contact with fish surfaces during processing and packaging.

- Employees with cuts, open sores, and respiratory problems will not work in the seafood department.

Seafood Cooler

- The cooler and other equipment used to store uncooked fish or fish products will not be used for other purposes.

- Blower, grills, ducts, condensation drip trays, and overhead coils will be cleaned and sanitized monthly.

- FIFO (first-in, first-out) rotation procedures will be followed in the seafood cooler.

- Floors and walls will be cleaned and sanitized daily and ceilings once a week. Tubs and pans used in handling fish and stored in the cooler will be cleaned and sanitized after each use. Drains will be clean and workable.

- Ice will be made from drinking water and will be handled and stored in covered containers to prevent contamination.

- Ice will not be used after it has been in contact with fish or fish products, or with contaminated surfaces.

- Containers used for storing or transporting ice will be cleaned and sanitized daily.

- Live fresh or thawed seafood will be held at temperatures below 38°F (3.3°C), as measured by a thermometer located in the middle of the cooler above stored products.

- Frozen fish will be stored at temperatures of –20° to 0°F (–28.9° to –17.8°C) or below.

- Cooked fish or seafood products will not be stored in the cooler with live or uncooked seafoods.

The Bakery Department

In the bakery department, the checking of raw materials in receiving is especially important since many bakery products, such as flour, meal, and sugar, are particularly attractive to rodents and insects. Packaging of these items is not always as strong as it should be and rough handling often takes place in the shipping process. As a result, the retail food store is often faced with contamination problems before the raw products arrive at the back door of the bakery. Each shipment must therefore be thoroughly checked before it is brought into your store.

Receiving is of prime importance in ensuring that raw products are free from insect and rodent infestation, and other contaminants when taking shipment from a supplier. It may be worthwhile to call your local or state regulatory agency to ask whether particular suppliers have had any significant violations over a period of time. If the agency provides a long list of violations, the supplier must be dropped immediately. Remember, your inspector will hold you responsible for any contamination in your facility.

Because many of the foods used in a bakery department are low in acid, such as cream fillings and dairy products, regulatory agencies keep an especially close eye on in-store bakeries as well as central chain bakeries. With the exception of brown-and-serve products, the items being purchased in the bakery are all ready-to-eat and present a danger if not handled properly.

Products must be properly covered at all times, whether in the cooler or waiting to be packaged in the processing area. This includes icings, glazes, and any fillings that are used in processing, as well as flour, sugar, nuts, crumbs, and other toppings used on the finished product. Glazes, fillings, and other dairy products must be held below 40°F (4.4°C) after opening, even though they may not require refrigeration in the first place due to the type of packaging used.

All cream and custard products must be refrigerated while on display and, if prepackaged, should have a label stating that the product should be refrigerated.

Although not always possible due to the design of the facility, holding flours and cereals below 50°F (10.0°C) will reduce the ever-present insect infestation problem in the bakery department. The fly population, a seasonal problem in many bakeries, can be reduced by keeping the area clean and sanitary. Other solutions to controlling flies are discussed in chapter 11.

Rodents also may be a problem in the bakery department since areas near ovens provide warm nesting places plus an abundance of easily accessible food. Contact a reputable pest-control operator to check your establishment at least once a month, and ask for a written report listing any problem areas or potential problem areas that should be corrected.

Finally, because bakery products are ready-to-eat, bakery personnel must be especially conscious of personal hygiene and work habits. A list of bakery department sanitation guidelines is provided in Table 14.5.

The Dairy Department

Although the dairy department does not, in most cases, involve nonpackaged products, the way dairy products are handled is still critical from a food-protection viewpoint. From an economic standpoint, a dairy department that sells fresh products can positively affect a store's reputation.

Table 14.5 Bakery Department Sanitation Guidelines (*7*)

Service Bakery Display Area

- All bakery products not in enclosed cases will be completely packaged.
- Doors on display cases will be closed except when products are being selected or displayed.
- Bakery items not packaged will be selected with a paper guard that will be disposed of following filling of each order.
- Cream- and custard-filled baked goods will be refrigerated at temperatures below 40°F (4.4°C) and will be identified as requiring refrigeration on store trays and consumer packages.
- Bakery display cases and equipment will be cleaned and sanitized each day.
- Floors will be cleaned and sanitized each day. Walls will be cleaned and sanitized monthly. Ceilings will be vacuumed quarterly.
- Hair guards and aprons or clean coats or smocks will be worn. Hands will be washed with soap and hot water after exposure to contaminated surfaces. Employees with cuts, sores, and respiratory diseases will not work in the bakery department.

Self-Service Bakery Display

- Non–potentially hazardous bakery products (products not requiring refrigeration or special care) will be wrapped and packaged at the place of manufacture using automatic machinery. Products are to be considered hazardous when exposed to contamination such as breaking of the package. All broken packages will be removed from display.
- Display racks and price tags will be cleaned and sanitized monthly. Walls will be cleaned and sanitized monthly. Ceilings will be vacuumed quarterly.

Bakery Preparation Area

- Utensils, including pans and mixers, will be cleaned and sanitized after use. The bread slicer will be cleaned daily and sanitized weekly. Space will be provided for small utensils and equipment to hang for air drying after sanitizing.

- All surfaces coming in contact with bakery products will be nonporous. These surfaces will be cleaned following each production activity and cleaned and sanitized upon completion of work for the day. Spilled ingredients will be cleaned from surfaces as observed. Work area will be cleaned and sanitized after handling potentially hazardous products, such as custards, and cream, nonacid, and low-sugar fillings.
- Retarders will be cleaned and sanitized weekly. Proof boxes and drains or drip pans will be cleaned and sanitized daily.
- Ovens will be cleaned every two weeks.
- The deep-fat fryer will be cleaned weekly or more often when changing cooking oil. The exhaust hood and filter will be cleaned each week.
- Surfaces on and around the fryer, including walls and the floor, will be cleaned and sanitized daily upon completion of frying activities.
- Glazer and doughnut trays with racks will be cleaned and sanitized daily.
- Baking and bread pans will be scraped and cleaned weekly. Crusted residue will be removed as necessary.
- Open dollies used for storing and holding trayed products will be cleaned and sanitized weekly, or more often as needed.
- All ingredients, fillings, and icings will be covered except when being used.
- Cream and custard fillings will be stored under refrigeration when not being used.
- Packaging workstations will be kept clean and orderly. Materials not being used will be completely covered or stored in an enclosed area.
- Floors will be scraped, cleaned, and sanitized daily. Spillage will be cleaned as observed.
- Walls will be nonporous and will be cleaned and sanitized monthly. Ceilings will be vacuumed quarterly.
- Sinks will be washed and sanitized after use and at the end of the production activity daily.

Table 14.5 (continued)

- Drains will be clean and workable.
- Clean hair guards, aprons, smocks, or coats will be worn. Fingernails will be clean. Hands will be washed with soap and hot water and dried by air or paper towel between production activities and after contact with contaminated surfaces.
- Employees with cuts, open sores, and respiratory problems will not work in the bakery department.
- All trash and garbage will be placed in a covered container and moved to the trash or garbage holding areas when full and each night following the completion of production activities. Trash containers will be cleaned and sanitized after use or daily if liners are used.
- Reusable or recyclable containers will be stored in a neat and orderly fashion away from high-traffic areas.
- No smoking or eating will be allowed in the bakery department.

Bakery Freezer

- Frozen bakery products will be delivered to the store in clean trucks with product temperatures at 0°F (–17.8°C) or below. All products will be moved directly into the freezer from the truck.
- A temperature of 0°F or less will be maintained in the freezer. Temperatures will be taken by thermometers located in the center of the freezer above stored products.

- Freezer temperatures will be recorded each morning and evening, with an abnormal temperature being reported immediately to the store manager.
- Frozen food will be stored on racks away from walls to provide free circulation of refrigerated air.
- Products will be dated on the outside of cartons and first-in, first-out (FIFO) rotation will be achieved.
- Floors, walls, ceilings, and blowers in freezers will be cleaned and sanitized at least once a year.

Bakery Ingredient Storage

- All products will be examined upon receipt for evidence of insect or rodent contamination. Evidence of either source of contamination will result in refusal to accept delivery.
- All products will be stored on racks or shelves 12 inches (30 cm) or more off the floor, positioned away from walls to help eliminate shelters for insects and rodents.
- Partially filled containers of ingredients will be tightly covered.
- First-in, first-out (FIFO) product rotation will be used for all products.
- Floors and walls will be cleaned monthly. Ceilings will be vacuumed quarterly.
- The bakery storage area will be constructed to inhibit the entry of insects and rodents.

Not too many years ago, some dairy department managers would say to employees, "Stack it high and sell it low. You haven't got time to be filling the case every half hour and we don't make any money on milk anyway." Of course, this kind of thinking did not consider whether the customer was going right home on a warm day or whether the milk had been left out during the shipping and receiving process and for how long.

The quality of milk and dairy products is definitely affected by temperature. These products should be kept in refrigerator storage and then properly stacked below the load line in display cases. Restocking the case should take place as product is needed. Milk should not be left in the aisle for long periods of time.

Milk that is handled correctly and refrigerated through the distribution chain at 40°F (4.4°C) will stay fresh for at least 10 days (see Figure 14.2). At 45°F (7.2°C), the maximum allowable under most state laws, milk will last about 5 days, while milk kept at 60°F (15.6°C) will last less than 1 day. For maximum product shelf life, the ideal milk storage temperature is between 33°F and 40°F (0.6°C and 4.4°C).

Figure 14.2 Temperatures for Milk and Milk Products

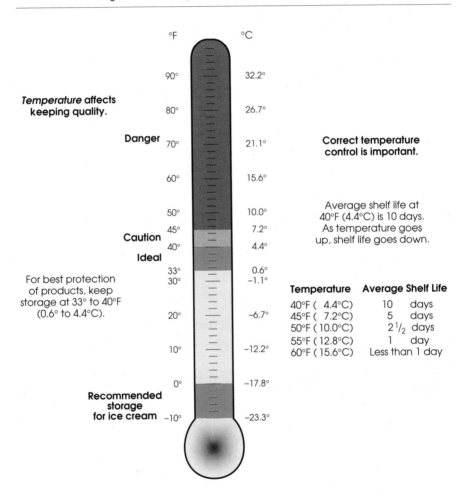

Source: New York State Dairy Foods, Inc.

Obviously, the most important aspect of dairy department sanitation and quality control is adequate refrigeration. Display-case thermometers should be checked for accuracy and monitored several times during the day to assure that the case is operating properly. In addition, the cooler and display cases must be cleaned and sanitized regularly. Customers will not buy products from dirty, smelly dairy display cases. Other important sanitation guidelines in the dairy department cover rotation of product (checking pull dates) and control of leakers and damaged merchandise. The NARGUS/USDA guidelines for dairy department sanitation are provided in Table 14.6.

The Frozen-Food Department

Frozen foods, like dairy products, come already packaged and in relatively good condition *if* they have been held at the appropriate temperatures throughout the distribution chain. The important points to concentrate on when handling frozen foods are

- *Receiving:* Quick handling of the product from the truck to an adequately controlled stockroom freezer is essential. This freezer should really be kept at –25° to –20°F (–31.7° to –28.9°C) (2). Incoming product should be checked for the following signs of thawing and refreezing:
    - frozen liquids in or outside the shipping cartons
    - large ice crystals on the packages or in the product itself
    - packages still soft—especially noticeable in high-sugar products

WEGMANS SUPERMARKETS

Frozen-food display cases must be clean and stocked below load lines.

Table 14.6 Dairy Department Sanitation Guidelines (1)

Dairy Display Area

- Display cases will be cleaned and sanitized weekly; milk sections will be cleaned and sanitized each day. All leakage and contamination will be cleaned and sanitized as observed.

- Drains and air ducts will be cleaned monthly or more often as needed. Coils will be defrosted periodically, allowing enough time for frost and excess moisture to be removed. The defrost cycle will be checked weekly and adjusted as needed.

- Dairy products, including milk, eggs, and dough products, will be displayed at temperatures below 40°F (4.4°C). The dairy case will be policed and temperatures checked each morning and evening.

- Dairy-case lights will be turned off when the store is closed. Milk and milk products will not be stacked adjacent to lights to prevent excess oxidation.

- Dairy products will not be stocked above load lines. Improper stocking can interfere with air flow and raise product temperature 15° to 20°F (8° to 11°C).

- Dairy products will not be stacked in the aisles. All products brought into the aisle for stocking will be moved immediately into the display case.

- Milk in paper containers will not be stocked by grasping the top of the container.

- First-in, first-out rotation (FIFO) practices will be followed. All items will be checked each day and those exceeding expiration dates will be removed. Torn, open, or inflated packages will be removed as observed.

- Floors will be cleaned and sanitized weekly, walls and ceilings vacuumed monthly.

Dairy Cooler

- Fruits and vegetables with strong odors will not be stored with dairy products.

- Temperatures in the dairy cooler will be below 40°F (4.4°C) and thermometers will be located in the center of the cooler above products. The cooler will be policed and temperatures checked each morning and evening.

- First-in, first-out rotation (FIFO) practices will be followed. All items will be checked each day and those exceeding expiration dates will be segregated in a "morgue" area for return to suppliers.

- Dairy products, including eggs, will be stored on easily cleaned, rust-resistant shelves and racks (away from walls to provide adequate circulation of refrigerated air).

- Blowers, grills, and condensation drip trays will be cleaned and sanitized quarterly or more often as needed.

- Racks and shelves will be cleaned and sanitized weekly.

- Floors, walls, and ceilings will be cleaned and sanitized weekly. Leakage and contamination will be cleaned and sanitized as observed.

- Drains will be clean and workable.

- Clothes and other contaminators will not be stored in the cooler.

Dairy Receiving

- Dairy items will be received in clean refrigerated trucks with product temperatures at 40°F (4.4°C) or below.

- Delivery trucks will have curtains or other devices to maintain desired temperatures within the truck during delivery operations.

- Dairy products, including eggs, will be moved immediately into the cooler, or refrigerated display or holding boxes. Orders will be checked in the cooler rather than on the dock.

- *Storage:* Correct rotation of product and adequate storage-freezer temperatures are necessary.
- *Display:* Make sure that the load lines are strictly observed and that the display cases are cold enough at all times. Bring only as much product from the storage cooler as can be stocked in a short period of time (approximately 15 minutes). Remember that even below 32°F (0.0°C) the quality of food still begins to deteriorate. For example, food quality is reduced several times faster at 15°F (–9.4°C) than at 0°F (–17.8°C). As mentioned in an earlier chapter, freezing food does not kill bacteria; it just holds most bacteria in a state of suspended animation. Keep frozen-food display cases a –10° to 0°F (–23.3° to –17.8°C). Ice cream display cases should be kept at –20° to –10°F (–28.9° to –23.3°C) (2).

When receiving several pallets of frozen food, product is often not moved directly from the pallets to the display case. It is important to put all items, except those that will be stocked immediately, in the freezer as soon as possible. Also, put the high-sugar products away first, if possible.

Frozen-food department sanitation guidelines are presented in Table 14.7.

Table 14.7 Frozen-Food Department Sanitation Guidelines (*1*)

Frozen-Food Display

- Frozen foods will be held at –10° to 0°F (–23.3° to –17.8°C) and ice cream at –20° to –10°F (–28.9° to –23.3°C) as measured in the refrigerated zone, except during necessary defrost cycles. The case will be monitored and temperatures will be checked each morning and evening.
- Frozen food and ice cream will be moved quickly from truck to freezer and freezer to display so that temperatures will not go above 0°F for frozen food and –10°F for ice cream.
- Broken packages and those with ice and discolored product will be removed from display. Residue from broken packages should be cleaned from the case as observed. Products will be rotated to assure first-in, first-out rotation.
- All products will be stocked below identified load lines.

- Display cases will be cleaned and sanitized quarterly; floors will be cleaned and sanitized weekly; walls and ceilings will be vacuumed quarterly.

Frozen-Food Boxes

- Floors, walls, ceilings, and blowers in freezer boxes will be cleaned and sanitized once a year.
- Temperatures of –10° to 0°F for frozen foods and –20° to –10°F for ice cream will be maintained in the freezer boxes. Temperatures will be taken by thermometers located in the center of the box above stored products at store opening and closing.
- Frozen food will be stored on racks away from walls to provide free circulation of refrigerated air.
- Products will be dated on the outside of cartons so first-in, first-out rotation will be achieved.

The Grocery Department and Front End

Many people tend to overlook the grocery department as an important part of a sanitation program. If not controlled properly, however, the grocery department can cause more problems throughout the store than any other department. Consider how often the grocery receiving door is opened during the day and how many possible sources of contamination can enter through that door.

Also, how is most grocery product damage handled? Is much of it stacked haphazardly in uncovered containers, where rodents and insects may find it as their source of food?

Is there adequate control of receiving doors and incoming products to ensure that these do not become major "avenues of contamination"? Receiving doors that are constantly open and unclean back rooms provide rodents and insects with a standing invitation to come in and sample the food you have for sale.

Products in the grocery department that are particularly attractive to rodents and insects include flour, nuts, grain products, sugar, cereal, noodles, and pet foods. These products can provide rodents and insects with enough food to allow them to raise many generations in your store. These pests, which can set up housekeeping under the bottom shelf kickplates, are very difficult to get rid of. Especially popular areas with rodents are the dry dog-food section and the bread rack. Bottom shelves in these areas should be removed and checked at least once a month, and more often should you suspect a problem.

The store manager can control most pest problems by enforcing strict housekeeping requirements in and around the entire store. A dirty, sloppy store that is attractive to rodents and insects will certainly repulse customers, especially those who may see one of the little creatures scurrying across the floor.

From an aesthetic standpoint, most customers do not care for a store with a parking lot strewn with papers, garbage, and broken shopping carts, or a sales area with floors that are dirty and in bad repair, dusty shelves, and filthy products.

Another forgotten area is the rest rooms. Many a customer has been unpleasantly surprised after asking to use the employee rest room in an emergency, usually for a child. They are shocked to find that a store that looks so clean in the sales area is so dirty behind the scene. Many regulatory-agency officials say they can often judge the level of sanitation in a store by starting their inspection in the rest rooms.

Other areas that should receive more attention are the vending-machine and drinking-fountain areas. These areas can be wet or sticky, dirty,

Table 14.8 Grocery Department and Front End Sanitation Guidelines (*1*)

Grocery Displays

- All products on display will be in good condition. Dented and swollen cans, and torn and cut packages will be removed from displays.
- All food items should be stocked to assure first-in, first-out rotation.
- Insecticides, rodenticides, and other hazardous chemicals that are potential contaminators of food will be displayed in areas at a safe distance from food in porous packages. Protective, nonporous bags with adequate warnings will be available for packaging these products.
- Dog-food will be displayed in areas away from food in porous packages. Torn and broken packages will be removed from display. Residue from broken packages will be cleaned as observed.
- Displays of products will be located so that the more perishable items, such as frozen foods and ice cream, will be late in the shopping pattern.
- Shelves and products will be dusted when restocking displays. All shelving will be cleaned and sanitized on a three-month cycle.
- Floors will be cleaned and sanitized weekly or as needed; walls and ceilings will be vacuumed quarterly.

Grocery Storage

- Floors should be vacuumed weekly and will be cleaned and sanitized on a quarterly basis. Residue from broken packages will be cleaned as observed. Walls and ceilings will be vacuumed on a semi-annual basis.
- A segregated area will be used for returnable bottles, and they will be placed in containers off the floor.

- All products will be on racks or skids off the floor. Racks and skids will be cleaned and sanitized on a quarterly basis. Potential contaminators will be cleaned and sanitized as observed.
- All damaged products ("morgue" items) will be placed in closed packages and will be removed within one week.
- Conveyors, stairs, and elevators will be vacuumed weekly and will be cleaned and sanitized monthly and cleaned of contaminators as observed.
- Dollies used in conveying products from the truck to the back room will be cleaned and sanitized monthly and will be cleaned and sanitized when contaminators are observed.

Checkout Areas

- All checkout personnel will be clean and dressed in clean clothing or uniforms.
- All checkout counters will be cleaned and sanitized daily. All leakage from meat, poultry, or milk packages will be wiped up with disposable towels, cleaned, and sanitized as observed.
- All observed leaking poultry and meat packages will be placed in plastic bags. All frozen foods and ice cream will be placed in insulated bags.
- Potential contaminators, such as hazardous chemicals and insecticides, will be bagged separately from food items.
- Shopping carts will be cleaned and sanitized monthly and cleaned of contaminators as observed.
- Floors will be vacuumed each evening and cleaned and sanitized weekly; ceilings and walls will be vacuumed quarterly.

and very unsanitary in appearance. Another neglected area is the employee lunchroom or eating area. If this room is cluttered and dirty, it will be a source of food for flies and other insects and an overall contributor to contaminating other areas of the store.

The last area of the store seen by the customer is many times the least taken care of—the front end. The front end must have constant attention since all traffic passes through the checkout area, creating a heavier-than-normal cleaning need. Constant checking for paper and trash is absolutely necessary, in addition to regular spot-mopping during the day. Checkstand belts should be kept clean; the area under the registers should not be a catchall for trash and junk but should be neat, clean, and orderly.

Sanitation guidelines for the grocery department and the front end are listed in Table 14.8.

References

1. Joint Committee of the U.S. Department of Agriculture and the National Association of Retail Grocers of the United States. *Total Food Store Sanitation Program.* Washington, DC: National Association of Retail Grocers of the United States, 1973.
2. Food Marketing Institute. *Food Handler's Pocket Guide for Food Safety and Quality.* 1989.
3. U.S. Food and Drug Administration. Center for Food Safety and Applied Nutrition. *Proposed Food Protection Unicode.* 1988.

15

Designing and Implementing a Sanitation Program

As you know, a strong sanitation program is one of the building blocks of an effective HACCP food safety assurance program. A strong and effective sanitation program *must* be an integral part of your store's standard operating procedures. This program should be in place and functioning well to ensure the success of your HACCP program. As you design and implement a sanitation program, there are certain steps that must be taken for the system to work properly and efficiently. These important steps are shown below.

1. Get top management commitment.
2. Survey present conditions.
3. Set objectives, goals, and priorities.
4. Assign program responsibility.
5. Educate and train personnel.
6. Acquire necessary resources.
7. Begin program implementation.
8. Stress inspection, evaluation, and feedback.
9. Follow-up and control.
10. Implement a rewards-and-incentives program.

Top Management Commitment

Without complete commitment from top management, a sanitation program is destined to fail. If top management does not make it clear to all empoyees that a food safety and sanitation program is of utmost importance to the entire organization, the program will not succeed.

Many companies get off to a good start with a sanitation program but find themselves unable to see it through for any time longer than a few months. How does this happen? In case after case, this failure is due to a lack of *complete* upper-management commitment coupled with poor short- and long-range planning, lack of implementation, follow-through, and control. Remember, it costs more money to restart sanitation programs than to sustain them over a period of time. The people in charge of a company sanitation program should report only to top management. Departments within the company must be instructed that in matters of sanitation, the people in charge of the program have complete authority.

There have been cases where top management has focused its attention on sanitation programs only after being penalized by regulatory agencies. Stiff fines and adverse publicity can make a believer out of the most hardened skeptic. Management must show its commitment to sanitation as a top-priority program and must continue its support for the program as an ongoing part of normal company activities. A memo from the owner or president of the company, such as the memo shown in Figure 15.1, would be invaluable in getting the sanitation program off the ground.

After the top executive has stressed the importance of the program through a memo or at a special meeting, it is then the job of the next level of management to set up orientation and training meetings to explain the program to supervisory personnel. Supervisory personnel must then follow the lead in their divisions, and so forth down the line. Any weak link will sabotage the sanitation program.

It also would be of great benefit to the program if the entire top-management team participated in an educational orientation program on sanitation. So many times, top management will commit its next lower level of management to such programs, assuming they already know all they need to know on the subject. This attitude can sometimes hurt the total commitment needed to make the program a success. Look at other programs in your company that have been successful. Did they have the total commitment of the executive level of management?

Figure 15.1   Sample Sanitation Memo from Top Management

To: All Company Personnel
From: J. Smith, President, Sunny Acres Supermarkets
Subject: Quality Control and Sanitation

From the beginning, the goals and objectives of this company have been to provide the consumer with safe and wholesome foods at the most reasonable prices. We have also taken pride in operating clean and sanitary facilities through the years.

In these times of increased consumer awareness and closer scrutiny by the media and regulatory agencies, I feel it is necessary that we strive even harder to adhere to our basic policy of maintaining a high level of food safety and sanitation in our company and of strict adherence to federal, state, and local laws.

I request *your* assistance in reaching and maintaining the highest standards of cleanliness and sanitation in our stores and distribution facilities. To achieve this goal, I have appointed Robert Jones to the position of Director of Food Safety Assurance. Mr. Jones will coordinate all food safety and sanitation activities for the company and report directly to me.

A survey of all facilities will be undertaken immediately by Mr. Jones. Corrective-action reports as a result of the survey will be sent to each division manager for action. Corrective-action reports will then be completed and returned to Mr. Jones who will, in turn, prepare a summary report for me to review weekly.

I consider this program one of the top priorities in our company and one that will continue to receive my personal attention. Let's continue to make sanitation a way of life at Sunny Acres.

I know that I can count on you to continue to do an excellent job. Thank you for your cooperation and support.

Survey of Present Conditions

The next step in the program is to assemble a small sanitation management team or committee to survey present sanitation conditions. This survey team should ask such vital questions as: What is the actual sanitation level of the facilities? Are there any deficiencies in our present program? What areas need to be corrected and improved? What are our sanitation goals?

Team members should talk to company personnel, including department heads, store managers, and the district manager or store owner. The company's size and structure will determine who is surveyed. The survey team should include a person with a thorough knowledge of sanitation, such as a sanitation consultant, a regulatory-agency inspector, or a company employee who has received the training and has the skills necessary to evaluate objectively a store's present sanitation conditions.

Using a checklist like those used by regulatory agencies that highlight critical and general deficiencies, make a complete inspection of each department. (Sample checklists are shown in Figures 15.2 and 15.3.) Note the processes used to complete each operation and make observations on the way associates prepare and handle foods. Watch how equipment and utensils are washed and sanitized.

A sanitation survey and inspection allows managers to identify and correct violative conditions before they become major problems. It also ensures that the sanitation program complies with federal, state, and local laws. The survey should focus on the following areas:

- temperature control of food and food-storage facilities.
- cleaning and sanitizing procedures for facilities and equipment: physical condition, cleanliness, and sanitation. Storage of cleaning and other chemicals, and type and condition of cleaning equipment should also be considered.
- personal hygiene and work habits, such as product-handling procedures.
- rodent and insect control.
- the condition of the building and facilities.
- miscellaneous areas, including waste disposal.

As a result of such a survey, the survey team may have a long list of items to be corrected in each area of the store. A priority system will have to be developed to determine which problems are most pressing, that is, those that need immediate attention as opposed to those that can be dealt with later. The investment factor in equipment, time, and materials also must be considered. This leads to the next step in developing a sanitation program—setting objectives and goals.

Figure 15.2   Sample Inspection Checklist of Critical Deficiencies

1. Food Received from Unapproved Sources
A. Unpasteurized milk/milk products used
B. Water or ice is not potable
C. Foods or ingredients from unapproved source
D. Meat, poultry, or game products are not from officially inspected plants
E. Shellfish from unapproved source
F. Liquid eggs, frozen eggs, or dried milk products are not from U.S.D.A. inspected plants

2. Food Products or Ingredients Adulterated or Unfit
A. Rodent-defiled foods or ingredients
B. Insect-infested foods or ingredients
C. Food products contain unidentified sulfiting agents or other unapproved additives
D. Other adulterated/unfit foods or ingredients

3. Food Not Protected from Contamination by Workers
A. Food handlers handle foods when ill with a disease transmissible by foods
B. Food handlers have infected cuts or burns on their hands
C. Food handlers do not wash hands thoroughly after contaminating them
D. Employee hand-washing facilities inadequate for establishments handling exposed foods

4. Food Not Protected from Contamination by Other Sources
A. Food-contact equipment, utensils, or conveyances for potentially hazardous foods: contact surfaces unclean or not sanitized and likely to contribute to contamination
B. Food-contact equipment, utensils, or conveyances are not cleaned or sanitized between use on different species or between raw and ready-to-eat foods
C. Ready-to-eat foods are subjected to cross contamination from raw foods, or cross contamination between species is likely to occur
D. Toxic chemicals are improperly labeled, stored, or used so that contamination of food is likely to occur
E. Food-contact equipment condition or design is likely to contribute to contamination

F. Insect, rodent, bird, or vermin activity likely to result in product contamination
G. Evidence of leakage or backup in sewage lines
H. Equipment cleaning or sanitizing facilities inadequate for establishments handling potentially hazardous foods

5. Critical Processing or Salvaging Parameters Are Noted
A. Pork products, which may be eaten without further cooking, are not treated to kill trichina
B. (Refer to Specialized Inspection Guidelines)

6. Potentially Hazardous Foods Improperly Cooled or Refrigerated
A. Potentially hazardous foods are not cooled by an approved method where the product temperature can be reduced to 70°F or less within two hours and 40°F or less within six hours
B. Potentially hazardous foods are not stored at safe temperatures

7. Potentially Hazardous Foods Not Adequately Cooked or Reheated
A. Poultry, poultry stuffings, stuffed meats, or stuffings containing meat are not heated to 165°F or above
B. All pork or any food containing pork is not heated to 160°F or above
C. Other potentially hazardous foods requiring cooking are not heated to required temperature
D. Potentially hazardous foods that have been cooked and then refrigerated are not rapidly reheated to 165°F or above
E. Equipment used for heating or reheating potentially hazardous foods is inadequate

8. Improper Hot-holding Procedures for Potentially Hazardous Foods
A. Potentially hazardous foods are being kept below 140°F during hot-holding (rare roast beef may be served at 130°F or above)
B. Hot-holding equipment improperly designed, maintained, or operated to keep hot foods above 140°F

Source: New York State Department of Agriculture and Markets, Division of Food Safety and Inspection Services, Albany, NY.

Figure 15.3   Sample Inspection Checklist of General Deficiencies

1. Improper or Inadequate Sanitary Facilities and Controls

A. Hand-washing facilities improperly installed or maintained
B. Suitable water temperature or adequate pressure for food processing; equipment, utensil, or container cleaning; or hand-washing in establishments that do not handle exposed foods, not available
C. Toilet facilities improperly installed, equipped, or maintained
D. Plumbing or sinks not properly sized, installed, or maintained: equipment or floors not properly drained
E. Lighting or ventilation is inadequate
F. Cleaning or sanitizing equipment, materials, or agents are not available, suitable, or properly stored
G. Sanitizing test devices not in use where required
H. Lack of certification of water potability or record for disinfection

2. Inadequate Sanitary Design, Construction, and Maintenance

A. Exterior of unsuitable construction or not in good physical repair
B. Establishment has insufficient space to accommodate operations
C. Interior floors, walls, ceilings, or fixtures are not of suitable construction, clean, or well maintained
D. Refuse containers not clean, covered, in good repair, or removed at sufficient intervals

3. Poor Hygiene and Activities of Food Handlers

A. Not maintaining a high degree of cleanliness or taking precautions to prevent contamination of foods from perspiration, cosmetics, chemicals, or medicants, etc.
B. Not wearing clean outer garments, effective hair restraints, or secure jewelry
C. Eating, drinking, or use of tobacco in exposed food areas
D. Locker or dressing rooms are not segregated from food areas, clean, or orderly

4. Inadequate Food Storage and Protection

A. Food not stored, conveyed, or displayed in a manner that prevents contamination, including marginal temperature deficiencies
B. Food or ingredient storage containers are not clean, covered, or properly identified
C. Bulk-food displays are improperly constructed, displayed, or handled
D. Street clothing or soiled linen stored unsegregated from exposed food or food-contact surfaces
E. Self-service food displays are improperly constructed, maintained, or supervised
F. Improper thawing procedures are utilized

5. Required Processing or Salvaging Procedures Are Not Followed

A. (See Specialized Inspection Guidelines)
B. Other required records are not maintained
C. Other coding requirements are lacking or inadequate

6. Insect, Rodent, or Vermin Activity

A. Evidence of rodents observed (not likely to result in product contamination)
B. Insects, birds, or other vermin observed within the establishment (not likely to result in product contamination)
C. Evidence of pets or other domestic animals in establishment

7. Equipment, Utensils, and Materials Adequately Utilized and Maintained

A. Food-contact equipment, utensils, or conveyances: contact surfaces unclean or not sanitized
B. Non-contact food equipment, utensils, or conveyances are not clean or in good repair
C. Food equipment improperly designed, constructed, or maintained
D. Thermometers not provided where required
E. Unused equipment or materials improperly stored or in an unclean condition
F. Storage cabinets or shelves are not clean or in good repair
G. Packaging materials unclean, improperly stored, or handled in an unsanitary manner
H. Air system or transfer lines are not clean, properly constructed, or in good repair

8. Other Sanitation

A. Chemicals or pesticides improperly labeled, stored, or handled
B. Outside premises or loading zones improperly maintained
C. Vehicles are not clean or in good repair
D. Morgue area or bottle-return area improperly maintained
E. Shellfish tags or records improperly maintained

Source: New York State Department of Agriculture and Markets, Division of Food Safety and Inspection Services, Albany, NY.

Objectives, Goals, and Priorities

Before implementing any sanitation program, it is important to establish what the program is intended to accomplish and why. Moreover, it is important to decide how long it should take to establish an effective sanitation program. If a sanitation program, or any other program that is attempted, is to be successful, attention must be given to the setting of objectives, goals, and priorities. This step is the backbone of the program, for it establishes the guidelines for the project.

The first step is to define the primary objectives of a sanitation program. Such objectives may be

- to protect public health
- to comply with federal, state, and local laws relating to sanitation and food protection
- to ensure that high-quality, safe foods are being sold to the customers
- to maximize profits

After agreeing on the basic objectives of the program, it is then necessary to set *specific* goals, which might include the following:

- Organize a strong sanitation program for each store.
- Reduce inspections violations by 50 percent.
- Reduce meat rewraps by 60 percent.
- Reduce all storage cooler temperatures to 34°F (1.1°C).
- Replace all outdated equipment.
- Train department heads thoroughly.

A list of specific goals should reflect exactly what you want to accomplish with your sanitation program. Of course, each goal would have detailed plans on how it would be accomplished.

As mentioned above, the survey of present conditions may yield a long list of items to be corrected in all departments. It will be impossible given the pressures of daily work schedules, however, to do everything at once. So, the next step in the overall planning of a sanitation program is the setting of priorities. This step is very important in keeping the program moving along its charted course.

Trying to correct everything at once will cause a great deal of frustration on the part of the staff and could cause the entire project to bog down and possibly fail. Taking too long to accomplish set goals could have the same effect. To help decide which items should receive the highest priority, consider the following criteria:

- *Priority I*—correct within one week. Falling into this category are those items that are of immediate concern to public health or could cause serious profit loss.
- *Priority II*—correct within 30 days. This category would include those items that, if not corrected within a reasonable period of time, could lead to serious public-health or profit-loss situations.
- *Priority III*—correct within three months. In this category are those items that need upgrading to make the program totally effective, but which are not necessarily sanitation problems relating to public health.

Assignment of Responsibility and Authority

The subtitle of this section might be "Who's in Charge." When something comes up concerning sanitation, every store associate must know whom to call or contact for information or action on a particular question or problem. If actions are not taken according to the planned schedule, top management must know where and with whom the responsibility lies. Therefore, it is very important to make clear exactly who is in charge and what his or her responsibilities are.

The next consideration must be to decide in what area of the company a sanitation program should be placed. This is a difficult question to answer because companies are so different in their organizational makeup.

Training and education must not be neglected in the total planning and management of a sanitation program.

WEGMANS SUPERMARKETS

A one-store owner might be the natural choice to lead the program, with subresponsibilities to each department head. A multistore operator might assign the primary responsibility to the district manager.

An ideal setup for almost any company would be to use the team or committee approach, with each area of company operations represented. Such a committee would be responsible for dealing with all sanitation problems within the company. It would meet on a regularly scheduled basis to plan, help implement, and follow-through on the program's progress.

If the company is large enough to have a director of security, it also should have a director or manager of sanitation whose sole responsibility is to coordinate sanitation activities. An effective sanitation department can be "worth its weight in gold" if given the opportunity to really function within a company. Proof of this fact is documented in chapter 3, "Sanitation and Store Profits."

One word of caution: If a particular person within a company is assigned to sanitation, the job duties should be clearly defined so that there is no antagonism between this person's department and others. For example, considerations that must be dealt with include

- Does the sanitation department take care of negotiations and follow-up for such jobs as window washing, trash pickup, and procurement of supplies?

- Is it the responsibility of the sanitation department to schedule cleaning hours in stores?

There are many such questions that must be considered and defined clearly to avoid confusion, hard feelings, and a shoddy job. One thing is certain, however—the success of the sanitation program depends on the assignment of responsibility to the right person or persons.

Training and Education of Personnel

Once these first steps have been accomplished, it is very tempting to get the program moving in high gear without first taking some time to train all personnel. Starting a sanitation program before all personnel have the knowledge and skills necessary to carry it out would be a real mistake! It will also be expensive in the long run.

The sanitation educational process must begin with top management and work down through store personnel. Training and education must not be neglected in the total planning and management of a sanitation program. A realistic goal is to train, or update and retrain store personnel at least every six months. This is necessary because of the high turnover rate in the retailing food industry and the constant shifting of job positions.

Personnel can be trained using a number of methods. Which method to choose depends on the trainer, the personnel needing training, the time available, and the type of training needed.

Sanitation training materials and programs are available from many organizations, including industry trade associations, colleges and universities, government agencies, chemical companies, food manufacturers, co-ops, and wholesalers. The Educational Foundation of the National Restaurant Association, for example, has many excellent slides, videotapes, books, and pamphlets which, although intended for the foodservice industry, can make excellent training pieces for the retail food industry. The Food Marketing Institute also has a wide variety of excellent training materials. The FDA state training branch in Rockville, Maryland, has a library of visual training aids that are available for loan. You may want to contact this FDA office and request a catalog of these visual aids. All of these materials, in addition to this Cornell Home Study course that allows personnel to complete the sanitation program at home or in a company-sponsored workshop, can help you build a strong sanitation training program.

Table 15.1 shows a general outline that can be used as a do-it-yourself formula for planning a sanitation seminar for various levels of management and other company personnel. By obtaining videotapes, slides, and written materials from some of the sources mentioned above, each part of the program outline can be easily planned and conducted. This outline is only a general guideline and can be reorganized to best suit the needs of each company and training group.

Necessary Resources

Prior to actual implementation of the sanitation program, the necessary resources must be acquired. These include the proper equipment and products with which the cleaning and sanitizing will be done, processing equipment that is easily cleanable, proper facilities conducive to cleaning and sanitizing, and the necessary hours to accomplish the job. Such resources should be acquired when needed according to planned objectives, goals, and priorities.

Starting an otherwise well-planned program without the necessary resources can be very damaging. It is very important to the success of the program that the necessary resources be supplied to store personnel as soon as possible.

Table 15.1 Program Outline for Training Supermarket Personnel in Sanitation

1. **Introduction and Orientation**
   - Program objectives: Why are we here?
     Our changing world
     Consumer demands
     Legislative demands
     Need for better profit structure
   - Importance of sanitation and food safety
   - Protecting public health—preventing foodborne illness

2. **Survey of Present Conditions**
   - Slides illustrating existing conditions
   - Discussion of biological, chemical, and physical hazards
   - Survey results
   - Reaction of group—why problems exist
     Lack of training
     Lack of management awareness
     Age and design of equipment
     People problems—resistance to change
     Lack of employee motivation
     Lack of follow-up and control

3. **Presentation of Model Program**
   - Top management down to worker level
   - System would consist of
     Training aids, manuals, notebooks, audiovisual aids
     Programmed instruction materials
     Survey and control checklists (involvement and motivational
       exercises)
   - Training materials—reviewed
     Guideline manual as backbone of system (semitechnical)
     Printed and audiovisual materials based on the manual and
       simplified (video, slide/tape, transparencies, charts, posters,
       exercises eliciting audience involvement)

4. **Presentation of Basic Sanitation Principles**
   - Video or slides
   - Examples, case studies, and problem-solving exercises
   - Quiz of materials
   - Group discussion
   - Review of materials covered

Table 15.1   Program Outline for Training Supermarket Personnel in Sanitation (continued)

5. **Present Good Industry Practices**
   - Slides showing examples of what two or three specific companies or groups are doing

6. **Economics of Sanitation**
   - Losses incurred by incorrect practices
   - Possible savings available
   - Actual studies documenting gains

7. **Specifics of In-store Sanitation—Need-to-Know Basis**
   - How to clean, sanitize, design, service, control, evaluate, etc.
   - Potential problems
   - Demonstration and practice of specifics

8. **Working with People**
   - Effective communication techniques
   - Motivation
   - Training the trainer

9. **How to Manage an Effective Program**
   - Setting objectives and goals
   - Assigning responsibility
   - Procuring resources
   - Training
   - How to motivate personnel through involvement
   - Evaluation
   - Follow-up and control

10. **Summary, Wrap-up, and Discussion**

Program Implementation

Although thorough planning is necessary for the success of a sanitation program, it is also imperative to get the program started as soon as possible, even if only minor changes are made for the first few weeks. Getting a start may include rescheduling cleanups for every four hours instead of once a day, acquiring single-service towels, using the appropriate detergent and sanitizer, and requiring associates to attend refresher training sessions. There is no reason to delay the sanitation program when there are so many actions that can be implemented in the short run while long-range planning is conducted.

Any delay in the program after careful planning and training could have an overall detrimental effect on the project. Target dates must be planned and adhered to for implementation of each step of the program. Of course, there might be delays in equipment orders and work done by service agencies from time to time, but these delays should be held to a minimum.

The main point to remember is that there is a great psychological advantage in getting the program "off the ground" as soon as possible. After the program has been in operation a while and most of the planned items have been implemented, it will be necessary periodically to inspect, monitor, evaluate, and give the store feedback.

Inspection, Evaluation, and Feedback

As a sanitation program becomes a normal part of everyday operations, it is advisable to begin periodic inspections of the facilities. These inspections should help in evaluating the program and give feedback to personnel so they can continue to move effectively toward project goals. The inspections and follow-ups should be performed by unbiased, objective company personnel not connected with the daily store operation or through outside services.

What exactly is inspection, evaluation, and feedback, and why are they necessary? Compare it to cutting a lawn. You begin the job, and after working at it for some time, you stop to see where you are. You are working towards a goal, which is to complete the cutting of the lawn and end up with a smooth, even job. Stopping at a point halfway through the task, you check what you have already accomplished (inspection). You consider the quality of the work already done (evaluation) and discover that some spots have been missed (feedback). The line that divides what has already been cut tells you how much further you must go to reach the planned goal, and the feedback that shows you what you missed on the first half tells you where you must backtrack to smooth over those areas not up to par.

This same principle applies to a sanitation program. At some point in the program, there must be a time for inspection, evaluation, and feedback. This can save a lot of backtracking in the long run as well as money and time that could be well spent in other areas.

Checklists similar to those in Figures 15.2 and 15.3 could be used for the inspection function. Records of inspections should be kept on file to check the store's progress over a period of time. But even the inspection, evaluation, and feedback mechanisms would be a wasted effort if they are not linked with effective follow-up and control.

Follow-up and Control

All the inspections, evaluation reports, and paperwork in the world will be useless if the suggested improvements or corrections are not implemented and followed up by management and store personnel. Herein lies the weak point of many programs, not only in sanitation, but also in many other areas of store operations.

One method of follow-up and control is the use of a corrective-action form like the one shown in Figure 15.4. The form requests corrective action to be taken by store management as a follow-up to the points noted on your inspection checklist (Figures 15.2 and 15.3). On the form are places for the person making the corrective action to initial that the work

---

Figure 15.4 Sample Corrective-Action Request

			Code		

Code

Maintenance Needed	M
Equipment Needed	E
People Problems	P

Sanitation
Corrective-Action Request

White Copy — Retained by Sanitation Dept.
Yellow Copy — Retained by Store
Pink Copy — Store Returns to Sanitation Dept. Noted with Action Taken

Facility __56__	Inspection Number __56__	Distribution _____
Date __3/15__	To Be Returned By __3/20__	
Time __9:00 A.M.__	Date of Audit __3/29__	Mr. Williams _____ Store Manager
Inspected By __BCD__		Ms. Johnson _____ District Manager

Department	Corrective Action Needed	Code	Date Completed	By Whom (Initial)	Further Action Needed OR Remarks
Front end	1. Clean entrance to store.	P			
	2. Clean around checkstands.	P			
Meat	3. Observe load lines in lunch-meat case.	P			
	4. Personnel must wear clean aprons.	P			
	5. Clean cooler fan guards.	M			
Bakery	6. Personnel must wear hair restraints—State Law.	P			
Deli	7. Obtain thermometers for display cases.	E			
	8. Clean walls.	P			
	9. Fill soap dispenser over hand-washing sink.	P			
Dairy	10. Observe load lines in display cases.	P			

was completed, indicate the completion date, and make any pertinent remarks. The report also allows for a follow-up audit to make sure the work is actually accomplished. If the corrections are completed, the report is filed; otherwise, rechecks are scheduled until the work is complete.

Constant checking and rechecking are important to make sure you are following the correct course of action. Lack of follow-up and control can lead to backtracking and a waste of time and money.

Many sanitation programs in food stores over the past few years have had good starts that bogged down after a few months due to a lack of planning, implementation, follow-up, and control. They eventually failed from lack of attention. Many times the programs are revived at a later date, costing vast sums of start-up money. A well-thought-out program having all the elements listed thus far will survive in the midst of the many other responsibilities required of today's retail food store employees.

A part of follow-up and control certainly must be keeping records of all regulatory-agency inspections, internal inspections, product tests, and any documents that can point to

- progress attained
- progress still needed

Records of an ongoing sanitation program that show steady progress could prove invaluable as evidence in a court of law should the need ever arise.

Rewards and Incentives

When trying to get people to do a little something extra or, in fact, any job at all, they must see a benefit—rewards and incentives. You might ask, why should we have to give rewards and incentives to associates to do the job they were hired for? That's a very valid question. Most people expect to do the job for which they were hired, but to get that something extra on a program such as sanitation, rewards or incentives can provide the necessary additional motivation.

Of course, there are many kinds of rewards and incentives that can prove effective. With some people, a kind word or a pat on the back will suffice, while others need more. There are natural benefits to a sanitation program that will provide rewards to employees for implementing a successful program. A successful sanitation program will mean less work in the long run for store personnel. Cleaning will be easier, equipment will last longer, less product will have to be reprocessed, the store image will be better, and people will have a cleaner facility in which to work. The safety of products prepared, stored, and handled will improve, and customers will appreciate the attention given to quality and safety.

But there are other incentives as well that may spark an even stronger desire to do the job. Some companies have used point systems and have awarded plaques to stores meeting certain standards set up by the company. Others hold contests between stores and districts, and award prizes to the winners. Ideas like the "Safe Food Award" or the "Department of the Month" have been used successfully.

Although sanitation effectively applied is really a reward in itself, it may be necessary to use other methods until this fact is understood by company personnel. Each operation is different and must build some sort of reward-and-incentive system into its sanitation program according to its needs.

Summary

This chapter has described the task of designing and implementing a company sanitation program that will provide a strong foundation for your HACCP program. The challenge is to take the information presented here, apply it to your store, and develop a successful sanitation and food safety assurance program.

Food safety and sanitation will always remain an important part of the total food store operation. The safety of the food sold in the grocery store must meet the highest safety standards so that customers can always be assured that the food they buy is safe and wholesome. The food safety and sanitation subjects covered in this book are all essential to store operations, company image, sales, profitability, and the health and welfare of your customers. Food safety assurance and the HACCP system require a commitment from all store personnel, from the top management on down, but the effort is well worth the results.

Glossary

Acid Detergents:

Detergents used for special applications—for example, in situations where minerals in foods or hard water leave deposits on equipment and other surfaces that cannot be cleaned with alkaline products. Acid detergents should supplement—not replace—alkaline detergents.

Additive

Any substance introduced to a food, whether directly (such as a preservative) or indirectly (such as material migrating from the packaging film).*

Adulterated Food

Food that contains any poisonous or harmful substance that may make it injurious to health. A product that does not conform to the standard or quality specified on its label or labeling.*

Aerobes:

Bacteria that require oxygen to grow.

Alkaline Detergents:

Detergents commonly used for regular cleaning of equipment, tables, utensils, glassware, floors, walls, ceilings, and general-purpose areas.

American Cockroach:

Also known as the Palmetto bug or the water bug, the American cockroach is among the largest of the cockroaches to be found in the U.S. They are reddish brown to dark brown, and although they have developed wings, they rarely fly. See *Cockroach.*

Anaerobes:

Bacteria that grow only in the absence of oxygen.

Angoumois Grain Moth:

A small buff or yellowish-white moth that attacks only whole, unbroken kernels of corn, wheat, and other grain and seeds. See *Moths.*

---

*The definition or description is from D. C. Cress, K. P. Penner, and F. M. Aramouni, *Food Safety—Common Terms, Acronyms, Abbreviations, Agencies and Laws* (Manhattan, KS: Kansas State University, 1993).

Anisakiasis:
An illness caused by the parasite *Anisakis simplex*, a roundworm found in some marine fish.

Anisakis simplex :
A parasite that can cause anisakiasis. See *Anisakiasis*.

Attractants:
Substances or devices capable of attracting insects or other pests to areas where they can be trapped or killed. When attractants are combined with poisons they are often referred to as "poison baits."*

Bacillus cereus (B. cereus) **Gastroenteritis:**
A spore-forming bacterium that produces two different types of toxin that cause two distinct forms of foodborne illness. These illnesses differ in the foods involved, the time of onset, and symptoms. One toxin causes a diarrheal illness, while the other causes a vomiting illness after the consumption of contaminated foods. The spores are common in soil, dust, plant products, bakery products, spices, animal products, and mixtures of ingredients, like puddings, soup mixes, and spaghetti sauces.

Backflow:
The flow of contaminated liquids and materials back into the approved water supply.

Backsiphonage:
Similar to backflow, backsiphonage occurs when the water level in a sink reaches a higher point than the water source or faucet and an accompanying drop in water pressure causes the contaminated water or liquid to siphon back into the line.

Bacteria:
Microscopic, single-celled organisms. Bacteria are found in the air, soil, and water, and on the skin and in the intestinal tracts of humans and animals. They can be found on almost all surfaces—vegetable peels, human hair, animal fur, and even on such nonorganic materials as unsanitized utensils, towels, and food-processing equipment. Bacteria "hitchhike" from one surface to another—for example, they can be carried from a person's hand to a ready-to-eat food product.

Bacterial Growth Curve:
The characteristic pattern of growth that bacteria will follow when they are introduced into a food and conditions are favorable. A bacterial growth curve has four portions: the lag phase, the log phase, the stationary phase, and the death (or decline) phase.

Bait:
A substance used as an attractant.* See *Attractants*.

Botulism:
A potentially fatal food poisoning caused by the toxins produced by the microorganism *Clostridium botulinum*. Toxin production occurs only under low acid, anaerobic conditions such as in improperly canned vegetables.*

Brown-banded Cockroach:
Similar in form to the German cockroach, the brown-banded cockroach does not have the two dark stripes running down its back. Rather, it is identified by two brownish yellow bands that traverse the body. See *Cockroach*.

Campylobacter jejuni :
The bacterium that causes campylobacteriosis. See *Campylobacteriosis*.

Campylobacteriosis:
A foodborne illness caused by the bacterium *Campylobacter jejuni*, which is found in soil, sewage, untreated water, and the intestinal tracts of chicken, turkeys, cattle, pigs, rodents, and some wild birds. This bacterium is found in undercooked meat and poultry, as well as raw milk.

Causative Organism:
Biological agent responsible for a case or an outbreak of a foodborne disease.*

Certified Applicator:
Person qualified to apply or supervise application of restricted-use pesticides as defined by the Environmental Protection Agency (EPA). (Individual states may have more restrictive definitions.)*

Chemical Foodborne Illnesses:
These illnesses are caused when people consume poisonous substances that occur naturally in some foods or that may be intentionally or accidentally added during harvesting, processing, transportation, storage, or preparation. There are five major types of chemical foodborne illness: metal poisoning, poisonous chemicals, intentional food additives, and poisonous plants and animals.

Chlorine Compounds:
A class of sanitizers that includes hypochlorite, commonly known as household bleach.

Ciguatera Fish Poisoning:
A foodborne illness caused by a neurotoxin called ciguatoxin, which is sometimes found in tropical and subtropical coral reef fish such as barracuda, snapper, grouper, amberjack, and sturgeonfish, among others.

Cleanliness:
In the food store, cleanliness refers to the visible agents that may transmit foodborne illness—for example, dirt on the floor, improperly cleaned countertops, or soiled food-preparation equipment.

Clostridium botulinum (*C. botulinum*):
The bacterium that causes botulism. See *Botulism*.

Clostridium perfringens **Gastroenteritis:**
A mild gastrointestinal illness caused by the bacterium *Clostridium perfringens* (*C. perfringens*). This foodborne disease is classified as a toxin-mediated infection or a toxicoinfection. The bacteria grow in the absence of air and produce spores, and are found in soil, dust, air, sewage, human and animal feces, and many food products. The most common foods involved include protein foods that have been boiled, stewed, or lightly roasted, like stews, gravies, casseroles, and bean dishes.

Cockroach:
One of the most common, chiefly nocturnal, insects in the world. Cockroaches can transport a number of disease-causing bacteria. There are four types of cockroaches that are commonly found in the U.S. See *American Cockroach, German Cockroach, Brown-banded Cockroach, and Oriental Cockroach.*

Critical Control Points (CCPs):
In a Hazard Analysis Critical Control Point (HACCP) food safety assurance program, critical control points are the points, steps, or procedures where control can be applied and a food-safety hazard can be prevented, eliminated, or reduced to acceptable levels.

Cross Contamination:
Contaminating one item with another item. For example, cutting raw chicken with a knife and then using the same knife (without first cleaning and sanitizing it) to slice a ready-to-eat product.

Danger Zone
Temperatures between which bacteria grow rapidly (40°F to 140°F).*

Death (Decline) Phase:
The final phase of a bacterial growth curve, the death phase occurs when nutrients are exhausted and/or metabolic by-products build up to levels high enough to kill the bacteria.

Detergent Sanitizers:
Detergents that also contain sanitizing agents.

Dinoflagellates:
The algae that cause paralytic shellfish poisoning. See *Paralytic Shell-fish Poisoning*.

E. coli 0157:H7:
The bacterium that causes hemorrhagic colitis. See *Hemorrhagic Colitis*.

Ectoparasites:
Parasites such as lice, mites, bedbugs, fleas, and ticks that may live in the feathers of birds and be transmitted to food products or humans.

EPA Establishment Number:
A number assigned to each pesticide production plant by EPA. The number must appear on all labels for a particular product.*

EPA Registration Number:
A number assigned to a pesticide product by EPA when the product is registered by the manufacturer of the designated agent. The number must appear on all labels for a particular product.*

Eradication:
The complete elimination of a pest from a site, an area, or a geographic region.*

Facultative Anaerobes:
Bacteria that can grow with or without oxygen.

First In, First Out (FIFO):
A system in which products are continually rotated through the purchasing, storage, and selling stages so that items can be sold when they are within the limits of freshness. All food items should be dated upon receipt so that older stock can be identified and used first.

Foodborne Illness:
An illness or disease transmitted to people through food products that results from ingesting foods which contain pathogens, microorganisms (or their toxins), poisonous chemicals, parasites, or viruses.

Food-Protection Program :
A store-wide system of assuring that the food products sold are safe and wholesome.

Food Safety Assurance Program:
A system that should be implemented throughout the food store to assure that foods processed, prepared, merchandised, and sold are safe and wholesome. See *Food-Protection Program.*

Fungicides:
Chemicals used to kill or suppress the growth of a specific fungus or group of fungi.*

Gastrointestinal:
Pertaining to the stomach and intestines.*

German Cockroach:
The most common of all cockroaches, the German cockroach is also known as the Croton bug. It is usually light brown in color, but it may be darker, and is easily identifiable by the two dark stripes running lengthwise behind the head. See *Cockroach.*

Good Manufacturing Practices (GMPs):
A collection of all of the correct procedures for processing and preparing food that need to be followed in a food store. They should be part of a company sanitation manual, and they are also the law.

Granary Weevil:
A blackish or chestnut brown weevil that is found in the northern states and feeds on a variety of whole grains. See *Weevils.*

Grease Marks/Smears/Rub Marks:
Darkened areas along walls and openings where rodents travel, these marks are made by the oil and dirt on the fur of rats and mice as they rub along the walls.

Hazard:
The potential for a substance or microorganism to cause injury under a given set of circumstances. It reflects both the inherent harmfulness of the substance or microorgansim and the likelihood that significant exposure will occur in a particular situation.*

Hazard Analysis:
A study of the dangers that exist in storing, preparing, and selling food products in the supermarket. The hazard analysis pinpoints circumstances in which the safety of foods may be compromised.

Hazard Analysis Critical Control Point (HACCP) Program:
A systematic, preventative approach to assuring the safety of food. There are seven principles of HACCP that should be applied to all fresh-prepared food departments in the store.

Hemorrhagic Colitis:
A serious bacterial illness caused by the bacterium *E. coli* 0157:H7, which is found in the intestinal tracts of animals, particularly cattle, chickens, pigs, and sheep. The bacteria flourish in raw or rare meats, especially ground beef, raw milk, and dairy products.

Hepatitis A Virus:
A virus that causes a disease of the liver called infectious hepatitis. Hepatitis A can be found in water that has been contaminated with raw sewage and in shellfish that have been harvested from fecally contaminated waters. It is also transmitted by infected workers.

Home Range:
The limited area within which rats and other rodents live.

Houseflies:
The most common insects to infest retail stores, houseflies breed in garbage, human and animal waste, sewage, and almost any kind of warm, moist organic material. They transmit disease-causing bacteria with their hairy bodies and sticky feet.

House Mouse (*Mus musculus*):
A small rodent that is common throughout the United States, the house mouse can be found in various locations throughout the food store, including not only walls and furniture, but also stored pallets of groceries.

Hypochlorite:
Also known as household bleach, hypochlorite is the most commonly used chlorine-compound sanitizer. See *Chlorine Compounds*.

Immune:
Resistant or not susceptible to a disease or poison.*

Indian-Meal Moth:
A moth that attacks grains and grain-based products, flour, seeds, powdered milk, and virtually all dried food products. The insect is tan and reddish brown with a copper luster. See *Moths*.

Infection:
The state produced by the establishment of disease-causing microorganisms (or an infective agent) in or on a suitable host. A foodborne infection occurs when food containing living pathogenic microorganisms is consumed. See also *Foodborne Illness.*

Insecticides:
Chemicals used to kill a wide variety of insects or a specific type of insect.*

Intentional Food Additives:
Vitamins, minerals, preservatives, and other compounds that are used to enhance the flavor, texture, nutritive quality, and appearance of foods, or to ensure their keeping quality. Additives to which some people have negative reactions are monosodium glutamate (MSG) and sulfites.

Intoxication:
The ingestion of poisonous substances present naturally in plants and animals, added intentionally or incidentally to foods, or produced by microorganisms multiplying in the food.*

Iodine/Iodine-containing Compounds:
A class of sanitizers, iodine is most often used in food stores when combined with a detergent or as a one-step germicidal detergent called an iodophor.

Iodophor:
A one-step germicidal detergent. See *Iodine/Iodine-containing Compounds.*

Irradiation:
The use of electromagnetic energy (ionizing radiation) at various levels to produce desirable objectives—from inhibition of sprouting to destruction of parasites and microorganisms and extension of shelf life—in food products.*

Lag phase:
The first phase of a bacterial growth curve, the lag phase is the one in which bacteria adapt to their new environment. During the lag phase, bacteria adjust their cellular machinery to break down food constituents, absorb the nutrients that are present in the food, and grow.

Listeria monocytogenes (*L. monocytogenes*):
The bacterium that causes listeriosis. See *Listeriosis.*

Listeriosis:

A foodborne infection caused by the bacterium *Listeria monocytogenes* (*L. monocytogenes*). Listeriosis can, under certain circumstances, be fatal. The bacteria are found in soil, decaying plant material, water, the intestinal tracts of domesticated wild animals and birds, and sewage. Among the foods that can be involved are raw vegetables, dairy products, raw meats, poultry, and seafoods.

Log phase:

The second phase of a bacterial growth curve, the log phase is the phase of maximum growth. Bacteria begin to absorb nutrients, grow rapidly, and increase in numbers during this phase.

Mediterranean Flour Moth:

A pale gray moth that feeds on flour, meal, grain, bran, cereals, nuts, chocolate, and many other food products. See *Moths*.

Mesophiles:

Bacteria that grow in middle or medium temperature ranges (77° to 113°F, 25.0° to 45.0°C). Most bacteria that cause foodborne illness and other human infections grow at these temperatures.

Metal Poisoning:

Excessive amounts of some metals can be toxic to humans, and metal poisoning can occur when quantities of metals get into foods through the use of equipment and utensils that are made from unsuitable materials. For example, when acid foods (such as fruit juice, sauerkraut, or carbonated beverages) are prepared or stored in equipment containing antimony, cadmium, lead, tin, or zinc, the metals dissolve in the food and if consumed, will cause illness.

Microbe:

An organism that cannot be seen by the naked eye. See *Microorganisms*.

Microorganisms:

Bacteria, molds, viruses, and other organisms so small that they cannot be seen without the aid of a microscope. Another word for "microorganism" is "microbe."

Misbranded Food:

Any food whose labeling or packaging is false or misleading.

Molds:
Larger than bacteria and yeasts, molds can be seen growing on the surface of a wide variety of foods. They are found everywhere and are easily spread by air currents, insects, and animals. Like bacteria and yeasts, molds are often involved in food spoilage, but they also have beneficial uses.

Monosodium Glutamate (MSG):
An intentional food additive that has been reported to cause illness when used in excessive amounts.

Moths:
Insects with antennae that are often feathery. Moths have a stouter body, duller coloring, and smaller wings than butterflies, and larvae that are plant-eating caterpillars. There are three types of moths that commonly attack stored food products: the Indian-meal moth, the Mediterranean flour moth, and the Angoumois grain moth.

Mycotoxins:
Toxins produced by certain molds and fungi multiplying on a food product. Diseases caused by these toxins are known as mycoses.*

Norway Rat (*Rattus norvegicus*):
The most widely distributed rat species in the United States, the Norway rat is also called the barn rat, brown rat, gray rat, sewer rat, water rat, wharf rat, and house rat.

Nosediving:
A situation that occurs in partially filled refrigeration cases in which the flow of chilled air is diverted into product voids, causing the product in front of the void to be cooled inadequately.

Nutrients:
Carbohydrates, proteins, fats, and other food constituents that cause organisms to grow. Bacteria and other microorganisms require nutrients to grow and multiply, just as humans and animals do.

Oriental Cockroach:
Also known as the black beetle or shad roach, the oriental cockroach is dark brown to black with a greasy sheen. See *Cockroach*.

Outbreak:
A situation in which two or more individuals experience a similar illness from consuming a common implicated food. For botulism or chemical poisoning, one case constitutes an outbreak.*

Paralytic Shellfish Poisoning:
A foodborne illness caused by a dangerous toxin produced by certain algae known as dinoflagellates. Mussels, clams, scallops, and oysters ingest these algae and then become poisonous to humans. The algae cannot be destroyed by conventional cooking, and it is for that reason that health agencies monitor the level of the toxins in the shellfish during the danger periods (May through October). See *Dinoflagellates*.

Parasites:
Organisms that rely on a living host to provide nutrients for growth and survival. There are several parasites that can live in animals used for food and can cause foodborne disease in humans.

Parts per million (ppm):
Number of parts of a substance (e.g., drug, toxin) in 1,000,000 parts of another substance. One ppm is equivalent to one inch in 16 miles.*

Pathogen:
A microorganism that can cause foodborne illness in humans.

Personal Hygiene:
Good health, careful work habits, and personal cleanliness are all elements of personal hygiene. Everyone who works with food must pay attention to the rules that cover this important element of a safety-assurance program.

Pest:
An unwanted organism (plant, animal, bacteria, etc.) that competes with people for feed, food, or fiber.*

Pest Control:
A program that is designed to keep rodents, insects, birds, and other pests out of the food store. Effective pest control should reduce or remove items that give pests food and shelter, and should also include systems for dealing with pests safely, quickly, and efficiently should they manage to gain access to the store.

Pesticide:
Any subtance used for controlling pests (weeds, fungi, insects, nematodes, etc.). Also includes attractants, repellents, growth regulators, defoliants, desicants, antitranspirants, sanitizers, and many others.*

pH (Acidity/Alkalinity):

pH is the measure of the acidity or alkalinity in a food product. It is expressed on a scale from 0 to 14, with 7 being neutral. Below pH 7 is considered acid (e.g., citrus fruits), while above pH 7 is defined as alkaline (e.g., peas or corn).

Poisonous Chemicals:

Chemicals that can cause illness or death in humans. Some chemicals are only poisonous if they are used incorrectly or unsafely.

Potassium Bisulfite:

One of the intentional food additives collectively known as sulfites. See *Sulfites*.

Potassium Metabisulfite:

One of the intentional food additives collectively known as sulfites. See *Sulfites*.

Potentially Hazardous Foods:

Foods that are able to support the rapid and progressive growth of bacterial foodborne pathogens. They usually are low-acid in pH, have a water activity (A_w) of > 0.85, and have a high protein content. Includes all foods that consist entirely or partly of meat, poultry, eggs, fish and shellfish, and milk and dairy products. These foods must be handled safely.

Psychotrophs:

Bacteria that are able to grow at cold temperatures (32° to 45°F, 0.0° to 7.2°C). These bacteria grow best at temperatures between 68°F and 86°F (20.0°C and 30.0°C). Most of these bacteria are responsible for food spoilage and cause off-flavors, off-odors, and off-colors in foods stored under refrigeration.

Quaternary Ammonium Compounds (Quats):

Among the most widely used sanitizers, quats are less versatile than chlorine, but they are highly stable, nonirritating, and noncorrosive.

Rice Weevil:

A reddish brown to black weevil that feeds on a variety of grains. The rice weevil can fly and is the insect that causes the most destruction to stored grains. See *Weevils*.

RODAC ® Plate:

A type of culture plate commonly used in carrying out a microbiological examination of food-contact surfaces.

Rodenticide:

A pesticide used for the control of rodents (rats or mice) and related animals.*

Roof Rat (*Rattus rattus*):

Most commonly found on the West Coast and the southeastern part of the United States, the roof rat is an excellent climber and commonly lives above the ground.

Salmonella:

Salmonella is a common bacterium that occurs in the intestinal tracts and fecal matter of animals. More than 2,000 types of salmonella bacteria exist. Their consumption by humans can lead to Salmonellosis. See *Salmonellosis*.

Salmonella enteritidis:

A type of salmonella that can be present in Grade A uncracked eggs. The bacteria can be passed to humans if the eggs are not properly stored and cooked. It is essential that eggs are stored under refrigeration and that they are thoroughly cooked before being eaten.

Salmonellosis:

An illness caused when food containing large numbers of salmonellae (living organisms) is consumed. It is one of the most frequently reported foodborne illnesses. A wide variety of foods have been implicated in salmonellosis outbreaks, including meat and poultry products, unpasteurized milk and dairy products, eggs and egg products, and meat and vegetable salads.

Sanitary:

In the context of food store sanitation, a microbiologically clean surface, utensil, or object is sanitary. Sanitary refers to the lack of invisible agents such as microorganisms that cause food spoilage or foodborne illness.

Sanitation:

A term that refers to all of the factors that promote personal hygiene and prevent foodborne illnesses by influencing the quality, safety, and wholesomeness of the food sold through a retail supermarket or other food outlet.

Sanitizers:
Chemical compounds used for sanitizing food-store equipment and utensils, and reducing the number of microbial contaminants to safe levels. See *Chlorine Compounds, Iodine/Iodine-containing Compounds, and Quaternary Ammonium Compounds (Quats).*

Sanitizing/Sanitization:
The procedure of reducing microorganisms on cleaned food-contact surfaces to safe levels.

Scombroid Fish Poisoning:
A foodborne illness caused by the products of bacterial action on the muscles of certain fish after they are caught. If improperly handled and stored, scombroid fish—tuna, mackerel, bonito, mahi-mahi (dolphin fish), and blue fish—can cause illness.

Shigella:
Several types of bacteria that can cause the foodborne illness known as Shigellosis. See *Shigellosis.*

Shigellosis:
A bacterial illness, also known as bacillary dysentery, caused by several types of bacteria known as shigella. These bacteria are found in the intestinal tracts of humans, and they are spread by food processors or handlers who have not practiced proper personal hygiene. Among the foods that can be contaminated are those that receive much handling, such as salads, and cut, diced, or mixed foods that are not cooked.

Shrinkage (Shrink):
The financial loss a supermarket suffers when food products cannot be sold and must instead be discarded.

Spores:
Special, thick-walled structures that are formed within the bacterial cell when unfavorable conditions occur. They are able to stay alive for many years, and when growth conditions are favorable, the spores change back into active bacterial cells.

Staphylococcal Intoxication:
One of the most common foodborne illnesses, staphylococcal intoxication is caused by the bacterium *Staphylococcus aureus (S. aureus),* also known simply as staph. The principal source of the bacterium is humans, but it can also grow in a wide variety of foods.

Staphylococcus aureus (*S. aureus*):
The bacteria that cause staphylococcal intoxication. See *Staphylococcal Intoxication*.

Stationary Phase:
The third phase of the bacterial growth curve, the stationary phase occurs when bacterial growth slows down and tapers off. In this phase, no growth occurs, but many cell functions continue.

Sulfites:
A class of compounds used as intentional food additives, sulfites (including sulfur dioxide, sodium and potassium bisulfite, sodium and potassium metabisulfite, and sodium sulfite) are used to maintain the freshness of vegetables, fruits, and certain wines. Sulfites can cause allergic reactions to individuals who are sensitive to them. The U.S. Food and Drug Administration prohibits the addition of sulfites to fresh foods and vegetables in retail food stores. See *Intentional Food Additives*.

Symptom:
An indication of illness or poisoning from chemicals or microorganisms such as skin irritation, nausea, sweating, headache, weakness, etc.*

Tail Drag Marks:
Distinctive marks left by rats and some mice, tail drag marks appear between the rodents' footprints.

Thermophiles:
Bacteria that thrive in hot temperatures (over 113°F, over 45.0°C). These organisms produce spores and are of major concern in the canning industry.

Toxicoinfection:
See *Toxin-mediated Infection*.

Toxin:
A poisonous substance produced by a living organism.

Toxin-mediated Infection (Toxicoinfection):
Illness resulting from eating food that contains large numbers of certain types of bacteria that produce toxins in the human intestinal tract.

Trichinella spiralis:
The parasite that causes trichinosis. See *Trichinosis*.

Trichinosis:
A foodborne illness caused by the parasite *Trichinella spiralis*, which is found in pigs, bears, walruses, rats, dogs, cats, and other domestic and wild animals.

***Vibrio parahaemolyticus* Gastroenteritis:**
A foodborne illness caused by the bacterium *Vibrio parahaemolyticus*, which is found in raw fish or inadequately cooked seafood, clams, shrimp, oyster, crabs, and lobster.

Viruses:
Genetic material inside of a protein coat, viruses are not complete cells. Because of their unique structure, they cannot carry out any functions outside of a cell or a living organism. They invade a living cell and then reproduce. They cause a variety of diseases in humans and can be transmitted through food.

Water Activity (A$_w$):
The availability of water in food. Pure water has a water activity of 1.00; most fresh foods have water activity values that are in the range of 0.98 to over 0.99. As the water activity is lowered, the ability of bacteria to grow is reduced.

Weevils:
A variety of beetle. Two types of this insect—the granary weevil and the rice weevil— attack foodstuffs in grocery stores.

Yeasts:
Single-celled organisms that are usually larger than bacteria. Although individual yeasts are invisible to the naked eye, large masses can be easily seen. Most yeasts are beneficial and are used in the production of beer, wine, bread, and other foods. However, certain yeasts can cause food spoilage.

***Yersinia enterocolitica*:**
The bacterium that causes yersiniosis. See *Yersiniosis*.

Yersiniosis:
An illness caused by the bacterium *Yersinia enterocolitica*, which is found in soil, untreated water, and the intestinal tracts of animals, especially pigs. The most common foods involved in this illness are meat and meat products (especially pork), milk and dairy products, seafoods, and fresh vegetables.

Abbreviations and Acronyms

AFDO:
Association of Food and Drug Officials

AMS:
Agricultural Marketing Service of the U.S. Department of Agriculture

ARS:
Agricultural Research Service of the U.S. Department of Agriculture

BATF:
Bureau of Alcohol, Tobacco and Firearms

CDC:
Centers for Disease Control and Prevention

EPA:
Environmental Protection Agency

FDA:
Food and Drug Administration

FSIS:
Food Safety and Inspection Service of the U.S. Department of Agriculture

FTC:
Federal Trade Commission

HACCP:
Hazard Analysis of Critical Control Points

HAZCOM (or HCS):
Hazard Communication Standard

HHS:
Health and Human Services

NMFS:
National Marine Fisheries Service of the U.S. Department of Agriculture

OSHA:
Occupational Safety and Health Administration

ppm:
parts per million

USDA:
United States Department of Agriculture

USDC:
United States Department of Commerce

USDL:
United States Department of Labor

Index